LIBRARY
ST. MARYS SEMINARY JU

W9-CJP-315

Dream and Reality

ASPECTS OF AMERICAN FOREIGN POLICY

Books by Louis J. Halle

DREAM AND REALITY: *Aspects of American Foreign Policy*

CHOICE FOR SURVIVAL

CIVILIZATION AND FOREIGN POLICY

SPRING IN WASHINGTON

DREAM AND REALITY

REALITY

Aspects of American Foreign

Policy • LOUIS J. HALLE

 HARPER & BROTHERS, PUBLISHERS, NEW YORK

DREAM AND REALITY

Copyright © *1958, 1959 by Louis J. Halle, Jr.*

Printed in the United States of America

*All rights in this book are reserved. No part of the book may be used or repro-
duced in any manner whatsoever without written permission except in the case of
brief quotations embodied in critical articles and reviews. For information address
Harper & Brothers, 49 East 33rd Street, New York 16, N. Y.*

FIRST EDITION

D-I

Library of Congress catalog card number: 59-7328

9998

9998

Contents

Preface   ix

Introduction   xiii

I • How the United States—like China, Japan, Russia, England, Switzerland, and India—has been suspended between the opposed impulses to seek isolation and to involve itself in international affairs.   1

II • How the sense of escape from a corrupted Old World reinforced the isolationist impulse.   13

III • How the Utopian myth or "the American Dream" was reinforced by the supposition that the great oceans cut America off from the rest of the globe.   23

IV • How the philosophic isolationism associated with the sense of escape came to be reinforced or replaced, in particular situations, by an isolationism arising out of ethnic circumstances represented by first-, second-, and third-generation Americans.   34

v

V • How expansion west of the Appalachians developed the independent American, without European ties; and how the position of the United States, like that of Russia, on the fringe of European civilization, poses the question whether we Americans are Europeans or belong to a species of our own. 47

VI • How, confronted by competing loyalties to civilization, nation, region, or parish, the breadth of our allegiance is determined by education. 59

VII • How, among Americans as among other peoples, the development of democracy has engendered the growth of nationalism. 70

VIII • How the successful assertion of our national independence, as a self-governing society, was made possible by an unmatched previous accumulation of practical experience in self-government during the Colonial period. 83

IX • How mercantilistic theories of empire held in eighteenth-century England conflicted with the actual position of the American community; how the conflict led to revolution; and how independence thereby came unsought. 95

X • How the Founding Fathers did or did not reconcile idealism and *Realpolitik* in their conduct of our foreign relations. 106

XI • How the French Revolution produced a division between our government and our people in which political theories and basic attitudes were at issue. 118

XII • How the doctrine of two hemispheres came to maturity under President Monroe, and what conflicts its self-denying aspects produced in American breasts. 132

XIII • How foreign policy may be constrained to serve domestic political purposes; and how the ideological impulses of the public confront strategically minded governments with a dilemma that they resolve by various devices.   145

XIV • How, in the twentieth century, we have still not been able to decide what our proper relationship is to the Latin American republics.   157

XV • How, without any intention of doing so, we acquired in the Philippines an imperial commitment on the other side of the world from which we would not be able to escape; and how we attributed such an unexpected development to destiny.   176

XVI • How—as our entanglement with the Philippines shows—the anatomy of destiny is related to the development of foreign policy by day-to-day improvisation.   189

XVII • How the obvious becomes obvious too late, so that—as our Far Eastern entrapment shows—prediction is easier in retrospect than in anticipation.   202

XVIII • How, after becoming committed overseas, we went for fifty years without an applicable foreign policy; and how, improvising relations with China and Japan from year to year, we set our feet on the road that led to Pearl Harbor.   215

XIX • How, in dealing with China and Japan, we advanced one step at a time on the road toward Pearl Harbor, and how the alternatives became progressively fewer.   229

XX • How we at last fell into the long-pending catastrophe and emerged triumphant, but with heavier and more dangerous Far Eastern commitments than before.   243

XXI • How the German submarine tested an obsolete foreign policy and found it wanting; and how, in spite of Woodrow Wilson, we failed to learn the lesson.   258

XXII • How the statesmen of 1919 failed to make a peace; and how the direction of our subsequent thinking about the failure led to its repetition by the statesmen of 1945.   273

XXIII • How, after fifty years, we were able to provide ourselves with an applicable foreign policy once more; and how that foreign policy found its expression in the Truman Doctrine and the Marshall Plan.   288

XXIV • How the problems presented by democracy and bureaucracy in the making of foreign policy have grown; the nature of those problems; the devices by which our leaders seek to meet them; and the present basis for hope, such as it is.

301

XXV • How the human mind, unable to encompass a vast, complex, and largely unknown reality, substitutes simple mythological views, to which foreign policy then addresses itself; and the challenge presented to our understanding.   315

Preface • Early in 1956 I was delighted to receive an invitation to teach for a year at the Graduate Institute of International Studies in Geneva, that honorable institution through which so many distinguished minds have passed. Given my choice of subject for a course of lectures, I chose (for reasons which I am about to explain) "Aspects of American Foreign Policy."

A man who found himself playing the violin in an orchestra, though he had never before had a violin in his hands, might come to wish that he knew more about the violin. It is in some such fashion that I came to take an interest in American foreign policy. Thirteen years in the State Department brought me to the point where I wanted to look into the subject. Then (to show that miracles still happen) the opportunity came. For two years as research professor in the Woodrow Wilson Department of Foreign Affairs at the University of Virginia I found myself a free man with daily access to the Alderman Library— in many respects, surely, one of the best university libraries in the country. I was like a horse too long in harness rolling in grass. Soon I had stacks of reading notes, but only vague notions of what I wanted to do with them.

The invitation from Geneva provided the occasion for developing the implications of this material in my mind, and for

ix

subjecting my consequent thought to the discipline of expression. Out of all this came a series of lectures, and out of the lectures the book to which this is preliminary.

Anyone who writes anything stands on other men's shoulders. For most of the information in this book I have relied on secondary sources, as any ordinary mortal must if he undertakes a broad enough approach to a large enough area. (Also, that is what secondary sources are for.) The dangers of such reliance are at a minimum when one deals with the history of American foreign policy, most of which has been thoroughly explored by a long list of scholars notable for their objectivity, competence, and conscience. I shall not name them here. Those I have drawn from are cited in every instance in which I have drawn directly from them. My bibliography, therefore, is in the footnotes.

In one area only have I made an extensive study of the primary sources. The first project on which I embarked, upon leaving Washington, was an examination of how the United States acquired the Philippines. Thanks to the hospitality of the Alderman Library and of the Sterling Memorial Library at Yale University, I was able to go over all (or virtually all) the documentary material on this subject that has been put into print. The product of this going-over is an unpublished study entitled "The United States Acquires the Philippines," which was awarded the Phi Beta Kappa Prize at the University of Virginia (1956), and of which three chapters in this book, (XV, XVI, XVII) represent, essentially, a drastic condensation. The temptation to incorporate the whole study was resisted, though not without effort. Its main conclusions, however, are here.

For the opportunity to live the scholar's life and do this work my gratitude to The Rockefeller Foundation and the University of Virginia is profound. But institutions are only the clothing of individuals. I therefore comprehend in my gratitude a number of persons, among whom I may mention Colgate W. Darden, Jr., president of the University, and John Gange, former director of its Woodrow Wilson Department of Foreign Affairs.

One acknowledgment remains. The test of any institution comes with the second generation. For a whole generation the distinction of the Graduate Institute of International Studies was closely identified with the personal distinction of Professor William E. Rappard, who left his enduring mark on it. To take his place as director would have been a formidable prospect for anyone. In Professor Jacques Freymond, however, the Institute has again found a man of the keenest intelligence, of an enterprising spirit, of energy and all-around ability, and of great personal charm. Again one man inspires a whole organization with his own personal quality, giving it a unique shape and stature.

It is proper for me to record this because the pages that follow were written at the Institute as well as being the product of lectures delivered there. The intangible influence of environment could not have been more favorable.

Before leaving America I had been told that the Institute had an excellent library in international relations. I was not disappointed, and I found in Mlle. Violette Fayod the kind of librarian to whom no researcher ever turns in vain. A good librarian is worth more than fine gold.

Finally, I am grateful for innumerable pleasant courtesies and helpful services to Mme. Alice Goebel and to Mlle. Nadine Galvani, whose typewriter worked overtime.

L. J. H.

Introduction • Truth may be invariable in itself,
but it is as various in the aspects it presents to an inquirer's view
as the approaches that may be made to it. The sea looks wrinkled
to the eagle but mountainous to the swimmer. The course of
action that outrages the critic who takes his stand on perfection
as the norm may elicit the admiration of the critic who looks
toward the difficulties to which it responds. I find myself capable
of being indignant at the ineptitude of American foreign policy
and, at the same time, of regarding it as a remarkable achievement. I could write an attack or a eulogy with equal honesty,
depending on where I chose to stand. Whoever undertakes to
examine a fixed object must first place himself in relation to
it. Let me make some general observations, then, that reveal
my own position.

American foreign policy is an expression of American history.
American history, in turn, is an integral part of the history of
mankind. The context is the historical record of all the nations,
that long and tragic record which Gibbon described as "little
more than the register of the crimes, follies, and misfortunes of
mankind." If, then, I have occasion in these pages to show "the
crimes, follies, and misfortunes" of my own countrymen, it
should not be thought that we Americans are thereby distinguished from others. Underlying these pages is the basic assump-

xiii

tion that we all partake of a common humanity, that Americans are only secondarily Americans. Primarily, they are sons of Adam. And how shall they, alone, escape the imprint of original sin? How shall they, alone, be without the mark of Cain?

In my own view men govern themselves badly at best. At the same time, I am constantly astonished that men are able to govern themselves as well as they do. Borrowing a simile from Samuel Johnson, I should say that our self-government may be likened to a dog walking on his hind legs: what is remarkable is not that he does it well but that he does it at all.

Most of my knowledge of government comes, so to speak, from having worked down in the engine room. In Washington, as in other great capitals, the engine room gives an impression of pandemonium. Especially in those times when major national policy has to be shaped, all appears to be uproar, all appears to be confusion. Ten thousand urgent voices assail the ears of those who have to make the decisions—with the result that no voice can be heard. Or, rather, everyone according to his own predilection will have the impression that only the wrong voices are being heard.

The President of the United States, today, cannot possibly do for himself all the thinking that must enter into the decisions of foreign policy which he makes. Neither can the Secretary of State. Consequently, they have great staffs of advisers and experts to do much of the thinking for them—whereupon the problem arises of communicating the thoughts of the subordinates to their masters, who do not always have time to read monographs or listen to lectures.

I shall not dwell on the infinite complexity of the problems which today present themselves for action by the governments of the great powers. There has never, I think, been anything like it before in the history of mankind. The problems are bigger than the men who have to deal with them, and perhaps the most serious danger today is that the men break down. (It is a question whether, at the end of the Second World War, any of our wartime leaders remained competent to make the decisions

xiv

that they still had to make.) Occasionally, as I look back critically at the policy decisions made in Washington over the first post-war decade, I have to remind myself that, while the issues involved seem clear to me now, they were anything but clear to me at the time, in the turmoil and urgency of the moment. For those who have to decide and act under the pressure of immediate necessity insight generally comes too late. Or too late to help any but their critics. Men act in the dark and live to survey the results of their action in the daylight that follows. "Alas!" says the old Greek tragedy. "How dreadful to have wisdom where it profits not the wise."

The difficulty is compounded in the foreign field by the relative unfamiliarity of the settings in which the problems arise. A farm problem in Ohio is one thing for Washington to solve. A crisis in Vietnam is quite another. How many Americans are in a position really to understand the cultural background and the physical environment which gives the Vietnamese crisis its peculiar character? Can we blame them if they tend to assume that the Vietnamese ought to react, in the situation, just as they, with their American background, would react? They have to deal with what they cannot understand—with what they cannot be expected to understand.

Finally, until recent days no other great power has conducted its foreign relations with anything like so great a degree of popular participation. Our American foreign policy, at least in its broad outlines, has been determined by the mass of the people—by their views, whether informed or not. For example, the question whether we will or will not assist countries far away from our shores to maintain their independence depends on the consensus of millions of little people—people who have not read books on diplomatic strategy or taken graduate courses in history, geography, international relations. People who never heard of Vietnam.

This element of democratic participation, however, is no longer unique in the United States. It has tended increasingly to prevail throughout the world in the twentieth century, although the devices and the ways in which it manifests itself vary from country to country.

Before the United States acquired roughly its present dimensions it was considered doubtful that democracy was at all possible on a scale larger than that of the Greek city-state. Alexis de Tocqueville, visiting the United States in the 1830's, believed that the country was doomed because of the incompatibility, as he saw it, of democratic processes with the effective conduct of foreign relations. "Foreign politics," he wrote, "demand scarcely any of those qualities which are peculiar to a democracy; they require, on the contrary, the perfect use of almost all those in which it is deficient. . . . A democracy can only with great difficulty regulate the details of an important undertaking, persevere in a fixed design, and work out its execution in spite of serious obstacles. It cannot combine its measures with secrecy or await their consequences with patience."[1]

This comment by De Tocqueville still seems to me to make sense today. By any ideal standard our American democracy, like other countries, has done badly in its foreign relations. If we Americans had conducted those relations with perfect wisdom, if we had at all times understood the implications of current events for the long historic future, if we had made the right decisions at every crisis, then two world wars might have been averted and the international scene, today, would have been in better shape than it is. By any ideal standard, then, we have done badly. But in the realistic terms of what one can reasonably expect of people we have done, I think, better than De Tocqueville anticipated. We have not gone under. And today we stand in the foremost rank among nations, bearing our new world responsibilities with a degree of determination and a vigor of understanding that are not altogether discreditable. So it is that, taking account of the "crimes and follies" referred to by Gibbon, I still find it remarkable that we have succeeded in doing no worse than we have.

When we see government up close we have occasion to be

[1] *Democracy in America* (New York, 1954), I, p. 243.

appalled; but distance may give a more favorable view. Nothing could exceed the fecklessness and disorder with which the statesmen of 1814 to 1815 approached the task of making a peace after the long crisis of the Napoleonic Wars. So far from reaching agreement among themselves, they were at crucial moments without any principles (let alone any plans) on which to agree. Time and again they merely drifted into decision or acted on whim. The so-called Congress of Vienna never assembled and constituted itself because the statesmen never succeeded in organizing it. The representatives of the European states came to Vienna and waited in vain. It was embarrassing. Social events had to be organized for them instead of a conference. Many despaired of any good result, and apparently had every reason for despairing. Yet one would have to search far through the record of human history to find another example of such an enduring peace as was made there. Far more thought and effort, far more intelligent planning, far more orderliness, went into the organization of the Paris Peace Conference and the Peace of Versailles in 1919, but with quite opposite results.

Today we cite the statesmanship of our Founding Fathers as the supreme example of political wisdom in action. But it did not look that way at the time, and the men themselves seemed less than monumental. The Secretary of the Treasury, in 1791 and 1792, maintained confidential relations with the British representative in Philadelphia and, in effect, conspired with him against the official policy of his own country, which the Secretary of State was trying to carry out.[2] The degree to which the members of the commission to negotiate a peace with Britain at the end of the Revolutionary War—Franklin, Jay, and Adams—allowed themselves to act independently and in conflict with one another would be almost unthinkable today. Bad faith toward one's colleagues, as well as one's allies, was commonplace. I have no doubt that if I had been there I would have concluded that, with so much intrigue and confusion, the

[2] B. F. Bemis, *The American Secretaries of State and Their Diplomacy* (New York, 1927), II, pp. 29-34.

future of the new nation was hopeless. How, I would have asked, can any government function without some basis for mutual confidence among its members?

Anyone who recalls the frustration and confusion of Washington from 1945 to 1950 may find grounds for a certain philosophical optimism in the increasing evidence, as time passes, that this was, in fact, one of the great constructive periods in the history of American foreign policy. There were times when no one would have believed it possible.

So the same spectacle, viewed from different positions, may provide occasion for irony and pity or may excite our admiration. The dog walking on his hind legs deserves alike our condemnation, our compassion, and our applause. He is to be congratulated even for doing badly.

What I have been outlining in the above observations belongs to "the tragic view of life"—or "the tragic view of history." As I have noted, the men who conduct the affairs of nations do so, for the most part, blindly. In formulating and developing a nation's foreign policy its leaders address themselves invariably to an imaginary situation which may approximate, or may not, the real situation; but which is never the same as the real situation. We live in the world of legend at least as much as in the world of historical reality, and we shape our policy accordingly. An individual of exceptional knowledge and insight may form in his mind an image of the external situation which is true in its prime essentials; but our modern bureaucratic governments are made up of vast numbers of persons among whom a consensus must be reached—and the collective mind of government is bound to be ordinary rather than extraordinary. When the consensus has to be extended to include the millions of minds involved in that collectivity of thought which we call "public opinion"—minds largely uneducated in history, geography, and anthropology; minds undisciplined by immediate responsibility; minds devoid of essential informaton—then the imaginary situation is likely to be imaginary indeed.

This separation between the image and the reality, between

what is ideal and what is actual, between the dream and the stern world of daylight, is the basis of the tragic view. It results in the constant defeat of the ideal, but also in its constant renewal, like the phoenix, from the ashes of defeat. So that human history is like a succession of Shakespearean tragedies, and the great societies of mankind rise toward divinity only to be consumed, at last, in defeat—in a defeat that sets the stage for a renewal of the divine hope and aspiration. This aspect of history has its illustration in the history of the United States, with its dream of Utopia and with the constant frustration of that dream by a recalcitrant reality.

What does the term, "American foreign policy," mean? Some of my colleagues in Washington used to argue that there was no such thing as American foreign policy. They said that there were, rather, a multitude of separate American foreign policies. There was our policy of extending long-term government credits to other free countries for their economic development. Or there was our policy of not recognizing the Communist regime in China. Or there was our policy of promoting West German rearmament. . . .

The people who insisted on seeing only this plurality of policies were the particularizers, the people whose preoccupation is with detail. If you asked them to write an account of American foreign policy they would present you with a catalogue.

I have undertaken something quite different here. I have undertaken to keep constantly before our eyes, in these pages, the large outlines of American policy. I have not been so much concerned with the individual points that are plotted on the graph paper as with the curve that manifests itself when they are looked at all together from a little distance. For if there is any order and sense in that policy, or any possibility of prediction, it is to be found only in the comprehensive view.

It will surprise no one, at this point, when I say that this whole subject presents itself to my mind in historical terms. American foreign policy is, above all, an aspect of American history. It is what it is today largely because of what has been in the past. This is so true that one might well say that the foreign policy of the momentary present is always, in a sense, an obsolete policy. It is behind the times. It addresses itself, this year, to the situation that challenged it last year. If you want to understand American foreign policy in 1958, you will learn more by studying the international situation in 1957 than by studying strictly contemporary events.

But here I am altogether too particular. Perhaps what I really ought to say is that, if you want to understand American policy in the twentieth century, you should understand the impression which the international scene made on us Americans in the nineteenth century.

I do not mean to be too literal about this. My only point is that a nation's policy is at least as much the product of its history as it is of contemporary challenges. The child is father to the man. We are what we are because of what we have been. It is the same in the lives of nations as in the lives of individuals. If we Americans suddenly take some action that, to others, appears wholly irrational and inexplicable, the explanation may lie in some experience of our infancy forgotten by others.

Therefore I have adopted, primarily and at the outset, the historical approach. I have looked at the beginnings of American foreign policy and the vicissitudes of its history with a view to understanding the consequent attitudes toward our external environment that have become established in the minds of us Americans, and that bear so largely on the development of our American policy in the present.

But I have not dealt with this history as an historian would, or as I would, myself, if I were writing a book on American diplomatic history. From the point of view of this particular book the historical facts have no importance in themselves. I present them merely as illustrations of the kind of experience that has shaped the nation we see today, or to explain peculiarities of our present foreign policy. Therefore I leave out more than I include.

The reader is now forewarned. In these pages I regard our foreign policy with the irony and pity, and with the occasional admiration, which seem to me proper to all the works of mankind. I seek the explanation of the present largely in the past. And I occasionally treat the historic experience of our own country as a sort of morality play, applicable to Everyman, to Everynation.

Dream and Reality

ASPECTS OF AMERICAN FOREIGN POLICY

I • One constant theme runs through the history of American foreign policy, from our first experiences as an independent unit in the world to the charged and revolutionary events of the twentieth century. It dominates virtually every debate and every significant decision throughout this period. It takes the form of a question which is aways being temporarily answered, with reference to transient circumstances, and which has never been finally answered until, perhaps, the 1940's. It takes the form of a tension, a polarity in our thinking, a conflict in our national desires or attitudes which at critical moments in history has divided our people, sometimes bitterly.

The tension is that between participation in world politics and withdrawal or aloofness or abstinence; between involvement and isolation, between alignment and neutrality. Throughout our national life we have been like a young man who cannot decide whether to enter the political arena or to retire into a monastery and forget this wicked world. You find precisely this question the subject of vehement debate among us in 1793 and 1939 alike. If one wishes to understand American foreign policy, then, one must understand how poignantly and persistently this single issue, in its various manifestations, has brooded over our councils and, occasionally, stirred the passions of our people.

Like Homer's old man of the sea, this single issue has taken a

1

variety of shapes. At one moment it appears as a question of whether we should remain neutral in a war between France and England; at another as a question of whether we shall or shall not become an imperialistic power with colonial possessions overseas. Then, again, it takes the form of a question as to whether it is our duty to liberate the enslaved peoples of the world—a question that goes back to the days when President Monroe wished to announce our support for the cause of Greek liberation in the same breath in which he announced the isolationist doctrine that bears his name—a question as fresh as Mr. Dulles' proposal to liberate the satellites of the Soviet Union. The issue has taken one form when we have looked across the Atlantic at Europe, another when we have cast our gaze across the Pacific. Sometimes, in fact, it has taken the form of a question as to which way we should face—toward the Far East, our backs to Europe, or toward Europe. This was a major issue with us as late as the election campaign of 1952, when the Republicans proposed, in effect, to substitute an Asia-first policy for the Europe-first policy of the Democrats. The same issue has taken still other forms as we have, from time to time, looked south toward Latin America, uncertain whether it was foreign territory, our parish, or our empire. It has been tangled in various and contradictory ways in the intellectual debates of recent years between "idealists" and "realists," between "moralists" and advocates of "expediency." It has often involved conflicts between political and commercial policy. Finally, it has involved us in all sorts of ironies—including what might plausibly be interpreted as an attempt to bring Tibet within the scope of the Monroe Doctrine.

Thus, while this issue has been most clearly recognized in the debates of the present century between our so-called "isolationists" and our so-called "interventionists," it is, in fact, more pervasive. Inevitably it becomes the major theme of the pages that follow.

The tension, the ambivalence between aloofness and participation, is not peculiar to the history of our American foreign

2

policy. On the contrary, it is common in the history of nations. Nowhere has isolationism been carried to greater lengths than in China, until the European powers forced themselves upon her in the nineteenth century. The agony of China's history from 1840 through the first decade of the twentieth century may be attributed to her hopeless effort to maintain the symbolic Chinese Wall, to resist the importunities of an external world that had become too powerful to be resisted.

A similar isolationism marked the history of Japan from the early seventeenth century to the second half of the nineteenth. Unlike China, however, Japan, when the West forced itself upon her, recognized the inevitable, abandoned the policy of isolationism abruptly, and embarked on a new policy of active participation and involvement in international affairs.

The whole long history of Russia, from its earliest beginnings in the ninth century to the present, may also be read in terms of a conflict between the respective appeals of isolation and involvement. Russia has never been able to make up her mind whether she is a part of the European world or a quasi-Asiatic power that stands outside and opposed to it. We see St. Vladimir at the end of the tenth century establishing cultural and religious bonds with Constantinople. In the fifteenth century we see Basil II and Ivan the Great following something not unlike an isolationist policy, at least in ecclesiastical matters, establishing the independence of the Russian Church from the West. The schismatic movement of the Old Believers in the seventeenth century represents a protest against a new attempt to westernize Russian Christianity. And at the beginning of the eighteenth century we see Peter the Great moving his capital to the western boundaries of Russia and plunging his country into the international politics and the cultural life of Europe. Russian writers of the nineteenth century suffered from an inner conflict over the identity of their country. They could not decide whether it was a European nation or a nation properly aloof from Europe and antagonistic to it. Gogol hardly regarded himself as European at all, while Turgenev was completely European. Dostoievski could not make up his mind whether his country should face east or west, whether it should be European or Asiatic. At one point he came to the conclusion that Russia should turn its face to Asia, because only in Asia would it be accepted as a European power! His dilemma was not dissimilar to the dilemma of the United States, confronted with the apparent choice between facing the Atlantic or facing the Pacific, turning its back on Asia or turning its back on Europe.

Even in the non-literary arts one sees this ambivalence and conflict. The music of Tschaikowski tells us that Russia is a province of Europe. The music of Moussorgski tells us that Russia is an Asiatic empire on the borders of Europe.

And in our own generation have we not seen this same ambivalence in Russian behavior? Did not Stalin, the Asiatic potentate from trans-Caucasia, pursue a policy of isolationism in erecting the barrier of the Iron Curtain—that modern version of the Chinese Wall? And is it not possible that his successors have at times been moved by an impulse to reverse that policy, to identify themselves as a part of the European community, pursuing European ways, wearing European sack suits instead of Russian blouses, renewing the exchange of persons and of information across Russia's borders, reducing the barriers?

Though the case is quite different here, even England has known something like this choice between isolation and involvement—knows it in fact today, when she must reconsider her relationship to a western Europe made up of states that are huddling more closely together. It was a British statesman, Viscount Goschen, who in 1896 used the phrase "splendid isolation" to describe the policy and the position of England with respect to continental Europe. From the point of view of our own modern times, it is hard to understand why the English of the fourteenth and fifteenth centuries did not see that England's involvement on the continent of Europe, the commitment of her military forces to adventures on the fields of France, was an immense obstacle to the achievement of her own independence, integrity, and welfare, or to the unification of the British Isles.

Joan of Arc should be as much the patron saint of the English as of the French—for it was Joan who put an end to the fruitless and costly English involvement, thereby establishing the conditions necessary for the development of the English nation no less than for the development of France.

England's later policy of manipulating the balance of power in Europe was certainly not isolationist in the sense in which we use the term when referring to China, Japan, or even the United States; but it did require a degree of aloofness, an abstinence from permanent, inextricable entanglements in continental affairs. English statesmanship was repeatedly having to make essentially the same kind of choice with respect to involvement in European affairs as Russia had to make, and as the United States has repeatedly made.

The neutrality which Switzerland has maintained with such determination and intelligence since 1815 represents another manifestation yet of an isolationist policy. Finally, the resistance of Nehru's India to any involvement in the international alliances of our day shows a desire to stand apart which has parallels in the early history of the United States.

I cite these examples to show that non-participation in international affairs is one of the classic possibilities open to national policy. It can rarely be absolute: the borders of China were always leaky, and the Dutch maintained a trading post near Nagasaki throughout the period of Japan's isolation. Typically, the non-participation is so limited that the term "isolation" is inappropriate and misleading. It means, merely, abstinence from involvement—or from permanent, inextricable involvement—in the political or military conflicts of other nations. It does not ordinarily mean, as it did in China and Japan, commercial and cultural isolation. It does not exclude trade or immigration. What it does exclude, typically, is peacetime alliance, any obligation to take sides in the quarrels of other nations. This is basic. Beyond this there may be other forms of non-participation practiced by particular nations, but the freedom from peacetime alliances or alignment is common to all the nations that practice this policy.

I suggest, therefore, that the impulse toward isolation or aloofness, so conspicuous in the history of American foreign policy, is not peculiar to Americans. It is a natural human impulse. In one respect it is simply the impulse to stay out of trouble. But I think it goes deeper than that. It represents the instinct for maintaining one's independence. Every agreement that a country enters into with another country abridges its effective sovereignty by giving the other country rights over it or claims upon it. Every agreement is a promissory note that reduces the independence of the nation that issues it. The natural desire of every nation, therefore, is to remain free of such pledges. The isolationist's ideal, says Francis Wharton, "is the non-juridical counterpart of sovereignty and, as regards its parentage, a blood-brother of sovereignty."[1]

In an address outlining and defending the policy of non-entanglement which he advocated, the late Senator Borah made the following statement: "This, it will be said, is isolation. It is not isolation, it is freedom of action. It is independence of judgement. It is not isolation, it is free government—there can be no such thing as free government if the people thereof are not free to remain aloof or to take part in foreign wars. People who have bartered away or surrendered their right to remain neutral in war have surrendered their right to govern."[2] One sees, here, how isolationism fits the spirit of nationalism, with its emphasis on national sovereignty.

This desire to remain uncommitted, however, comes into conflict with other considerations. Promissory notes are not issued for their own sake. Each is issued on the basis of a *quid pro quo* which may represent either necessity or a temptation not to be resisted. A nation enters into a binding agreement with another nation because its survival may require it to pay in this fashion

[1] "The Historical Meaning of the American Doctrine of Isolation," *American Political Science Review*, XXXIV, 3 (1940), p. 540.

[2] "American Foreign Policy in a Nationalistic World," *Foreign Affairs*, Vol. 12, No. 2 (Jan., 1934), p. xi.

for that nation's indispensable co-operation—as when it depends on the other nation for protection against attack by a third power. Or it enters into such an agreement in order to gain the help of the other nation in realizing some ambition of its own, such as the conquest and absorption of a third nation. But it never enters into such an agreement out of mere good fellowship or because it likes commitments as such. Any state in a position to abstain from such commitments is naturally impelled to do so.

What has been peculiar to the United States is not the impulse to practice such a policy but the nature of the opportunity. Setting up a new nation in a New World beyond the seas, we Americans found ourselves in a good position to stand apart from the entangling alliances of the Old World. What is equally significant is that, throughout most of our history, we have thought that we were in an even better position than we actually were to stand thus apart. We have thought of ourselves as occupying an island continent, cut off by vast seas from the rest of mankind, made virtually impregnable by nature.

In our own history, then, the tension between isolation and involvement, which is the main theme of its foreign relations, also takes the form, on occasion, of a conflict between dream and reality. We Americans have constantly dreamed of isolation and have repeatedly experienced involvement. We have dreamed of security behind our watery ramparts only to awaken belatedly, time and again, to the approach of danger across those very seas to which we had confided our protection.

Let me exemplify this contrast between the dream and the reality. First I shall quote some words spoken by a matchless American statesman—a man who stood, I think, above all his contemporaries in wisdom. This is what Abraham Lincoln said in an address which he delivered in 1837: "All the armies of Europe, Asia, and Africa combined, with all the treasure of the earth (our own excepted) in their military chest, with a Bonaparte for a commander, could not by force take a drink from the Ohio or make a track on the Blue Ridge in a trial of a thousand years. . . . [Danger] cannot come from abroad. If destruction be our lot we must ourselves be its author and finisher. As a nation of freemen we must live through all time, or die by suicide."

We should not be too hard on Mr. Lincoln. He was twenty-eight years old when he spoke these words, a young man whose direct experience of the world was confined to the deep interior of our continent. But the fact is that in these words he was expressing the common mind of America, the belief that it held throughout the remainder of the nineteenth century and through the twentieth century as well, despite the experience of the First World War, until the Japanese bombs fell on Pearl Harbor in December of 1941. Lincoln was not really thinking when he made this assertion. He was merely uttering a commonplace in the approved rhetorical manner of the day, and undoubtedly gaining the applause of his audience for it. Since politics began, the support of the majority has gone to those who have spoken what everyone believed to be true, rather than to those who spoke what was true. Like most political orators, Lincoln was engaging in cant. If he or any intelligent man of the time had subjected the statement he made to a critical testing, he could hardly have failed to see that it was flatly false. "All the armies of Europe, Asia, and Africa," commanded by a Bonaparte, could have proceeded quite freely to make tracks in the Blue Ridge and to take drinks from the Ohio River. They would have found virtually no military obstacle to oppose their progress. One would be tempted to say that Lincoln's statement was obviously untrue, if it were not for the fact that it remained the belief of every American, unquestioned because unconsidered, then and for generations to come.

So much for the dream. What of the reality?

A mere quarter of a century before Lincoln spoke, within his own lifetime, an army from across the seas had invaded Washington almost unopposed and had burned down both the Capitol and the White House. England had done this in 1814, at a time when her main military power was engaged in a desperate struggle against Napoleon. She had done it with her left hand, with the meager forces that she could spare from this effort—and we who had no other military challenge to cope with, we who had both hands free, had been unable to prevent her. The truth was that mere detachments of British forces, all alone, without the armies of Europe, Asia, and Africa, and with a Bonaparte in opposition rather than in command, had little trouble doing what was substantially more revealing of our vulnerability than merely making a track in the Blue Ridge or sipping water from the Ohio. Yet Lincoln and the majority of his audience had been alive when that happened. So great is the capacity of all of us men to depart from plain and even self-evident reality into the dream!

The fact is that, from as early as 1689 to the present date, America has found itself involved, as an active belligerent, in every general European war—that is, in every European war which has not been confined and enclosed, like the Franco-Prussian and Crimean Wars, within the interior of the Continent. The War of the League of Augsburg was fought on American as well as European soil. So was the War of the Austrian Succession. So was the War of the Spanish Succession. So was the Seven Years' War, which reversed the pattern by beginning in America and spreading to Europe. So was the great war between Napoleon and the rest of Europe, during which our capital, as well as Russia's, was burned. So were the two European wars that became the world wars of the twentieth century.

Lord Macaulay, referring to Frederick the Great's invasion of Silesia, described the ineffectiveness of oceanic barriers to war in a memorable phrase: "In order that he might rob a neighbour whom he had promised to defend, black men fought on the coast of Coromandel and red men scalped each other by the Great Lakes of North America."[3]

I don't want to make more of this cosmopolitanism in warfare than the facts warrant. Sir J. R. Seeley pointed out long ago[4] that England's three great wars in the eighteenth century were

[3] From Sir J. R. Seeley, *The Expansion of England* (London, 1925), p. 28.
[4] *Op. cit.*, p. 34.

9

all with France, that essentially they were incidents in what he called a second Hundred Years' War, and that the real issue was the possession of North America. The English colonists had at least as great an interest in this issue as the Englishmen at home. They were not really being exploited; they were not really giving their blood for Silesia. And in the last of the three eighteenth-century wars France was the ally of the Americans, fighting with them for their independence. But it does remain a sheer physical fact of American history that, from the beginning, the battle-ground of war embraced the great ocean, diminishing it to the dimensions of a lake around and about and across which the conflicting forces maneuvered and struck at each other.

This actual experience of American involvement in the quarrels of Europe, continuing through to the present century, has been largely disguised and hidden from our understanding by the geographical isolation of the American sector from the main theater of war, before the twentieth century, and by the custom of calling the American phases of these wars by names different from those applied to their European phases. Nominally, we used to have our own wars, distinct from those of Europe. Thus, when the English were fighting the French in the Seven Years' War, we Americans were fighting them in what we called the French and Indian War. Again, on the face of it we were not engaged in the Napoleonic Wars, we were engaged in something else called the War of 1812. But there would have been no War of 1812 if there had been no war in Europe. Then and on every other occasion we have not succeeded in keeping out of any general European war, despite the famous breadth of the Atlantic Ocean.

Up to 1815 it would surely not have occurred to anyone to claim a natural impregnability for the United States, a natural invulnerability to external aggression. This dream became possible only during that long period of European and world peace which began in 1815 and lasted, almost unbroken, for a century. It was a dream from which we Americans found the greatest difficulty in awakening. It was a dream from which any people would have found equal difficulty in awakening.

It was also a dream which the world once shared. In the politics of the European powers it took form as the principle of "peace beyond the line." According to this principle, though the European powers might war against one another in Europe, their warfare need not and should not pass an imaginary line that separated the metropolitan Old World from their colonial domains in the New World. The European wars should be limited and contained within the European sphere, while peace continued its undisturbed reign "beyond the line," in that distant and almost legendary sphere which no European statesman had ever seen for himself. This principle was formally enshrined in the Treaty of Whitehall concluded between France and Britain in 1686, one clause of which read: "It is furthermore declared and agreed that if ever any rupture shall occur in Europe between the said crowns (which God forbid), no act of hostility, whether by sea or by land, shall be committed by any garrisons or soldiers of the Most Serene Most Christian King [i.e., Louis XIV] or any subjects of islands, colonies, fortresses, states, and governments which now are or hereafter shall be under French rule in America against subjects of the Most Serene King of Great Britain [i.e., James II] dwelling or sojourning in any colonies of America, and reciprocally that in the aforesaid case of rupture in Europe no act of hostility, either by sea or by land, shall be committed by any garrisons or soldiers of the Most Serene King of Great Britain or by any subjects of islands, colonies, fortresses, states, and governments which now are or hereafter shall be under English rule in America against subjects of the Most Serene Most Christian King dwelling or sojourning in any colonies of America. But true and firm peace and neutrality shall continue in America between the aforesaid French and British nations, in the same manner as if no such rupture had occurred in Europe. . . ."

Here, in the form of a treaty between European powers, is the perennial American dream. On the other hand, in the form of repeated armed conflict between France and England, which

11

invariably spread across "the line," one sees the intractable reality.

This is the tension between isolation and involvement in one of its aspects, in the opposition between such wishful thinking as arises during long periods of peace and the strategic realities which contradict that thinking when, at last, the peace fails.

II • The American dream of isolation had deeper and more ramified roots than those of ordinary human inclination. It had special cultural, historical, and even religious roots as well.

From the establishment of the first colony at the beginning of the seventeenth century until well into the present twentieth century the population of North America was supplied by refugees from the Old World, people who conceived of themselves as escaping from wickedness and frustration in Europe to a new and better life across the seas. The sense of escape, consequently, has dominated the attitude of Americans toward Europe, toward the Old World. Europe was the dungeon from which they had fled to the wide-open American continent, where all men were equal, where all men were free, where opportunity was unlimited. Europe was the ancient prisonhouse on which they had so gladly turned their backs—forever.

As late as the 1930's, Nazi persecutions drove many of the best German scholars and teachers to America. With the overthrow of the Nazis and the establishment of the West German Republic they had the opportunity to return to their native land —but few returned. Following the established pattern, they had become Americans and had turned their back on a Europe in which such bitter experience had come upon them.

This attitude, if it was not universal, was at least typical

13

throughout most of our history. The first colony in North America, founded at the beginning of the seventeenth century, was established by Englishmen who were attracted by the expectation of freedom and opportunity in what Michael Drayton called "Virginia, Earth's only Paradise."[1] That the settlers, at first, found it more a hell than a Paradise is beside the point. We shall continue to have occasion to note how attitudes and policies are shaped more by dreams than by actuality. The legend of the founding of Virginia is the legend of escape to a better world.

About this same time the increasing persecution of the English Puritans by James I and Charles I confronted them with either of two alternatives, if they were not to give up their religious beliefs and practices. One was rebellion; the other was escape to a new world. Those who remained undertook by rebellion, in the Civil War, to reform the old England, to transform it into a new England that should respect the freedom of the God-fearing to worship according to the authority of the Bible and their own consciences rather than the authority of bishops. On the other hand, those who emigrated founded, around the shores of Massachusetts Bay, a "New England," apart from the old rather than by transformation of the old, as a refuge for the God-fearing from the oppression and persecution of the worldly.

This choice which the English Puritans made between reform and withdrawal is a choice that has appeared repeatedly to confront American foreign policy. Under the administration of President Wilson the United States undertook to reform the wicked external world, making it "safe for democracy." Under the succeeding administration of President Harding the United States, having failed in this attempt, withdrew from the scene of its failure into a renewed isolation. The choice between reform and withdrawal is one manifestation of the conflict between involvement and isolation.

Few events in American history loom larger in our folklore or have a more heroic quality for the American mind than the

[1] S. E. Morison and H. S. Commager, *The Growth of the American Republic* (New York, 1954), I, pp. 38 and 43.

escape of those Puritans, the Pilgrim Fathers, in the *Mayflower* from the corrupt Old World, and their landing at Plymouth Rock, in what became Massachusetts, on November 11, 1620.

Note, now, another ambivalence that runs throughout the record of American history. It is fair to say that both the Virginia settlers and these Massachusetts settlers crossed the Atlantic in search of freedom. But freedom for what? The Virginia settlers appear to have had in mind chiefly the freedom represented by greater economic and social opportunities, the freedom to rise on the economic and social scale. This they found, for the famous "first families of Virginia"—the Byrds, the Washingtons, the Randolphs, and the rest—had not, for the most part, been first families when they left England. They achieved their wealth and their status as great landed gentry after their arrival in America.

But the freedom that the Pilgrim Fathers came in search of was freedom of belief—freedom, at least, to believe as they believed, if not freedom to believe otherwise.

To this day, when we Americans talk about our traditional freedom we sometimes mean freedom of opportunity and we sometimes mean freedom of belief. We sometimes mean that any American can rise to be President of the United States, or to be a millionaire, however humble his origin, and we sometimes mean that any American is free to believe what he wants and to worship as he pleases. By contrast with the eighteenth century, however, the twentieth century has seemed distinctly more favorable to the former kind of freedom and perhaps not quite so favorable to the latter. The concept of freedom takes more account of the material standard of living today than it used to—in America as everywhere else.

It is as well that the Pilgrim Fathers had their minds fixed on the things of the spirit, for they could hardly have found a more inhospitable material environment than the barren coasts of New England in November, at the beginning of the long New England winter. Imagine these churchly people—men, women, and children—brought up in a civilized and even an urban environment, landing on this wintry coast, with no shelter for their heads, with only meager supplies of food, and with the best part of a year to go before they could expect a harvest, even if they did survive the winter to clear the ground and plant it!

"For summer being done," their leader, Governor Bradford, wrote, "all things stand upon them with a weatherbeaten face; and the whole countrie, full of woods and thickets, represented a wild and savage hue. If they looked behind them, there was the mighty ocean which they had passed, and was now as a maine barr and, golfe to separate them from all the civill parts of the world. . . . What could now sustaine them but the spirite of God and his grace?"[2]

And they were indeed sustained by "the spirite of God and his grace," although half of them died that first winter. For "they knew they were pilgrimes," as Governor Bradford later said, "and looked not much on those things, but lift up their eyes to the heavens, their dearest countrie." Another of the survivors wrote back to one of the sponsors of the expedition in England: "It is not with us as with other men, whom small things can discourage, or small discontents cause to wish themselves at home again."

Our first American holiday, Thanksgiving, was celebrated in November of 1621 to give thanks for the Lord's mercy in seeing the little band through its first year of escape. That first year was, perhaps, in material terms, the worst that Americans have ever suffered—yet I doubt that they ever gave thanks to God more fervently than at the end of it. It is not in prosperity but, rather, in the mitigation of adversity that we men appreciate God's mercy.

We Americans have celebrated the Feast of Thanksgiving ever since, for almost three and a half centuries of increasing prosperity, as one of our two principal national holidays. I mention this because it shows how deep an impression this experience of our forefathers made on our national consciousness. The land that was won with so much suffering would not be easily given

<hr>

2 *Ibid.*, I, p. 53.

16

up; the ocean that had been crossed at such a price would not be willingly recrossed. That ocean was, as Governor Bradford said, "behind them." England, Holland, Europe, the Old World with all its corruption, was behind them. They had turned their backs on it forever. They were done with its tyrannies, its politics, and its wars forever. They had escaped to return no more. That sense of escape, which is a part of the experience, has been handed on, generation after generation, even to us Americans of the twentieth century.

As the years have passed, it is true, the tradition has in some respects weakened and faded, has taken on the color of new times. The freedom to amass this earth's riches has gained on the freedom of the spirit, in the estimation of us Americans as well as of others. In the 1930's the President of the United States, responding to the appeal of the business community, proclaimed that the nation should, thereafter, thank God two weeks earlier each year, so as to avoid overlapping between the commercial boom that accompanied Thanksgiving and the commercial festival which is Christmas. This, happily, was one of the most unpopular measures ever taken by a popular President; and today, however much the commercial interests may complain, we again celebrate Thanksgiving as we did before, on the last Thursday of November. Few of us now thank God, on that day, as the Pilgrim Fathers did, but at least a vestige of the ancient reverence remains.

"Thus," said Governor Bradford, "out of small beginnings greater things have been produced by his hand that made all things of nothing . . . ; and as one small candle may light a thousand; so the light here kindled has shone unto many, yea, in some sorte, to our whole nation."[3] This light, whether burning bright or flickering low, is part of the illumination by which the American nation has since set its course. It has drawn our eyes away from the old world to our own new-found land. It has been a light made in America, contrasting with what we have

[3] *Ibid.*, I, p. 54.

conceived to be the darkness of an unregenerate and abandoned Europe.

The sense of escape from the Old World with which those who were to become Americans arrived in the New World was reinforced by a pervasive Utopianism in their thinking. This Utopianism is perhaps the main philosophical factor that has shaped American foreign policy from the first colonizations to our own time.

The Pilgrim Fathers, and the others who followed them to populate New England, were sustained in their hardships by that dream which they were about to realize. They had fled from the Babylon of the Old World to found the City of God in the New. And the ideological tyranny which they imposed in their newly founded City responded to the desperate necessity of excluding the corruption of that environment from which they had escaped, of insulating their City against it, of isolating it.

Isolation, insularity, is a precondition of every Utopia. It is no coincidence that most of the Utopian dreams in European literature have their setting on a distant island, removed from the worldly world and protected by formidable surrounding seas.

The discovery of the New World was accompanied by a great renaissance of Utopianism in the literature of the Old World; and there is a logical connection between these two developments, a connection of cause and effect, a connection that has its place among the roots of American foreign policy. Sir Thomas More's *Utopia,* first and most famous of them all, appeared twenty-four years after Columbus first sighted an island off the shores of what later turned out to be a new and unsullied continent. "First among the thinkers who discerned the wider opportunities opened up by the discovery of the New World," according to Professors Rose and Salter, "stands Sir Thomas More. While the successors of Columbus prepared to exploit [the discovery] the eager brain of More discerned in the New World a new heaven wherein might dwell righteousness. His vivid imagination first brought together in fruitful union the

18

world of Plato and the world of Columbus and Cabot. With quick intuition he saw that the ideal Republic of the Greek sage might be founded in the fertile wastes possessing the two essentials hitherto always denied to mankind—space and security. All down the dark vistas of the past, land hunger had been the parent of war, war of cruelty, cruelty of countless vices undermining the social order. . . . The introduction [to *Utopia*] reveals a soul in revolt against the grim actualities of his age. He sees the European States in a condition of veiled or actual hostility; rulers waging wars of aggrandisement; wars breeding other wars and leaving behind a loathsome progeny of hatreds and hardships. . . . Such is the old order, the aftermath of the long civil strifes—a weary waste of selfishness, extravagance, injustice and misery.

"Over against the hopeless welter of the Old World he throws up in sharp relief an ideal commonwealth spaciously framed in the lands discovered by Amerigo Vespucci. There . . . he discerns a home where mankind may start afresh. He pictures Utopia as a larger England, remote and safe from invaders. . . . As for government, philosophers either rule or counsel the ruler, who holds office for life unless deposed for tyranny. . . . Social well-being is assured by peace and security, prosperity by thorough tillage of the soil, and culture by a six hours' day which leaves scope for the 'free libertye of the minde and garnishing of the same.' . . . To lessen the risk of war they make no alliance. . . . This is the moral of More's message. It sets forth the two forces which were to draw myriads oversea—the lure of a new life and discontent with the old life."[4]

More's was only the first of many Utopias which appeared in the following two centuries, almost all of them inspired, directly or indirectly, by the vision to which Columbus's discovery gave rise. Bacon's *New Atlantis* came out in 1626. Harrington's *The Common-Wealth of Oceana*, which appeared in 1656, suggested to those who later wrote the constitutions of the individual

[4] J. Holland Rose and F. R. Salter, in *The Cambridge History of the British Empire,* "The Old Empire" (Cambridge, 1929), I, pp. 93-95.

states and of the United States Utopian features which they incorporated in their designs. Prospero's Utopian Island, in Shakespeare's *The Tempest*, was set in the New World, as was Sir Thomas More's—corresponding, to be precise, with Bermuda. Later Voltaire, in his *Candide*, was to describe another Utopia, called the land of Eldorado, this one isolated by impassable mountain ramparts, but also situated in the New World. And did not Jean-Jacques Rousseau have the New World in mind when he dreamed of a land in which the noble savage was unspoiled by the political and social institutions which afflicted his native Europe? Note the expectation implicit in these Utopian attitudes that human nature would have a different manifestation in a New World that was free of those ancient social institutions which virtually imposed corruption on it in the Old World.

"Since the days when the fleet of Columbus sailed into the waters of the New World," wrote the historian of the American frontier, Frederick Jackson Turner, "America has been another name for opportunity . . . each frontier did indeed furnish . . . a gate of escape from the bondage of the past; and freshness, and confidence, and scorn of older society, impatience of its restraints and its ideas, and indifference to its lessons, have accompanied the frontier."[5]

Turgot, the French statesman who tried in vain to introduce reforms into the French government that might have staved off the approaching French Revolution, wrote a letter to the American, Dr. Price, in 1778, two years after the American Declaration of Independence (and also two years after Turgot had been dismissed by Louis XVI for his attempted reforms). The American people, he wrote, "is the hope of the human race. It may become the model. It ought to show the world by facts, that men can be free and yet peaceful, and may dispense with the chains in which tyrants and knaves of every colour have presumed to bind them, under pretext of the public good. The

[5] "The Significance of the Frontier in American History," in *The Turner Thesis*, G. R. Taylor (ed.), (Boston, 1949), p. 18.

Americans should be an example of political, religious, commercial and industrial liberty. The asylum they offer to the oppressed of every nation, the avenue of escape they open, will compell governments to be just and enlightened; and the rest of the world in due time will see through the empty illusions in which policy is conceived. But to obtain these ends for us, America must secure them to herself; and must not become, as so many of your ministerial writers have predicted, a mass of divided powers, contending for territory and trade, cementing the slavery of peoples by their own blood."[6]

And how was America to secure to herself those blessings of Utopia that would set the example for and thereby encompass the salvation of Turgot's France and the rest of the Old World? Dr. Price, printing Turgot's letter in 1785, gave his own opinion. "The Atlantic," he pointed out, "must be crossed before [the American states] can be attacked. . . . Thus singularly happy, why should they seek connexions with Europe, and expose themselves to the danger of being involved in its quarrels?—What have they do with its politics?—Is there anything very important to them which they can draw from thence—except *infection*?—indeed, I tremble when I think of that rage for trade which is likely to prevail among them."[7] The kind of isolation for which Dr. Price asked was a Chinese isolation, an isolation that excluded foreign trade as well as foreign politics—and all in the name of Utopia.

The notion that we Americans could best benefit the world by realizing an ideal among ourselves, a notion which surely has much validity, crops up as a justification of isolationism, whether noble or selfish, throughout our history, down to our own day.

Today again, or today still, men feel a disgust with the great machine civilization that darkens their lives and persists precariously from year to year under the brooding threat of thermonuclear destruction. Suppose, in these circumstances,

[6] Quoted by Morison and Commager, *op. cit.*, I., pp. 320-321.
[7] *Ibid.*

that someone should discover a new and accessible planet on which the sun shone benignly, a planet which abounded in lush fields and meadows, in fruit and nut trees, in milk and honey—an eighteenth-century dream planet, a pastoral and idyllic planet, unpopulated, unspoiled, far-removed from our own crowded, scarred, blackened, and chaotic earth. Would we not all dream of moving there to realize that ideal of peace, of plenty, and of godliness which had become impossible on earth? This imaginary new planet is what America, the New World, was in reality for Europeans and for its own settlers alike in the centuries after its discovery.

III • The Utopian ideal, sometimes called "the American Dream," was the inspiration that in large part motivated every settlement in North America, not only that of the Pilgrim Fathers. For three centuries a vast population was drained off from Europe, with its ancient miseries, to fill up the wilderness of the new continent, to cultivate its riches, and to enjoy its egalitarian freedom. The exodus from Europe was an exodus of the dissatisfied, like the exodus of the Jews from Egypt. America was the asylum, the land in which their ancient frustrations would come to an end.

The American Dream, which drew this population across the ocean, is the predominating intellectual or ideological fact in the history of America. It has shaped the thinking and the politics of us Americans, making it almost sacrilege for any of us to take a gloomy view of the future or to recognize the possibility of disaster in the present. It has equated patriotism with self-congratulation and the hope of an imminent millennium. It has made us, at times, look back on the Old World with pity or with scorn or with a willful disregard.

You can trace this American Dream throughout our political oratory from Jefferson to Eisenhower. Here is how President Jefferson, delivering his Inaugural Address in 1801, described the position of Americans: "Separated by nature and a wide

ocean from the exterminating havoc of one quater of the globe
. . . possessing a chosen country, with room enough for our
descendents to the hundredth and thousandth generation . . ."
the only thing "necessary to close the circle of our felicities" is
"a wise and frugal government, which shall restrain men from
injuring one another, shall leave them otherwise free to regulate their own pursuits of industry and improvement, and
shall not take from the mouth of labor the bread it has earned."

Note Mr. Jefferson's reference to America as "a chosen country." I am not sure what that means. It could mean the country
of its inhabitants' choice, since they had chosen it as the scene
of their experiments in leading the good or the abundant life.
But it could also mean the country of God's choice, and I must
say that in our accesses of ardent patriotism or in our patriotic
songs we, like other peoples, have not always blushed to claim
God's special favor. This "chosen country" is, in Mr. Jefferson's
phrase, "separated by nature and a wide ocean from the exterminating havoc of one quarter of the globe." It may be that,
in the view of some of us Americans, God had abandoned that
distant quarter of the globe when he chose America—abandoned
it as he abandoned Sodom and Gomorrah, abandoned it as he
abandoned all but the Ark and its inhabitants to the Great
Flood. We Americans were the family of Noah.

Finally, "chosen" may mean chosen for the erection of the
City of God, chosen for the New Paradise, chosen for the establishment of the Kingdom of Heaven on earth. Or it may
merely have a generalized meaning, as when we talk of a choice
cut of beef. In any of these cases, it represents that sense of
separation and escape, and of a heavenly future, which has
animated us Americans through the generations, even into our
own times. And who shall say that, in material terms, in terms
of the standard of living produced by modern science and
technology, it has not been justified?

The experience of the twentieth century, it is true, especially
that of the great depression, has tended to deflate our complacency and our optimism. If one doubts, however, that the

24

Dream continues dominant in our political thinking, one has only to listen to our political orators in an election year. Every nation is best known by its cant. According to our orators, the final realization of our American Dream is still just about to be. Read President Eisenhower's address accepting the nomination as Republican candidate for President in San Francisco on August 23, 1956. In it, like every American orator in such circumstances, he pictured the "brave and shining new world" which was now almost within our grasp. "Science and technology," he said, "labor-saving methods, management, labor organization, education, medicine—and not least, politics and the art of government—all these have brought within our grasp a world in which back-breaking toil and long hours will not be necessary. . . . The fear and pain of crippling disease will be greatly reduced. The material things that make life interesting and pleasant can be available to everyone. Leisure, together with educational and recreational facilities, will be abundant, so that all can develop the life of the spirit, of reflection, of religion, of the arts, of the full realization of the good things of the world.[1] And political wisdom will ensure justice and harmony."

The Dream has, to be sure, changed in its emphases since the days of the Puritans. It shows the impact of the Industrial Revolution, of democracy, and of materialism. One gets the impression that the modern demos to whom its appeal is addressed is disposed to put leisure and luxury ahead of "the life of the spirit, of reflection, of religion, of the arts." The demos is more likely, perhaps, to vote for a six-hour day than for a renaissance of poetry. But there was much of this materialism even in our early beginnings. The settlers of Virginia and Georgia were more concerned with the standard of living than with the freedom of belief, and the New England Puritans themselves, as their history unfolded, showed no contempt of commerce.

[1] This harks back all the way to 1516, to that vision of Sir Thomas More's Utopia in which husbandry, limited to a six-hour day, leaves scope for the "free libertye of the minde and garnishing of the same."

Through most of our American history this Utopianism has powerfully reinforced our isolationist tendencies, for we have thought of our Utopia as a promise that could be realized only if we kept our distance from the contagion of an irremediably corrupt Europe. At other times, as in Woodrow Wilson's day, it has impelled us to see if we could not reform the Old World overnight, making it over in the image of our own dream.

In these historical antecedents, all promoting a contrast between the Old World and the New, one finds a prime cause of that disposition which we Americans have occasionally manifested to regard ourselves as the elect, as paragons of political virtue, and to look upon old Europe as the ancient and doomed repository of all wickedness. In these antecedents one may find a prime cause of that fear of having any dealings with the European Old World which has occasionally marked our policy. One weakness of all Utopians lies in their necessarily low opinion of the external world, and in an anxious hostility toward it.

The sense of escape reinforced the isolationist disposition which is natural to all nations, and so it tended to make isolation a cardinal objective of American foreign policy. Under the circumstances we took a view of the world's geography that supported our independence. We fondly regarded our Western Hemisphere as physically remote from the rest of the world, isolated by barriers of heaving salt water. In our imaginations we made ourselves another planet, establishing a terminology of two separate worlds, the "Old World" and the "New." Ours was an entirely New World, detached, separated by interplanetary space from the Old World. We emphasized its physical separateness in our minds. "All the armies of Europe, Asia, and Africa combined" might leer with envy at us from the Old World shores, but there was no way in which they could reach us across the gulf of oceanic space. Our "chosen world" had been removed by a provident Nature from their reach.

When we attempt to understand international politics we have always to consider the factor of geography in two distinct aspects: the physical body of the earth as it is, and the image of that body in men's minds. We must distinguish between what the geography is, as a matter of measurable fact, and what men see when they look at it. Again we have the opposition of fact and legend, with the latter exerting a superior appeal.

A man from Mars, one supposes, would have considerable difficulty with our common enumeration of the continents. Europe, we would tell him, is one of the continents and Asia is another. But when he had studied earth through his telescope on Mars, before coming to visit us, he had not seen them as two continents. Having the innocent eye of the child in Andersen's tale of "The Emperor's New Clothes," he might wonder how what was plainly a peninsula of Asia could be considered a separate continent by people in their right minds.

It would hardly do to answer that Europe, if it is not separated from Asia by water, is in fact separated by some difficult or extensive terrain. In that case India would have a better claim to full continental status than Europe. Are the Urals, which the traveler can hardly find when he has come to them, greater than the Himalayas, which he can hardly cross? Or is Europe really cut off from Asia Minor by the Bosporus, over which the Persian King Xerxes threw a bridge on his way to the Battle of Thermopylae and the sack of Athens—across which, in a moment of informality, an American ambassador swam in the late 1940's, thus duplicating with ease the overestimated feat of Leander?

The nearest thing to a satisfactory answer which we could offer the Martian is that the concept of a continent called Europe represents the importance which Europeans have always attached to their own part of the earth, and that it does have an historical and anthropological meaning. The peoples of the two areas, beginning with the Greeks and Persians respectively, have considered themselves different. The continent of Europe exists in the mind, if not on the map, but is no less important for that.

Again—are the Americas one continent or two? Generally

we have regarded them as two. But with the inauguration of President Roosevelt's "Good Neighbor" policy in 1933 we began calling them one. From that date, until about the end of World War II, all official documents refer to "the American Continent," singular. This enabled us to talk about "continental solidarity." But at the conclusion of the war the United States began to associate more closely with Europe, and thereupon, quite unconsciously, we reverted to the two continents in our language—North America and South America. Politics, apparently, makes geography as much as geography makes politics.

Throughout American history, as I have mentioned, we have regarded the Atlantic Ocean as a barrier, or as we might regard the space between two planets. But, with the creation of the "Atlantic Community" after the Second World War, it radically changed its character and became a lake which made close neighbors of all who lived on its shores.

These political concepts are vividly reflected in the work of map makers, who always have the choice of what projection to use for their maps, and what angle of vision. Throughout the days of our isolationist thinking Mercator's projection dominated our minds. It gave an exaggerated importance to the Atlantic as a barrier by doing away with its diminution from the Equator to the North Pole. Today we see maps of the Atlantic Community that emphasize this diminution and really do make the Atlantic and Arctic Oceans look like one enclosed lake.[2]

This, however, is a novel and still a rather odd concept to us Americans, like a clever paradox formulated *pour épater le bourgeois*. Those of us above forty, at least, have all been brought up on the traditional view of an Old World and a New World separated in space, on the concept of the two hemispheres.

The fact is that nature never created the two hemispheres

[2] Cf. Richard B. Morris, *Encyclopedia of American History* (New York, 1953), p. 395.

of our imagination. There may be an American continent or American continents, but there is really no such thing as a "Western Hemisphere" opposed to some other hemisphere, presumably an "Eastern"—just as there are no eastern and western sides of a globe if one picks it up and examines it. The globe does have a north, extending hemispherically from the Equator to one of the poles, and a south extending from the Equator to the other pole. One knows where the northern and southern halves of the globe begin and end, and one could explain the distinction to the man from Mars. But where does the East begin, and where the West? The man from Mars, in his ignorance, might think we were talking nonsense if we tried to explain to him that, for anyone standing on the coast of California, the East is in the direction of the setting sun. The International Date Line has a meaning quite different from that of the Equator. It is political and arbitrary. Its position was determined by the accidental location of a human settlement, a suburban town called Greenwich now enclosed by the expanded city of London. It is a product of politics. It was deliberately drawn at the antipodes of a national capital, and as such has no standing comparable to that of the Equator, which represents nothing human but might have been drawn by the dividers of the divine architect.

Now what kind of a division is it that lumps the English and Spanish with the Chinese and Indonesians, but separates from them the present inhabitants of North and South America? Can we even say that this is based on anthropological, historical, and cultural realities? It seems to me that if we are going to divide the world into two halves on the basis of anthropology and history, then we must revert to the old distinction between Orient and Occident. Here is a distinction which would be readily perceptible to the man from Mars if he knew even the rudiments of anthropology and world history.

But this distinction destroys American isolationism by lumping America and Europe. One can see why we Americans found it not uncongenial to our thinking to picture, instead, a Western

Hemisphere from which Europe was quite excluded.

Today, however, since our postwar revolution in foreign policy, we talk of "the West," giving it a meaning that associates Europe and America, that brings them together in an Atlantic solidarity paralleling the "continental solidarity" of the Good Neighbor policy.

Nothing lends itself more readily to paradox than this play on geography, this adaptation of geographical distinctions to political or cultural preconceptions. But one must guard against exaggeration. Even on a globe it is plain that the two great oceans of the world, running almost from pole to pole, do divide it into two perceptibly distinct land masses: the two Americas, not quite severed from each other, on the one hand; on the other, Eurasia and Africa. This physical distinction, however much it may have been exaggerated in the past, is not altogether imaginary.

It is, moreover, reinforced by history, since, in a rough manner of speaking, until a few centuries ago it distinguished the inhabited and historic part of the world from the uninhabited part of the world which remained outside of history. Still, this is a rough manner of speaking. There were teeming populations in parts of America, and cultural developments that, around the eighth and tenth centuries, were superior to anything in western Europe, at least. The Middle American and Peruvian civilizations stand outside of history chiefly from a European point of view. The parochialism is evident. But this view is not altogether delusory. One must exaggerate neither way. It may be that, in the time of Columbus, the entire population of North America north of the Rio Grande was no more than a million—which is tantamount to saying that the continent above Mexico was empty—and the Indian civilizations left no real historical records.

We are concerned, here, chiefly with the geographical notions of North Americans. The colonizers and settlers and other immigrants who left Europe to populate North America were stepping out of a crowded continent into an illimitable wilderness, and were stepping out of an historic world into a world unblemished by any previous history. The distinction between Old World and New World must have had the most vivid reality for them—a reality more vivid for them than it can possibly be for us, now that the primeval wilderness has been replaced by a crowded and essentially European civilization, now that history has scarred and damaged the land.

Moreover, to those who had endured the months of danger and hardship required to cross the Atlantic, that ocean was a considerable barrier. The present new generation, overflying it in a few hours of luxurious ease, can hardly recapture this sense of its magnitude. I first crossed it as a child, and my most vivid impression, which is still with me (since adult experience does not erase the strong impressions of childhood), was of its immensity. When the ship I was in finally reached the opposite shore, after ten days and nights of plunging through the heaving surface of this no man's land, I felt as if I had indeed arrived at another planet. Our ancestors took six times as long to cross it, and therefore had even better reason to think of Europe and America as lying "worlds apart."

From the point of view of the military strategist, however, an ocean is not a barrier in and of itself. It does not, in and of itself, protect the land which it surrounds. On the contrary, it is a clear and unobstructed highway to the nation which can dominate it. During the nineteenth century, when the English navy dominated the Atlantic, it provided easier accessibility to North America for the English than if it had been the best of dry land. It opened the way for English power to move at will and virtually undetected along our boundaries, to strike where it pleased. So far from being a barrier to the power that controlled that ocean it was the broadest of avenues. It left us virtually defenseless. Where, in that watery waste, could we erect our forts? Where could we build a Chinese Wall or a Maginot Line?

In like manner, England had been defenseless against the Romans, the Saxons, the Danes, and the Normans when these people were successively able to dominate the waters that separated her from Europe. The English Channel did not become an effective moat until England, herself, was able to dominate it—and then it became an avenue by which the English could invade the Continent at will. Since oceanic travel became possible an ocean has constituted a defense only when it has been dominated by the defending nation or by some other nation willing to protect it.

From 1805 until the end of the century the English navy was virtually unchallenged in the Atlantic—from the shores of Europe to the shores of America. The Atlantic Ocean, therefore, offered no defense at all against the English. That is why the British, for all the interplanetary space we have been talking about, found it easy in 1814 to ascend Chesapeake Bay and burn the capitol.

This had not been the case a generation earlier, when the American colonies had been able to make good their independence in warfare against England simply because the French navy, allied with the colonists, overcame the English navy off our shores. But by 1814 the French, under Napoleon, had turned their backs on the Atlantic and given up any ambition to make it serve them. They had surrendered it to England, which exercised a now unchallenged sway over it.

If, then, the Atlantic constituted a barrier after 1815, protecting the New World from the Old, it was only because it was under the naval domination of an Old World power which made it a matter of general policy, in its own interests, to protect the independence of the New World. Our real shield was not the Atlantic Ocean but the English navy. By one of the greatest and most significant strategic misconceptions in modern history, however, we Americans universally came to believe that it was the ocean in and of itself. We recognized no dependence on England at all. As a matter of national pride we would have scorned to acknowledge such a dependence. God had made the ocean to safeguard the independence of the chosen land. Even England was held helplessly at bay by it.

This was not only true when Lincoln was a young man, when he could make, unchallenged, the remarkable statement which I quoted in the first chapter. It was true, still, when I was a young man. In the period between the First and Second World Wars, when isolationism enjoyed an ascendency among us Americans, and when it was considered patriotic to be anti-British, the common mind of America appeared virtually agreed that the mere existence of the Atlantic Ocean rendered us independent of any balance of power in Europe, that it afforded in itself a protection which would be unaffected by the extinction of England or by the rise of a militaristic and aggressive Germany to hegemony in the Old World. Even if an aggressive Germany should conquer France and the British Isles, the worst she could do would be to snarl at us in impotent frustration across the impassable Atlantic. To those who thought this way, and it was surely a majority of the Americans who had any opinion at all, the United States had, out of a quixotic chivalry, made a terrible mistake in 1917, when it went to the rescue of the English and the French—returning across the ocean to the Old World in disregard of its own properly independent national interests. Any of us who protested that our security depended on British sea power was likely to be regarded as a soft-headed Anglophile. The English, he might be told, were looking after themselves, not us (which was perfectly true), and we ought to learn to do likewise. Hadn't our forefathers succeeded in throwing the English out of our continent—at any rate south of Canada?

So, again, examining the divergence between the dream and the reality, we see the classic ingredients for the tragedy of human history.

IV • The chief point I have made so far is that the sense of escape which attended the formation of the American nation is one of the prime causes of the isolationist impulse that has played so great a role in the development of American foreign policy. This is simple and logical. It seems plausible. But is it entirely true? Is human nature really as simple as that? Does the human mind have such a crude and monolithic character? Can it simply reverse itself, once and for all time, when the gears are shifted? Is it really possible for people, constituted as they are, to break with the past like this, by one act of severance to reject it forever?

I suggest that it is not. The endless challenge and the fascination of historical studies lies in the fact that all the great generalizations are true and, at the same time, are not true. Simplicity and complexity dwell together, combining, I have no doubt, to form some grand consistency beyond the reach of human thought, but conflicting with that "foolish consistency" which Emerson declared to be "the hobgoblin of little minds."

The sense of escape felt by the population of America, in its formation and growth, is a massive fact making for isolationism. Another fact, less massive but great and substantial, is the persistent affinity of the American people for the respective lands from which they or their ancestors came. And in the latter-day history of the United States this affinity, even more than the sense of escape, has made for isolationism. Thus truth is found among contradictions; it emerges from the accommodation of opposites; and any conscientious interpretation of human history becomes an exercise in the representation of paradox. The human mind, itself, is never consistent in any narrow sense. It is always composed of contraries, a living paradox in which love and hatred, sympathy and antipathy, the spirit of mercy and the impulses of cruelty, humility and pride, are identical or seek a common reconciliation. It is quite possible for a man to resent being identified as a national of his abandoned country at one moment, and to resent equally, the next moment, any slight cast upon it. It is possible to love mankind so much that one hates people. The reason why history is marked by paradox is that human nature, itself, is endlessly paradoxical.

Let me begin with an introductory sample. I said that the Pilgrim Fathers came to America to escape the corruption of the world they left behind them. That is true only as far as it goes. Unable to practice their religion in England, the Pilgrims emigrated in 1608 to Holland. Here they found what they wanted, religious freedom. But as the years passed they continued to be discontented, and a principal reason for their discontent was that, living in Holland, they were bound eventually to lose their character as Englishmen. A new generation would grow up that was no longer English. It was largely to avoid this denationalization that the Pilgrims in 1620 changed their place of refuge from the Netherlands to lands in which they would once more dwell within the circle of the English crown.

Were the Pilgrim Fathers escaping from England? Surely they were. But they were also returning to it. They were breaking their ties, and they were reaffirming their allegiance. The theory of escape is true, and it is not true.

This paradox is repeated everywhere. I daresay that at no point in the history of the thirteen American colonies does one

35

find such frequent assertions of loyalty to the Crown as in the period leading up to 1776, when the colonists, straining against it increasingly, finally broke with it. This is the nature of man, and history must take account of it.

With so much by way of introduction, let me now look at how the American population actually was supplied by the Old World over the period from 1606 to the end of the nineteenth century—and look at it in terms of the attitudes that influenced American foreign policy.

We begin, in 1625, with something under two thousand Englishmen, nine-tenths of them in Virginia, one-tenth in New England. During the next century the Dutch settle in the intervening area, on Manhattan Island, along the river discovered by Hendrick Hudson and named after him, in the Delaware Valley. One finds Swedes settling on the Delaware, Rhinelanders and Palatines (the ancestors of our present "Pennsylvania Dutch") in the hills of what is now Pennsylvania. The Huguenot refugees alight at scattered points from Massachusetts to South Carolina after having been flushed from France by the Revocation of the Edict of Nantes. With the triumph of the Anglican Church in England's Revolution of 1688, and the deposition of the Stuart dynasty, dissenters and Jacobites from Scotland and Northern Ireland begin to swarm in, escaping from the alien or hostile authorities who had made the conquest of their native land. When, in 1704, the English Parliament passes an act barring Presbyterians from public office, they come to America, where they suffer no such bars. In 1710, again, more than three thousand German Palatines, made homeless by the War of the Spanish Succession, are resettled in the general vicinity of New York. Through most of the eighteenth century come successive increments of Scotch-Irish or Germans, fleeing from persecution, high rents, or excessively onerous restrictions of one sort or another. Whenever Ireland has a famine, up goes the American population. Fourteen hundred settlers come all in a lump from Minorca, Livorno, and Greece in 1768, establishing a colony in Florida and eventually dispersing. By 1790 the population of the erstwhile English colonies, now newly federated as the United States of America, have a total population of something under four million—still hardly more than half the population, over this large area, of the present city of New York, though half their history up to the present has already elapsed. Sixty per cent of it is English; almost 78 per cent is English, Scotch, and Irish combined. The next largest percentage figure, German, is only 8.6.

But now begins the great movement from the coastal plains of North America westward. The barrier of the Appalachian Mountains gives way before the pressure of population. The Mississippi gives way. Across the ocean from Europe, packed into their ships, come immigrants from all nations, landing in Boston, New York, Philadelphia, Baltimore, or Charleston, quite overwhelming the original population, proceeding to fan out, swarming over the mountains, pushing the frontier westward. Europe is spilling over and the empty spaces of North America are beginning to fill up. The nineteenth century has arrived, the age of the falling death rate, and population pressures will soon have the effect of leaving no habitable part of our globe uninhabited. Those who spill across the ocean are the marginal people, the people who have found themselves pushed out by the old societies. Persecution of Jews and other minorities, the denial of opportunity, or economic frustration, bring millions to America from Germany, Russia, Poland, Austria-Hungary, the Slavic countries, and Italy, as the nineteenth century draws toward its end and the twentieth comes in. These refugees, figuratively and sometimes literally, fall on their knees when they reach port, thanking God for having brought them safely to this new land, where some now expect to see the streets paved with gold. The welcoming torch held aloft, night and day, by the Statue of Liberty in New York harbor represents the new freedom and the new abundance. It stands as the equivalent of St. Peter at the gates of Heaven, presiding over the portals of Utopia, over the gateway to the American Dream.

"This immigration from the Old World to the New," say Morison and Commager, "represents the greatest folk movement in history, ancient or modern."[1] The population of 1790 has doubled by about 1815. It has tripled ten years later, quadrupled in another ten years. By 1870 it has increased tenfold, and from now on the decennial increment for sixty years rises from eleven or twelve million to seventeen million. But by about 1890 the frontier has already disappeared, the whole land has been brought under rule, and after World War I the bars of the law are raised against further mass immigration.

This increase of population represents immigration and domestic procreation alike. For the decade from 1820 to 1830 the immigration contributes somewhat less than 130,000 to a total of three and a quarter million, or 4 per cent. In the 1870's it contributes almost two and a half million to a total of eleven and a half million, or almost 22 per cent. In the first decade of the present century it contributes almost eight and a quarter million to a total increment of seventeen million, a jump to almost 50 per cent of the total increase. Picture, now, one immigrant arriving for every two children born in the United States. In this decade immigration reaches the record of 1,285,-349 in a single year, 1907. It is interesting to note that seven years later, in the historic year 1914, this record is almost equaled by one million two hundred and eighteen immigrants who must have thanked their lucky stars to have escaped from Europe at that moment, and who may have been less than eager to go back and participate in its turbulent affairs.

So the population of the United States increases by immigration and by the procreation of immigrants or their children far more than by the proliferation of the early settlers. The old population is quite overwhelmed in the second half of the nineteenth and the first quarter of the twentieth centuries.

Where does all this new population come from? We have seen

[1] *Op. cit.*, II, p. 175.

a rich contribution of Germans and Scotch-Irish in the eighteenth century. In the eighty years from 1820 to 1900 almost four million Irishmen arrive, more than ten for every Scotchman. (Incidentally, the population of the Irish Republic and North Ireland together was hardly over four million in the mid-1950's.) England sends us almost two million of her population; the three Scandinavian countries a million and a half. But the record immigration comes from Germany: five million. In the entire period of the nineteenth century and the first half of the twentieth, the German immigration is distinctly the most important, in its numbers and in terms of its impact on the foreign policy of the United States during a century that saw America twice drawn into great coalition wars against "the old country."

What we have, here, is two periods of immigration. The first, from the beginning of the seventeenth to the end of the eighteenth century, fills the eastern seaboard with a population in which the stock of the British Isles is overwhelmingly preponderant. The second, spanning the nineteenth century, represents settlement across the Appalachian Mountains, in the Middle West, predominantly by German immigrants who reinforce the numbers of eastern Americans moving westward and who establish large Germanic colonies across the northern part of the area, from Ohio to the Dakotas. But Russians, Poles, Slavs, Czechs, and others are also well represented. The inflowing Irish, with their anti-British tradition, take to the cities and come to dominate municipal politics in parts of the East. Toward the end of the nineteenth century the flow from eastern and southern Europe, from Italy, Greece, and the Balkans, begins to be more prominent.

All this produces a problem of assimilation. Those who are already Americans are concerned that the newcomers be promptly Americanized. The newcomers are also determined to transform themselves into Americans, if only because of the pressure upon them by those who came earlier. Remember that they are escaping from purgatory into the American Dream. Assimilation takes place at a remarkable rate, Germans, Poles, or Italians becoming typical Yankees in hardly more than a generation. This is less true where you get mass settlement and concentration, as among rural communities of Germans or Scandinavians in the Middle West, or of Italians or Jews in the big cities. But the homogeneity of the American mind, considering this demographic history, is remarkable. It has long been noted, for example, that the popularity rating of coast-to-coast radio programs (and I suppose it applies to television as well) does not vary appreciably from one part of the country to another. The inhabitants of the Northwest have the same attitudes and tastes as the inhabitants of the Southeast, three or four thousand miles away. It appears, at times, that the dynamics of assimilation may threaten an excessive standardization or uniformity of the American mind, that the pressure for conformity may go too far.

One effect of the drive to assimilate is the emphasis on Americanism as the prime virtue of Americans. We are proud of that Americanism which, by definition, we alone have. Another and related effect may be noted in a tendency to regard the quality of foreignness or any features of foreign culture as a sort of malady to be overcome as quickly as possible. It is too bad that foreigners should be foreign, that they should have foreign ways, but if they will escape to America we can cure them. Out of our native kindliness we have been doing just that for many years now, and we are expert at it.

This, in a sense, is a counterpart of the European belief that Americans are barbarians. Where nationalism prevails, nations always tend to regard one another with pity, contempt, or resentment.

The subject of immigrant attitudes toward the old country and the new has been discussed most shrewdly by the American historian, Marcus L. Hanson, in a paper called "The Problem

40

of the Third-Generation Immigrant."[2] The sons and daughters
of immigrants had rough going. They were mocked and criticized for the foreign accent in their speech or for their foreign
ways. At the same time—and this slightly qualifies part of
what I have said—they were under conservative pressure from
their parents in the home. "Even the immigrant father who
compromised most willingly in adjusting his outside affairs to
the realities that surrounded him insisted that family life, at
least, should retain the pattern that he had known as a boy.
Language, religion, customs and parental authority were not
to be modified simply because the home had been moved four
or five thousand miles to the westward. . . . How to inhabit
two worlds at the same time was the problem of the second
generation."

"That problem," says Mr. Hanson, "was solved by escape.
As soon as he was free economically . . . the son struck out for
himself. He wanted to forget everything," the foreign language,
the religion, the family customs. He wanted to get away from
the old environment into a new and wholly American environment in which everyone would look upon him as a perfectly
good "hundred per cent American." You would not find such a
man showing allegiance to the old country, but you would be
very likely to find him expressing contempt for anything that
was not American, or that was "unAmerican." He would be
against alliances with foreign countries. In other words, he
would be an emotional isolationist.

To return to Mr. Hanson, however, and to the *third* generation which is the topic of his paper: the son of the son of the
immigrant. "Anyone," he writes, "who has the courage to codify
the laws of history must include what can be designated 'the
principle of third-generation interests.' The principle is applicable in all fields of historical study. It explains the recurrence
of movements that seemingly are dead. . . . The theory is

[2] This originally appeared in 1938 as one of the Augustana Historical Society
Publications and has now been reprinted in Edward N. Saveth's *Understanding
the American Past* (Boston, 1954).

derived from the almost universal phenomenon that what the son wishes to forget the grandson wishes to remember." While the second generation is generally not minded to study history, the third generation is. The grandson is completely American, without any traces of foreign origin left. He does not have to protect himself from the scorn of his neighbors. He does not have to take a defensive attitude or pretend that he is different from what he is. Typically, he has not only become an American but he has prospered. Now a substantial landowner or merchant, he "looks about him and says: 'This prosperity is our achievement, that of myself and of my fathers; it is a sign of the hardy stock from which we have sprung; who were they and why did they come?' "[3]

So the grandson picks up, again, the now exotic thread of the past which his father had dropped. He looks back sentimentally upon the family history and the old country which he has never seen, idealizing it. If he can find time for a vacation in Europe, he is likely to search out the old family graveyard and the town records in Bavaria, or Poland, or Slovenia. He may see if he can find any relatives still living there, perhaps old people who will throw up their hands in surprise that this rich American should be the great-nephew of old So-and-So, dead now these many years. Such a third-generation American is not likely to vote in favor of having the United States join any international combination against what he thinks of affectionately as "the old country."

We have accepted the fact that the second generation's desire to forget its past leads to isolationism. Does it not follow that the pride which, by contrast, the succeeding generations take in their foreign past is adverse to isolationism? Indeed it does. And the descendants of two or more generations in America vastly outnumber the second-generation isolationists. A country thus populated by immigration ought to be the reverse of isolationist, once the second generation no longer predominates.

[3] Saveth, *op. cit,* pp. 478-79.

42

In keeping with the paradoxical nature of history, however, the very loyalty which these descendants of immigrants feel toward "the old country" may make an isolationist foreign policy all but imperative.

The best example I know is to be found in isolationist Switzerland, with its population divided among those with French, German, or Italian cultural affinities. In this context I quote the following from an article entitled "Switzerland in Present-Day Europe" by Professor Jacques Freymond:[4] "The Swiss have learned to know the peculiar conditions of Swiss neutrality, conditions which have not been imposed on them from abroad, but which arise out of the opposition of interests and the conflict of religions in the bosom of the ancient Confederation. They recall that on this neutrality their unity, and therefore their national existence, has depended, during the First World War as well as during the seventeenth and eighteenth centuries. . . . [The great majority of the Swiss have concluded] that neutrality is one of the premises of their national unity. One of the first consequences of abandoning their neutrality would be . . . a major domestic crisis. . . . The country would, in such circumstances, find itself divided, where today it is closely united."

One might also cite the experience of Argentina in World War II. After the Axis attack at Pearl Harbor, Argentina had international obligations with which a policy of neutrality could hardly be reconciled. Swiss neutrality has been accepted by all for more than a century. But Argentina had aligned herself. She had made commitments. She had pledged herself to solidarity with the other American republics, including the United States. She had agreed to respond to any such attack as took place at Pearl Harbor as if it had been an attack directly on herself. Yet, when the time came, Argentina adopted a policy of neutrality that was actually benevolent to the Axis powers, and she persisted in that policy, in spite of great pressure from

[4] Translated from *Réforme*, Paris, No. 534, June 11, 1955.

43

her neighbors in the American Hemisphere, until after the defeat of Italy. For a major proportion of the Argentine population was of Italian descent, with third-generation loyalties to the ancestral land. These loyalties conflicted with the vital strategic interests and the obligations of Argentina in the international arena. Her interests and obligations pulled her one way, her Italianate population pulled her the other. So she remained neutral until after the elimination of Italy from the war ended this particular dilemma.

The existence of a large American population with third-generation affinities for Great Britain has obviously not made for American isolationism or neutrality in the twentieth century. Here the affinities have been in harmony with the strategic situation. Personal loyalty and national interests have marched together. But the existence of a large American population with third-generation affinities for Germany has given rise to such a conflict between loyalty and national interest as makes for non-participation or neutrality. For ambitious and tyrannical German rulers have twice in this century threatened the security of all the Atlantic nations, and our national interest has impelled us to take arms against the threat. Interest, here, has countered third-generation loyalty and, in the upshot, has won out. But the isolationist sentiment that delayed our action, in both instances, until the eleventh hour, coincided essentially with the nostalgic loyalties of those beyond the second generation of descent from German immigrants.

Finally, I quote again from that plea of Senator Borah for a policy of isolation which I quoted in the first chapter. "This country has within her boundary," said the Senator, "people from almost every land under the sun, still conscious under certain conditions of the 'mystic chords of memory.' Every civilization has made its contribution to the American civilization. How easy to transfer the racial antipathies and political views and controversies of the Old World into our very midst. Once abandon our policy of aloofness from European controversies,

44

and we bring these European controversies into the American home and into our national life."[5]

It is no coincidence that Theodore Roosevelt, the great activist in American politics, the opponent of isolation and the advocate of participation all over the world, should have inveighed passionately, time and again, against what he contemptuously called "hyphenated Americans," Americans with loyalties divided between the United States and the country of their forefathers. For the existence of these Americans was a prime factor in enforcing a policy of isolation.

Samuel Lubell, some years ago, made a study of modern isolationist sentiment in the United States, the results of which appear in his book, *The Future of American Politics*.[6] "By far the strongest common characteristic of the isolationist-voting counties," he writes, "is the residence there of ethnic groups with a pro-German or anti-British bias. Far from being indifferent to Europe's wars, the evidence argues that the isolationists actually were oversensitive to them." Mr. Lubell goes on to question the survival of any powerful isolationist sentiment in the United States under present circumstances. "If Germany were overrun by the Red Army," he asks, "would the German-Americans favor a policy of not 'intervening in Europe's quarrels'?" He then answers himself: "None of the ethnic resistances which obstructed our getting into war with Germany would be raised against war with Russia. On the contrary, they probably would obstruct the making of peace if a settlement with the Soviets ever became possible."[7]

So we may make a distinction between what might roughly be called "ideological isolationism," based on a sort of ideological distaste for the Old World as a whole, and the ethnic isolationism which we find Mr. Lubell analyzing. Mr. Lubell recognizes but tends to discount the ideological isolationism, the isolationism which I have identified with our historic American

[5] *Foreign Affairs*, Vol. 12, No. 2, Jan., 1934, p. ix.
[6] New York, 1952, p. 132.
[7] *Ibid.*, pp. 154-5.

sense of escape, and I daresay that it has diminished markedly in the present century, perhaps to the point where it is not of major importance today. But I note how the Franco-British military adventure in Egypt, during the fall of 1956, brought forth from such right-wing Republicans as Senator Knowland statements that evoke, once more, the traditional and almost legendary bases of American isolationism. Again the American people were offered, in the form of England and France, the spectacle of the wicked and imperialistic Europeans with whom they had better not be involved.

However, the Senator Knowlands do seem to be speaking for a minority opinion of constantly lessening importance in our day. Ethnic isolationism has undoubtedly gained in proportion to ideological isolationism in this century, but there is mutual support and the deep currents of traditional thinking do not die easily. Chaos in Europe or European political recalcitrance on a large scale, from the American point of view, would undoubtedly bring these currents to the surface and show that they are still running. However, if one wants to know why it was that, in 1947, the United States finally abandoned the policy of isolation, one must certainly give substantial weight, among the several reasons, to the facts that it was now the Soviet Union which had come to loom as the threat to the Atlantic nations, that we had no Russian population with third-generation affinities for this successor to the Czarist Empire, and that we did have a large population of third-generation descendents of immigrants from those Baltic, Balkan, and other east European nations which had fallen beneath the power of Soviet Russia. Here, again, loyalty and national interest marched together, with loyalty lending an emotional force to our policy which, at times, threatened to push us into what might have been an excessive degree of participation or involvement.

V • There is no relation between ethnic isolationism—the isolationism that addresses itself only to particular and transient events, the isolationism that is only a tactic—and philosophical isolationism, the isolationism in principle, which was predicated on the American Dream. The ethnic isolationism was fortuitous. It was evoked by a particular coincidence of circumstances, domestic and international, which happened to repeat itself twice in this century but which no longer appears to be in prospect.

By contrast, the philosophical isolationism was profound and meaningful. It represented the purpose for which America was created. It represented the national outlook, the dream of Utopia which had brought so large and hopeful a population across the seas from the Old World. Therefore, the passing of this traditional isolationism, in its degree, can mean nothing less than the defeat of the dream. It represents that triumph of reality over the ideal which we see repeated over and over throughout history. It re-enacts, in other words, the tragedy of history.

America, now, is no longer to be conceived of as Utopia, the Land of Peace and Plenty, the Paradise set apart by God for the salvation of the elect—perhaps eventually of all mankind. America is no longer Noah's Ark lifted above the Flood by God's

47

mercy. America has become entangled in the toils of international power politics, of this sordid preoccupation which it had been her whole purpose to avoid. The gulf of ocean has failed her and she finds herself no longer on another planet but sharing, instead, the common doom of mankind. The price of original sin is hers to pay too. Isolationism has become impossible. Utopia has been absorbed into the corrupt community of the world. *Finis* is written on the American Dream.

At this point I had better make some distinctions. In the first place, it is clear that whether American isolationism has passed away or not, American isolation is over. If that isolation ever was possible, it has become physically impossible today. Hydrogen bombs can be flung upon our cities from Europe or Asia; and the air we breathe could be poisoned from far outside our borders. What has happened to our position, in a sense, is what happened to the position of the medieval castle and the walled town when artillery was developed. They became obsolete. Not only did they become obsolete in themselves, but along with them the feudal way of life and the chivalric ideal became obsolete. Gunpowder not only knocked down walls, it knocked down philosophies and ideals as well. It destroyed the immunity of the noble knight from the attacks of the basely born who did not share his code of ethics; and thereby it destroyed that code of ethics. It substituted the ethics of Machiavelli for the ethics of Bayard.

America, too, has lost such protection as it once had. Our own navy or a friendly navy dominating the Atlantic cannot intercept the high-flying ballistic missiles. We no longer have a wall behind which we can organize our domestic life to suit ourselves and approach our ideal way of life. The world, now, can enter our domain at will. Consequently, we must go outside to deal with it. We have been forced from our fortress now and are a part of the great world, sharing its good and its bad, its successes and its failures.

We must make some distinction, however, between the total loss of our isolation and the degree in which we may have

48

abandoned our isolationism. The abandonment of isolationism should follow logically upon the loss of isolation; but logic is never supreme over the human mind, and in any case it needs time to produce its effect. There is always a lag between new realities and the logical conclusions which men draw from them, however obvious the logic may later appear to be.

If we want to understand the present attitudes of Americans, we should not look at the situation that confronts us today but at the situation which challenged us yesterday. I have no doubt that our school children, learning American history, still learn the lesson of our successful escape. They learn about the oppressions of King George III, and how we drove his redcoats out of our land so that we could establish liberty within it. They learn about our successful struggle to disentangle ourselves from the dynastic rivalries, the power politics, and the constant wars of European sovereigns. An image of the Old World, contrasting with the New, becomes fixed in their minds. On the other hand, the magnitude of recent changes has not yet been properly mastered by the historians for inclusion in grade-school texts. This is as it should be and I make no complaint. We all understand the past better than the present and we must wait, consequently, for the present to become past. But we have here a fact that explains the lag in drawing conclusions from the present.

The loss of our physical isolation, however, is not new. It has been increasingly manifest for some two generations now. I shall have later occasion to deal with the revolutionary events that, as early as the 1890's, changed America's position in the world. Let it suffice here to say that the long sway of the British navy over the oceans was, at that time, coming to an end and we, ourselves, almost fortuitously, acquired an empire overseas that was bound to involve us in the world's affairs. At the time, however, only a handful of persons understood this.

The First World War gave a thumping demonstration of the fact that we were not isolated, convincing enough people to set off, among us, a debate which lasted for a score of years, until the Second World War. But it was still possible to say that we need not have become involved in the first war. Only with the attack on Pearl Harbor in the second war did a clear preponderance of our people come to accept the fact that isolation had become impossible. The hydrogen bomb and intercontinental ballistic missiles have since tended to complete our education.

American isolation, such as it was, having died about the turn of the century, our traditional isolationism has been in decline ever since. It has been in a decline promoted by the strategic realities of the shrinking world in which we live. But there is another major factor as well, I think. It is the disappearance of the contrast between the Old World and the New, that contrast on which our philosophical isolationism was based. Generations have passed, now, since Europe has been a continent enthralled by powerful dynastic lords whose personal ambitions and mutual rivalries were the cause of war. Politically, Europe has rather generally followed the lead of the United States, developing democracy and popular self-government. It has come to know other evils, but the Louis XIV's and the George III's are no longer to be found on the scene.

On the other hand, America, itself, is no longer a virgin continent. It has lost that innocence which we thought of as a precondition of Utopia. It is no longer what Sir Thomas More or Turgot or Rousseau had in mind. It, too, now, has been hardened and scarred by the impress of history. Today it is crowded by restless masses of people; its skies are darkened by the smoke of factory chimneys; through the North American night in which Audubon once listened to migrating geese one hears the roar of the trucks on the highway. A forest of television aerials has taken the place of the aboriginal forest. The land has at last been civilized, urbanized, macadamized. And the civilization which has transformed it is essentially the same civilization which we find in Europe. What we have, in fact, is one area of civilization interrupted by some ocean that hardly impedes communication. Where, then, is the contrast which so impressed our ancestors, on both sides of the ocean, with the possibility of realizing the Utopian dream? It is gone, and with it the main philosophical reason for our isolationism.

But the American people are not an absolutely homogeneous mass, in spite of the pressures for standardization of which the need to assimilate immigrants has been such an important cause. There is a spectrum of American opinion from total isolationism at one extreme to the advocacy of world government at the other. Moreover, and perhaps more important, there are the inner strains and conflicts, which may manifest themselves within the mind of one individual, between the logic of our present situation and the atavistic or nostalgic impulses that go with our heritage. No one can understand our attitudes toward international affairs without understanding this conflict.

In the first chapter, I mentioned that Russia, historically, has been torn by an inner conflict over the question whether she was a representative of European civilization or a quasi-Asiatic nation that stood outside the frontiers of Europe. Throughout the history of America we see the same dilemma; and just as we may still see it in Russia today, so we may still see it in America. Are we a member of the European family of nations? Are we a European nation? Do we belong to that Western civilization which is nothing more than European civilization writ large, European civilization expanded beyond the borders of Europe? Or did we escape from it to found our own American civilization, which is distinguished by the contrast which it makes with the old European civilization? Did we or did we not escape?

Considerations of our internal American geography have something to do with the degree in which we feel, or have in the past felt, an identity or lack of identity with the civilization of Europe. Though this can be and generally is exaggerated, it is probably true that one finds more identification with Europe among the inhabitants of the eastern seaboard than among the inhabitants of the West. But there may be more fundamental reasons than distance for this. Up to this point I have argued as if the historic escape from Europe was completed when the refugee landed on the western shores of the Atlantic Ocean, our own eastern seaboard. But I could make just as good a case for it that the escape really took place when the refugee crossed the Appalachian mountain ranges into the inner wilderness of North America, leaving the coastal area behind him. The eastern seaboard, the coastal plain that is confined between the Appalachian Mountains and the sea, remained for centuries bound to Europe and to European ways. As a group of agricultural communities which did not even pretend to self-sufficiency, its population depended on European industrial production and on European markets for the sale of its own products. Because the East bordered the sea and preoccupied itself with maritime commerce it had much of the cosmopolitanism that such circumstances imply—and this is still true today. The men and women of Virginia, the men and women of New York or Massachusetts, wore European clothes, whether denims or silks and satins, whether three-cornered hats or "stovepipes."

But those who crossed the Appalachians and cleared the land beyond quickly lost their European contacts, their direct economic dependence on Europe, and even their European education. Their lines of communication with the past and with what lay behind them (the same thing) became tenuous. The point where isolation really began, then, was at the Appalachian barrier.

"At first," wrote Frederick Jackson Turner, "the frontier was the Atlantic coast. It was the frontier of Europe in a very real sense. Moving westward, the frontier became more and more American. As successive terminal moraines result from successive glaciations, so each frontier leaves its traces behind it, and when it becomes a settled area the region still partakes of the frontier characteristics. Thus the advance of the frontier has meant a steady movement away from the influence of Europe, a steady growth of independence on American lines. And to study this advance, the men who grew up under these conditions, and the

52

political, economic, and social results of it, is to study the really American part of our history.[1]

Mr. Turner's "terminal moraines" are still visible today. One such moraine may be found in the environs of the present city of Washington, located as it is on the fall line of the Potomac River, the limit of navigation. Below Washington the Potomac is a stately river, an aristocratic river, broad, placid, cultivated, and refined. From its spreading shores carefully tended green-swards sweep up to the mansions of the gentry on the upper slopes overlooking it—the Mount Vernons and the Gunston Halls. Here colonial ladies and gentlemen in powdered wigs were served on silver plate and followed the latest fashions across the Atlantic. The shipping from European shores came past their front lawns on its way in and out.

But face up the Potomac from Washington instead and a different scene presents itself. Here the river is a wild cataract between wooded mountain gorges. Those who cleared the bits of flatland here and there along these upper reaches were never gentry. They were, as they are today, American dirt farmers who never saw a ship coming from Europe. Instead of satin breeches they wore buckskins; instead of tricorns they wore racoon-skin caps. Here you get into the land, not of the Fairfaxes and Washingtons and Lees, but of the Daniel Boones and Davy Crocketts. The mountains rise above Washington, ridge after ridge, through what is now West Virginia, to Cumberland Gap, where one looks down into the interior of the continent, into what was once the wild Northwest Territories, into what is now the Middle West. Communications to the rear are broken at Cumberland Gap, at this watershed. The only highways, here as elsewhere, are rivers, and beyond the Gap they all flow westward and southward, into the Mississippi, the mouth of which lies within Spanish America, pointing toward Mexico and the Indies. On the coastal plain people still face east, toward Europe, and have their communications in that direction. Beyond the Appa-

---

[1] "The Significance of the Frontier in American History," 1893—in *The Turner Thesis, op. cit.*, pp. 2-3.

lachians they face away from the coastal plain and away from Europe alike. Here they are on their own. Here they forget, at last, that they are Europeans—if they are Europeans.

It was certainly true in our earlier history, and it may remain true today, that the Americans of the eastern seaboard were more European in their thinking and their affinities than the Americans of the trans-Appalachian interior. But this difference, as I have said, was more than a function of the distance from Europe. It was a new kind of man that you got on the other side of the Appalachians, a man whose economic, social, and political interests had relatively little to do directly with Europe and even tended to throw him into conflict with the dominant groups of the eastern seaboard. I shall have something to say in a later chapter about the economic and political conflict between the old East and the new West, a conflict so profoundly based that one wonders what miracle prevented the West from splitting off altogether from the East and establishing a separate nation, as it almost did. Here, however, I shall discuss only one of the roots of the difference that was made by the crossing of the Appalachian barrier, the effect which that migration had on the character and degree of education.

I think it can be said that the more fully educated an American is, especially in history and literature, the more he feels a kinship with Europe, a personal participation in a grand common civilization reaching back to ancient Greece and Rome. For his education is bound to be essentially a European inheritance conferred upon him.

What I am doing here is simply applying to the American scene a principle of general validity. The totally uneducated man lives in a world that is bounded by his immediate physical horizons. He lives in his native valley and knows nothing of the great world beyond or of the past. He has not read books about these worlds, or attended lectures on them, or visited museums where their cultural achievements are displayed. He knows only one way of life, which is his own, and other ways of life would

54

seem to him abnormal if not perverted.

One recalls the conversation in Mark Twain's *Huckleberry Finn* between Huck, who has had some schooling, and the runaway slave, Jim, who has had none. Jim has just discovered, from something Huck said, that the French don't talk the same language as Americans.

"Why, Huck, [he says] doan' de French people talk de same way we does?"

"*No,* Jim; you couldn't understand a word they said—not a single word."

"Well, now, I be ding-busted! How do dat come?"

"*I* don't know; but it's so. I got some of their jabber out of a book. S'pose a man was to come to you and say Polly-voo-franzy —what would you think?"

"I wouldn' think nuffn; I'd take en bust him over de head— dat is, if he warn't white. I wouldn't 'low no nigger to call me dat."

"Shucks, it ain't calling you anything. It's only saying, do you know how to talk French?"

"Well, den, why couldn't he say it?"

"Why, he *is* a-saying it. That's a Frenchman's *way* of saying it."

"Well, it's a blame ridicklous way, en I doan' want to hear no mo' 'bout it. Dey ain' no sense in it."

The totally uneducated man, then, may hear rumors of another world beyond his horizon, in which people speak strange languages and practice abnormal customs, but his reaction to that other world is almost bound to reflect that fear of the unknown which expresses itself in antipathy. Like Jim, he is outraged by the thought of it.

The world to which such a man's loyalties are naturally confined is the small world that is bounded by his physical horizons. He may even consider the people who live in the next valley, across the mountains, as foreigners and enemies. There are people in the mountains of Tennessee still, I believe, who have such a restricted allegiance. Their loyalty is to their immediate community, the only one they know, rather than to the United States of America. Americans who come from other parts of the country are not regarded as compatriots.

I suppose the same thing might have been true until recently, or may even be largely true still today, in parts of Europe. Imagine a Frenchman living at some isolated spot in the Vosges Mountains, unlettered and unread. He knows nothing of François Villon, of Racine, of Voltaire, of Baudelaire, or of Sartre. He doesn't know who the English are and he has hardly more than heard of Jeanne d'Arc. He could not tell you who the President of France was. This hypothetical Frenchman, perhaps, is less a European than he is simply brute man. His country, too, does not extend beyond the valley in which he lives. Contrast him, now, with the learned member of the Académie Française who has received, in his upbringing and education, the heritage of European civilization, from its antiquities to its developments in the most recent past. Such a man is likely to feel an allegiance to Europe that our hypothetical peasant cannot feel to anything greater than his parish in the Vosges.

What, after all, is the function of education except to transmit to successive generations this larger heritage of a common civilization? Education is the basic conservative force in any society, large or small. It is the vehicle of civilization, which does not survive without it. It imparts a larger allegiance to supplement local ties. Can one not lay it down as a rule that the less educated a man is the smaller the world in which he lives, both as regards space and time; the less educated he is the more he is confined to the present and the immediate?—and, conversely, that the more truly educated a man is the larger the world in which he lives, for other worlds of the past are opened up to him and other worlds in the present? I suspect that if we ever have the "One World" of our idealists, or of our ideals, it will not be by the devising of international lawyers and constitution makers but by the education of all mankind.

The colonists on the eastern seaboard of America were educated as Europeans. The language they spoke and the books

they read were European. The Puritans, especially, had emphasized education. In secondary schools Latin and Greek were
taught. The boys at Harvard "studied the same seven arts and
three philosophies as at Oxford, Cambridge, or Dublin, using
the same Latin manuals of logic and metaphysics, Greek texts,
Euclids, and 'Hebrew in Twenty-four Hours,' as in European
universities."[2] The descendants of these Puritans and of the
Virginia settlers consulted, in philosophy, Montesquieu and
Locke. In poetry they recited, I suppose, Shakespeare, Milton,
Alexander Pope. In law they read Vattel. The study of Greek
and Latin greatly enlarged their world, and they reverenced a
biblical text drawn up under the supervision of a European
monarch and officially authorized by him. They played European music on their European flutes, viols, and harpsichords;
they danced European dances. And like true colonials everywhere they were in most respects more conservative than the
people at home, more jealous of the cultural heritage, more
insecure with respect to it, and therefore more determined to
transmit it intact to the new generations.

But the break in communications which occurred when these
people crossed the Appalachians was accompanied by a break in
education. Latin and Greek, Montesquieu and Locke, Shakespeare and Pope, Bach and Mozart, were not included in the
baggage with which they crossed the mountains. These were
all left behind on the coastal plain, together with powdered
wigs and lace handkerchiefs. "Even in the 1880's," Morison and
Commager report, "one could find in log cabins of the Kentucky
mountains calf-bound volumes of Pope and Johnson that 'great-
grandpaw toted over from old Virginny'; but that great-grand-
son could not read. The Southern pioneer often had to descend
to the redskin's level before he could rise again; . . ."[3]

Thus the break in communications at the Appalachian watershed was also a break with the past, a break with the heritage
of European civilization which the colonists had brought across

[2] Morison and Commager, *op. cit.*, I, p. 57.
[3] *Ibid.*, I, p. 365.

the ocean with them. In descending to the level of the redskins, these pioneers ceased to be European and took the first step toward becoming American. For a generation or two they commonly became illiterate, and the experience left its imprint when education came back. In their education the colonists of the East were jealously preserving their European heritage. Like the Pilgrim Fathers striving to remain Englishmen, they were striving to remain civilized Europeans. But the sons of illiterate fathers, when schooling came back, no longer regarded themselves as European. They had not this sense of heritage. The umbilical cord had been broken. They were something new, something without a past. In this sense they were the first true Americans.

VI • Education enlarges the temporal and spacial world in which man lives. An illiterate mountaineer can hardly see beyond his valley; but an Emerson regards the whole globe as his oyster. Let me apply this principle to the question whether Americans regard themselves as members of European civilization or as members of a new American civilization opposed to it. Perhaps the best way to do this is to sketch the portraits of two imaginary Americans who represent, respectively, types that are not imaginary.

One is a man born of parents who were able and disposed to give him the available educational advantages. In childhood he became familiar with London through the pages of Charles Dickens, with Paris through the pages of Victor Hugo. He learned something of English history at an early age by reading Kipling's *Puck of Pook's Hill* and *Rewards and Fairies*. These stories acquainted him with the Roman occupation of Britain, the Anglo-Saxon invasions, the Danish raids, the Norman Conquest, the development of English constitutionalism at Runnymede, the conflict between England and Spain, the Napoleonic Wars, and so forth. He learned some more English history from Kingsley's *Westward Ho!*, and the *Tale of Two Cities* introduced him to the French Revolution. *The Odyssey* was read aloud to him in translation, and in Hawthorne's *Tanglewood*

Tales he gained a further sense of the presence of ancient Greece. From books of history and legend he became familiar with such events as the defense of Thermopylae by the three hundred.

This boy had some French lessons at home or at school and was taught the Fables of La Fontaine. As he grew up he read Molière and discovered for himself Voltaire's *Candide*. He also read some Goethe, or had it thrust upon him. Shakespeare was first presented to him in the form of Lamb's *Tales from Shakespeare*, but eventually he became familiar with the plays themselves, by reading them and perhaps also by seeing them performed. Incidentally, this added something to his knowledge of English and Roman history. He knew, from the plays, who Richard II was, and Henry V. Plutarch's historic heroes, Coriolanus, Mark Antony, and Julius Caesar lived again for him. Octavian and Cleopatra became more than names. In fact, the reading of Shakespeare led to the reading of Plutarch. He also read Browning and Tennyson, acquiring from Browning the nineteenth-century Englishman's love of Italy. Then, too, he read about Charlemagne and Roland, about the heroes of the Arthurian legends, and about Robin Hood—not history, to be sure, but something that nevertheless carried a sense of the past, of the ideals which men had once held.

It is possible that the boy who grew up in these circumstances spent at least one summer vacation in Europe, visiting its historic sites, seeing its historic monuments. In museums he came to know what the Italian Renaissance was, for example, by seeing the works of Giotto, Fra Angelico, Botticelli, Verrochio, and Michelangelo. Perhaps he visited Pisa and its Leaning Tower, standing self-consciously on the very spot where Galileo once stood to conduct a scientific experiment.

In college this lad then learned his European history more formally and intensively. He studied French socialism in the nineteenth century, let us say, and wrote a paper on the career of Louis Blanc.

I need not describe him further. Here is an American who

has been brought up to the European heritage. The cord is still attached. When the possible destruction of European civilization confronts him he is deeply moved. He sees all civilization as one, and that a basically European or, as we call it today, Western civilization. When he looks at the liberal parliamentary institutions of India or Japan, for example, he sees this civilization just as clearly there as at home. If it is destroyed in Europe it will almost surely disappear everywhere, in the United States too. We Americans, as he sees it, belong to European civilization, which is the glory of the world. The educated man I have described feels an allegiance, not just to his native city, not just to New England, say, or the South, or Texas, not just to the United States, and not just to the New World. He feels an allegiance to historic Christendom. In the final analysis, if he has to make a choice between Europe and Asia, or rather that part of Asia which is in rebellion against Europe, he will feel under a compulsion, whatever the merits, to choose Europe. This, after all, is the civilization to which he belongs.

It is true that many Americans who conform to this type— perhaps I could even say typical examples of the type—have in the past shown themselves belligerent, in a nationalistic way, toward the European Old World. One thinks of John Quincy Adams, of Theodore Roosevelt, of the elder Henry Cabot Lodge. But these gentlemen did not have to make a choice between the collapse and the survival of European civilization. They assumed its survival and their relationship to it. Their differences with Europe were family differences. Essentially, their position was that of the growing son who rebels against the continued pretensions of parental authority and parental superiority. They wanted America to live its own life now. They were determined that it should make good its independence. But that determination would have been meaningless if the relationship had not been close, if the independence had been a fact. That determination also revealed the child's assurance of his parents' vigor and powers of survival.

All this has been changed now. Whether we like it or not,

61

America's relation to Europe is more like that of the grown man to his ailing parents. The educated American's ancestral tie no longer manifests itself so much in defiance, but more in the disposition to cherish and protect. I remember how many outspoken American Anglophobes, in 1940, when the survival of Britain became questionable, suddenly changed their tune and put on lapel pins (with the lion and the unicorn rampant) reading, hopefully: "There will always be an England." In many respects the relationship of dependence has been reversed, and today's educated European may feel toward America a resentment not altogether dissimilar to that which educated Americans once showed toward Europe. We share, as well as a civilization, a common human nature.

Having sketched the first of my two imagined Americans, let me now offer up the second. This man, today, might be born in either the East or the West of the United States, since the original disparity in education between the two regions disappeared generations ago. Let us say, however, that his father had been, first a ranch hand, then an oil prospector. He had made some money "wildcatting" in oil, and had increased it substantially by real estate speculation. He was proud of the wealth he had acquired and used to tell his son that he had been brought up in the best of all schools, the "School of Hard Knocks." The son was taught a suspicion of "book learning" that may, itself, have been a heritage from generations of ancestors going back to the first family pioneer who crossed the Appalachians, leaving his European schooling behind him. The boy acquired a feeling that there was something unmanly, if not unhealthy, about studying books. It was like playing the piano. His father would be proud of his accomplishments in baseball, but he would be worried if he found him taking any great interest in music—at least in good music.

In school this boy learned rudimentary reading, writing, and arithmetic. He also learned elementary American history—and the heroic history of his native state loomed as large as anything

62

else in his curriculum. When such a man thought of foreigners he might, if he came from the Southwest, think of Mexicans, whom he regarded as inferior to his own breed. If he was, say, a Texan, he might have quite a clear pattern of history in his mind by the time he had finished his schooling. Just as the United States had sent King George and his redcoats packing, so Texas had sent Santa Anna and his rabble of Mexican *soldados* packing. The two greatest men in history were George Washington and Sam Houston.

You may sometimes recognize this man, when you see him, by his clothes. Just as in Russia, which is half in Europe and half out, some Russians wear native Asiatic blouses while others wear sack suits, you will find many Americans dressing rather differently from Europeans, perhaps wearing wide-brimmed sombreros and cowboy boots.

This second type I am sketching is a "hundred per cent American." A "hundred per cent American" is one whose patriotic allegiance is exclusive. The cultivated man whom I described first may, I am sure, be a good patriot with a profound allegiance to his country. But this is not all. He also feels some ties to the civilization of which his country is one member and which includes a preponderance of foreigners. Henry Adams, for example, included Mont St. Michel and Chartres Cathedral within the circle of his loyalties. My "hundred per cent American," however, is disposed to scorn any extrapatriotic allegiance at all. He doesn't think too much of foreigners and their ways, and he'd just as soon not have anything to do with them. Like Senator Borah, he may even boast that he has never been outside the borders of the U.S.A. and doesn't intend to be. Why should any good American want to go some place else?

In the era of nationalism all countries have their share of these superpatriots, and of the xenophobia that distinguishes them. We all tend to vaunt ourselves at the expense of our neighbors, commonly equating patriotism with a scornful attitude toward foreigners. When one finds this xenophobia in the United States, however, it sometimes takes a peculiarly out-

63

spoken form for historical reasons which I have already discussed. The experience of assimilation through which our ancestors went, and which their descendants imposed on later immigrants, promoted the flag-waving kind of patriotism. There was the need to demonstrate overtly that one had broken with one's European background. During the last war, more often than not, one would find that the shops which displayed American flags in their windows were owned by people with German names. Perhaps Mr. John Jones did not feel that he had to demonstrate the fact that he was an American, but Mr. Hans Finstermacher did. This compulsion is, after all, what has made us a nation instead of a conglomeration of nationalities. But as a by-product it has set off this competition among some Americans to outdo one another in demonstrations of patriotic exclusiveness.

Thus we have the portraits of two extreme types, the educated cosmopolitan, belonging to European civilization, and the "hundred per cent American." Today one can find little if any geographical basis for the distinction which they represent. It is true that the bonds of education were loosed when the easterner crossed the Appalachian range to become a westerner. But that was a long time ago. If he descended to the cultural level of the redskin, the descent was only temporary. The break in communications was eventually repaired. Railways, which flow up and over mountain ranges, took the place of rivers as the main channels of communication. Eventually, Shakespeare and Gibbon, Victor Hugo and Dickens, Goethe and Schiller, also surmounted the Appalachian barrier and descended upon the West. Families from which literacy had disappeared for one or two generations recaptured it. Land-grant colleges were established, emphasizing the practical arts, perhaps, but adding culture as time passed. Finally great universities were founded, the equals of the best eastern universities. The proportion of highly educated people today is, I suppose, roughly even in its distribution from coast to coast, varying more with the distribution of great urban centers than with reference to the Appalachian Mountains. They cluster in Chicago and San Francisco as much as in New York or Boston.

Still, there is something in Turner's statement, which I quoted in the last chapter: "As successive terminal moraines result from successive glaciations, so each frontier leaves it traces behind it, and when it becomes a settled area the region still partakes of the frontier characteristics." In the descendants of the pioneers one finds the persistence of attitudes proper to pioneers—for example, the emphasis on what is practical, on utilitarian knowledge; the contempt of style in behavior, action, or expression—of mere manner or manners; the disdain for abstraction, generalization, and theory; the consequent suspicion of book learning; and the assumption that culture is for women, to be acquired as a social grace or an ornament.

These are, perhaps, typical attitudes of the uneducated everywhere, and they surely have their value. They inhibit, by social compulsion, the tendency of all cultural activity to become too refined, too rarefied, too precious, too abstract, too insubstantial, and too pretentious. They keep it from becoming effete, from losing virility, from abandoning the earth. They do in fact save it from mere fashion and foppery. I am glad that all Americans don't go around discussing the cosmic significance of Picasso's art or the exquisiteness of their own aesthetic sensibilities. But if the American Dream is ever realized—and it could be realized now only on a world-wide basis—it will find our population generally possessed of the breadth and maturity which one finds in the truly educated man anywhere, in Justice Oliver Wendell Holmes, say, or in George Santayana, or in Winston Churchill—to take three contrasting personalities. When that happens in the United States and everywhere else—and hardly until then—we shall have that cultural unity on which a peaceful international order, world-wide in scope, can be based.

At the beginning of this chapter the subject was isolationism. Now it is nationalism. By an easy and natural transition I have slid from the one to the other. It is significant that I should have been able to do so.

Nationalism is a universal phenomenon in our day. Indeed, most students of world history would say it is the dominant characteristic of our day, that it is, at least, the most important factor in present international relations. I find myself of the same opinion. Under the circumstances I shall not forbear to engage in some examination of it as a whole. For me to seek the explanation of nationalism in America only would be too parochial, since the phenomenon is essentially the same everywhere. If we understand it everywhere, then we shall understand it in America as well.

For most practical purposes it is enough to note that something called "the spirit of nationalism" is rampant in the world today, and to regard that spirit as a self-generated and independent fact. This demon has, in modern times, entered into peoples and moved them so powerfully that today it tends to control their actions. For strictly practical purposes we need not ask why or how this has happened. The fact that it has happened is what we have to deal with.

If we seek a deeper understanding, however, we cannot rest content with a tacit assumption that nationalism simply happened to the world without any cause, that it was not the consequence of something else. As I have already suggested indirectly, I think it is, in fact, the consequence of something else. I think it is the consequence of democracy. Nationalism is natural to that great majority of the people in every country whose education has not equipped them to feel at home in any world larger than the national state. It is the consequence of the transfer of political power to these people.

I have mentioned the inner and outer circles or boundaries of personal allegiance: the smallest that of the Tennessee mountaineer's home valley; a somewhat larger circle containing the subnational state—Tennessee itself or the Canton of Geneva; a still larger circle embracing a major section of the national territory—the South in the United States or French Switzerland;

66

a still larger circle bounding the nation-state; then perhaps a continental circle, such as defines the loyalty of some Latin Americans; and finally the circle of allegiance that embraces a world-wide civilization.

At one end of this scale the progress of popular education, which has accompanied both the growth of democracy and the improvement of communications, has tended to diminish parochial loyalties. The Tennessee mountaineer or the Vosges mountaineer has almost disappeared, if he has not in fact disappeared. At the other end of the scale, the transfer of political power, in recent times, from a cosmopolitan governing class to the rank and file of people has reduced the effectiveness of supranational or cosmopolitan thinking in government. By a falling away of parochialism at one end and of effective cosmopolitanism at the other, that median allegiance to the national state—greater than the parish and less than the civilization—that median allegiance which is consonant with the degree of education possessed by what have become the broad ruling groups of our world, has risen to dominance. Loyalty tends to be concentrated here, in the middle of the spectrum. This makes for an unprecedented degree of national unity and of international disunity alike.

Recognizing that this is true all over the world, one can see how much America is part of the world, and the world part of America, today. We all share one history; and the historian of the future may find it increasingly hard to write simply a history of Europe, or a history of India, or a history of the United States. It is all becoming world history.

We all live in the zone between legend and reality, and one of the tensions under which we labor comes from the compulsion to reconcile the two. Occasionally, however, the legend is diametrically opposed to the reality. The case I have in mind is the old Marxist doctrine that nationalism is natural to capitalist or feudal ruling groups while internationalism is natural to the masses, to the "workers of the world," to "the people." This, it seems to me, is part of the misconception of popular attitudes which has prevented the Communists, in particular, from basing their movement on popular consent. It is because "the people," from the time of the October Revolution in 1917 to the Hungarian crisis of 1956, have not reacted as Marx and Lenin were sure they would, that the Red army has had to play so much larger a role than had been projected for it. It is this contradiction between legend and reality that has made it so hard, at last, to distinguish Communist "liberation" of the people from their enslavement.

I would not have anyone think that I have a better opinion of kings than of commoners, or that I prefer the rule of a hereditary nobility to democracy. I think that every form of government is bad: monarchy by divine right, oligarchy by birth, tyranny by usurpation, the rule of a single political party, or constitutional democracy. They are all bad. They all have great evils and dangers inherent in them, and some also have their good points. My own ideal choice among these evils would be a sort of constitutional liberalism in which popular influences were dominant, perhaps, but not unchecked.

I could put this another way by saying that a prime test of any system of government is the degree in which it tends to place the direct powers of government into the hands of those best qualified—best qualified in terms of character, mental qualities, and sense of responsibility toward their fellow men. I think that by this test the record of democracy is bad, but rather less bad than that of other systems. I shall even say distinctly less bad. But I am not untroubled in this belief; because it is certain, as a matter of historic experience, that democracies easily degenerate into corruption, confusion, and impotence. Athenian democracy under Pericles was one thing; under his immediate successors, Cleon and Alcibiades, it was another. And in our own times we have seen how dangerous demagogues can rise to positions of ominous power by playing on the emotions, the prejudices, and the gullibility of masses of people who are not gifted, any more than the rest of us are, with godlike wisdom. We have seen the people entrust their supreme politi-

68

cal power to those who should not be entrusted with a toy pistol. Democracy seems to me dangerous. But then, so does every other system of government, and even more so. Therefore, on balance, and where the minimum conditions exist, I prefer democracy—or democracy, at least, of the representative variety.

But if the conduct of international relations were the sole function of government I think perhaps I would not prefer democracy.

I have felt it necessary to make this personal confession because I am now launched on a special topic that will require me to examine some of the weaknesses of democracy in comparison with what appear to be occasional advantages of aristocratic or oligarchical rule. Pointing to the weaknesses of democracy is like saying that one's wife wears a wig, which might give the impression that one does not really love her, though one had said nothing of the sort. If, then, I come to the common conclusion that an oligarchical government may be better able than a democracy to conduct its international relations in a responsible fashion, it must not therefore be assumed that, the whole balance sheet considered, I would prefer the oligarchy. Perhaps what I would prefer is something in between, democracy tempered with oligarchy, as we had it in the first generation of our American republic.[1]

[1] "So two cheers for democracy: one because it admits variety and two because it permits criticism. Two cheers are quite enough: there is no occasion to give three. Only Love, the Beloved Republic deserves that." (E. M. Forster, in *I Believe* [anthology] [London, 1940], p. 98.)

VII • The basic problem is to reconcile legend and reality in the world as it presents itself to our minds. All of us are born into the lands of legend. A small child, so far from distinguishing between legend and reality, can hardly conceive of a distinction to be made. Dragons are as real as tigers. The house is as likely to be attacked by an extraordinary giant as to be entered by an ordinary thief.

The progressive achievement of maturity represents a progress from this imagined world toward the world of reality. As the child grows up he acquires a critical faculty. He begins to ask: Is this really so? Did this really happen? Only in the most exceptional cases, however, is this process carried anywhere near to completion. Virtually all of us represent a development arrested midway. We complete our formal education and our minds cease to grow when we are still far from emerging fully into the world as it is. We remain halfway within the egg. The fact that the world of legend is easier to live in undoubtedly contributes to this premature discontinuance of the process. It takes a degree of courage and character, as well as knowledge and experience, to live by oneself in the real world—though I suspect that the real world, ultimately, is the more rewarding, if the more difficult, of the two.

One trouble with being half educated, and thus suspended

between two worlds, is that it puts the individual under psychological strains which may exceed his tolerance—and so he ends by having a nervous breakdown, or by taking to drink (which helps keep out the real world), or by going to pieces some other way.

I search my mind for the simplest and most intimate example I can find. In Anglo-Saxon societies, at least, every boy grows up with some image of ideal womanhood in his mind—the girl of his dreams. He gets this from magazine fiction, from the movies, from television—all the media by which the standard boy-meets-girl legend is fixed in his consciousness. A generation ago, if not so much today, the girl of the legend was a pure spirit, more fit for the ranks of the angels than for the grossness of life on earth. She was, of course, too good for the boy, who had in him that quality of the beast which is exclusively male—or which, at least, is lacking in nice girls. But, as the legend has it, by some miracle she consents to an earthly love, the boy is elevated by her purity, and so they live happily ever after.

In my real example the boy falls in love with a real girl, but what he sees in her is another girl, the girl of the legend. Falling in love, in this context, means the achievement of this illusion. If, now, they get married, what a strain is imposed on them both! He must be constantly striving in his own mind to retain the dream in the face of what has become an intimate and continuous contact with the reality; while she must struggle to live up to an image of herself in his mind (if not in her own as well) that does not represent what she really is. They both try to live a pretense. The consequence is that they cannot be relaxed together. They cannot be themselves. The strain between legend and reality ultimately breaks them. They fall into contention and bitterness; they are "disillusioned" with each other and with themselves; the marriage ends in failure, dashing their callow dreams into dust.

My illustration is inadequate in one respect. The legend, as I have said, can hardly survive the intimate and continuous exposure to reality that goes with marriage. In most aspects of life and society, however, reality has no such advantage. It cannot impose itself. It cannot force the victim of legend to confront it squarely and finally to acknowledge it, as he ordinarily must in marriage.

A girl I once knew, who had been reading romantic accounts of the luxuriance which makes tropical lands so spectacular, went to Mexico City on her first trip south of Cancer. Writing home to a friend, she referred in terms of awe to the "incredibly fertile and luxuriant" Valley of Mexico. When the friend replied, unkindly, that the Valley was, if not a desert, as least quasi-desert, she could only comment indignantly that it did not seem so to her. It did not seem so to her because what she saw was what she had been conditioned by fiction to expect that she would see, and the physically observable fact could not prevail against it. Only, perhaps, if she had had to make her living by growing vegetables in the Valley would she have been forced, at last, to acknowledge the reality—like the romantic boy who gets married. Most people, however, do not have to put the legend to any test so severe.

For society in general, the world of legend expresses itself in prevalent intellectual fashions and cant. What we believe in is not the observable truth but that putative image of truth which expresses itself in what everyone says is so. Something quite absurd may be universally accepted as true, at a particular time, simply because everybody says it is true, and everybody says it is true because that is the fashionable thing to say, because that is what everybody else is saying. Whoever denies it will be an object of scorn at best; at worst he will have to drink the hemlock.

Later, however, when the fashion has passed, when it has given way to new fashions, we wonder how anybody could have believed such nonsense—conveniently forgetting that at the time we believed it ourselves. It is this that makes hindsight so much more reliable than even the physical sight of our uneducated eyes.

A few years ago the program of technical assistance for the

development of the Latin American states was being justified, in Washington, by the argument that lack of economic and social development was the prime cause of Communism, or that it provided the essential conditions for the proliferation of the virus. Conversely, the greater a society's development, the more resistant it was. Now we all knew that this was true because everybody said it was true. We testified to it repeatedly in Congressional hearings, and there was no danger that we would be challenged. Yet, at the time, any examination of the reality would have suggested, at least, that something rather like its opposite might be the truth. The Latin American countries in which the Communist movement had penetrated least, or not at all, were also the least developed: Haiti, Honduras, Paraguay. The countries in which it had achieved its greatest strength were, in general, the most developed: Chile, Brazil, Mexico, Cuba.

The fact is that our societies, our governments, and we as individuals are constantly under the sway of a legendary world against which the real world can hardly prevail. Only half educated, only half matured, we live in that world and, responding to the instinct of partisanship, give our allegiance to it, so that the truth which emerges from the critical observation of reality may even, on occasion, become a sort of treason, calling for such punishment as was imposed on Socrates, on Christ, on Abelard, on Galileo, and on any number of other great figures throughout history.

It seems to me that, at least since the Middle Ages, there has been no such demonstration of the power of legend as the sway which Marxist doctrine has gained over so many minds. The masters of the international Communist movement, speaking in the name of Marxism, have been able to enslave multitudes of people while persuading observers that they were, in fact, liberating them. Making war, they have persuaded observers that it was peace. Forcibly suppressing virtually a whole people, as in Hungary, they have made it seem that the suppressed were "enemies of the people." So great is the power and

73

the magnetism of legend! So great is man's desire to believe in it! So fierce is his allegiance to it!

And this brings me back to where I was in the last chapter, when I referred to the legend that internationalism is the mark of the masses while nationalism is confined to their capitalist rulers. I suggested that, in fact, the opposite was true, that the oligarchies or governing classes of the past tended to be more cosmopolitan or international in their thinking than the masses of the people whom they governed and who represented the lower common level of education.[1] I identified the growth of nationalism with the democratic shift of political power to those who stood at this level. This, in turn, called for an examination of what education does to men, and it was essentially as an introduction to such an examination that I was moved to equate the degree of maturity in individuals with their capacity to live in the world of reality.

This equation is borne out by the degree in which the teachings of the great moral leaders have remained without effect even on those who have claimed to be their followers. The classic example is the morality of Christ, which in a test of twenty centuries has proved too sophisticated for acceptance by a Christendom made up of such semimature people as ourselves. Nothing is more prominent in the career of Jesus than his running fight with the scribes and Pharisees, with those who represented the fashionable or the established morality of society,

[1] Long before Marx, Goethe told Eckermann: "You will always find [nationalism] strongest and most violent where there is the lowest degree of culture. But there exists a degree of culture where national antagonism vanishes altogether, and where one stands, so to speak, above nations, and feels the weal or woe of a neighboring people as if it had happened to one's own" (quoted by Hans Kohn in *The Saturday Review,* June 8, 1957, p. 11). Marx's contemporary, Walter Bagehot, wrote: "Nations touch at their summits. . . . It is always the highest class which travels most, knows most of foreign nations, has the least of the territorial sectarianism, which calls itself patriotism, and is often thought to be so" (*The English Constitution,* London, 1867, p. 152). What Bagehot said was true but out of fashion, and it had no appreciable influence. What Marx said was untrue, but it conformed to the growing legend of democracy and had a revolutionary influence.

then and ever since. In what outspoken terms he denounced this pharisaical or self-righteous morality; the morality that advertises itself by the public performance of prayer; the morality that wears virtue as a robe for all to admire; the legendary and fashionable morality which assumes perfection in oneself and one's kind, wickedness in others; the morality that consequently addresses itself to the denunciation or reform of others rather than the improvement of oneself. All this, Christ said, was a false morality, the antithesis of true morality, which was represented instead by the humble publican of the parable. And so it was chiefly against the self-proclaimed men of virtue and professional moralists, not against the self-acknowledged sinners, that he preached his morality of tolerance, compassion, and humility. Yet from his time to the day in which we live, Christendom has been dominated by the very morality which he denounced so unmistakably, because his own opposed morality was too sophisticated for the generality of men. And in the claims of a self-righteous nationalism itself, in the disposition of nations to regard themselves as paragons in a world of sin and to shake their fingers at others, we see the triumph of the Pharisees, who remained alive and predominant after Christ, himself, had been crucified.

I return, now, directly to my theme. The foreign policy of a nation must address itself to the world as it is in reality, rather than to the legendary world which competes so successfully with it in men's minds. Those who make a nation's foreign policy, therefore, must be able to distinguish the reality of the situations with which they have to deal from the legend. If they deal with those situations as they are fashionably supposed to be, but as they are not in fact, then they are bound to produce such confusion and failure as is virtually the standard daily product of international relations. If their minds are governed by the prevalent legends—whether the Communist legend, or the legend of nationalism, or the legend that America is invulnerable to attack—if their minds are governed by these legends, they cannot master the challenges of reality but must, rather, succumb to the caprices of chance or to an unforeseen destiny against which they did not arm themselves. Nothing is more dangerous than for a nation to base its actions on what is fashionably held to be true, what everyone says is true. Yet this is the basis on which all nations act—in greater or less degree.

"In greater or less degree" is an important qualification, since the degree is what concerns us here. What, then, determines the degree?

I have already given my answer. What determines the degree is the degree in which those who make policy have achieved that maturity or sophistication which frees them from legend and enables them to apprehend, beyond the fog of fashion, the realities of the world in which they must make their decisions.

Until the middle of the nineteenth century, the international affairs of the European world were in the hands of men who, by their education, were Europeans more essentially than they were Frenchmen, Germans, Dutch, English, or any other nationality. They all spoke French to one another as the lingua franca of the governing classes, the language of educated Europeans everywhere, a language that (outside of France at least) excluded the lower orders. They had all been brought up on the same Latin and Greek classics; they listened to the same music, attended the same theater, read the same books, enjoyed the same scandals, made the same small talk, had the same weaknesses for much the same women, and were distinctly more loyal to their social class, which was international, than to the national societies for which they nominally spoke. There is no more outstanding example of this than the determination of the statesmen who made the Holy Alliance to work together for the suppression of the democratic elements in their own countries, elements which they regarded as alien.

It is startling in our day to note the extent to which the national identity of rulers and statesmen used to be disregarded.

It was all right in 1689 for the Dutch Stadtholder, while continuing to be Stadtholder, to take on the additional job of being England's ruler as well. With the establishment of the coalition against Louis XIV at the beginning of the eighteenth century the Duke of Marlborough became, in effect, the leading figure in Dutch domestic politics as in English. It is as if Sir Winston Churchill had been virtually Prime Minister of France as well as of England.

If family ties are more intimate than the bonds of nationality, then the sovereigns of Europe, again, were supranational. They belonged to European families which, in turn, belonged to no single nation. The House of Hapsburg was not Austrian, the House of Romanov was not Russian, the House of Bourbon was not French or Spanish, the House of Orange and the House of Hanover were not English. None of these dynasties had any single or exclusive nationality. They all had a common European cosmopolitanism based on consanguinity, the French language, a common culture, common standards of polite behavior. They and their ministries were composed of gentlemen first, nationals only second.

When Gibbon proposed that Europe be considered as "one great republic" on the basis of the common "system of arts, and laws, and manners" which distinguish Europeans from the rest of mankind,[2] he was presumably thinking of Europe as the political expression of its governing class, rather than of those politically inert elements which submitted to the sway of that governing class in each country.

What was true of the princes was essentially true of their employees, the diplomats. The diplomats, so far from being controlled by strong ties of national or dynastic loyalty, had a strong disposition to conduct themselves as mercenaries, serving whoever paid them best. Just as any sovereign might hire an army abroad—Henry VIII of England hired the Holy Roman Emperor's army, George III hired the Hessians—so the sovereign

[2] Quoted by Hans Morgenthau, *Politics among Nations* (New York, 1955), p. 194.

could and did recruit his diplomats from abroad. Imagine the French government, today, hiring an American Foreign Service Officer away from the State Department! Imagine the State Department recruiting outstanding German diplomats for its own service by paying them more! But until relatively recently (until the triumph of democracy) this sort of thing was accepted practice. ". . . the Austrian Ambassador to France," Professor Morgenthau tells us,[3] "felt more at home at the court of Versailles than among his own nonaristocratic compatriots. He had closer social and moral ties with the members of the French aristocracy and the other aristocratic members of the diplomatic corps than with the Austrians of humble origin. In 1757, the Comte de Stainville was Austrian Minister in Paris, while his son, later (as Duc de Choiseul) Prime Minister of Louis XV, was French Ambassador at the Court of Vienna. At the same time another son was Major of a Croat regiment in Hungary. It was not surprising that in such circumstances the diplomatic and military personnel fluctuated to a not inconsiderable degree from one monarchical employer to another. It was not rare that a French diplomat or officer, for some reason of self-interest, would enter the services of the King of Prussia and would further the international objectives of Prussia, or fight in the Prussian army, against France. . . . In 1756, shortly before the outbreak of the Seven Years' War, Frederick the Great sent the Scottish Earl Marischall as his Ambassador to Spain in order to get information about the Spanish intentions. The Scottish Ambassador of Prussia had a friend in Spain, an Irishman by the name of Wall, who happened to be Spanish Foreign Minister and who told him what he wanted to know."

In the remnants of the old ruling classes today one still finds this quality of a common cosmopolitan background that reduces distinctions of nationality to minor significance. Until about the time of the last war, the Argentine government was dominated by a class of wealthy landowners, most of whom were virtually indistinguishable from the landed gentry in England.

[3] *Ibid.*, p. 222.

I mean this literally. I have been a guest at more than one great *estancia* on the Argentine pampas where I thought my hosts and the neighboring landowners actually were English people, until I discovered that they had all been four or five generations in Argentina, considered themselves altogether Argentinian, and spoke Spanish among themselves when alone. As a rule, these people managed to spend at least a month or two in London or Paris each year, they were likely to send their children to European universities, they read the latest books from Europe and the United States and followed the latest fashions, and they maintained the closest contacts with the fashionable people of the European capitals, with whom they had far more in common than with the masses of their fellow countrymen. During the nineteenth and early twentieth centuries, when these people governed Argentina and their equivalents governed England, Anglo-Argentine relations were conducted with an ease and an intimacy to which the nearest approach, in our own day, is to be found in the relations between the United States and Canada. There was understanding and the most constructive kind of business partnership between the two countries.

All this was radically changed by the Argentine revolution that brought into power governments which, if they had any other base than the military, rested on the so-called *descamisados* of the streets of Buenos Aires. Immediately a frenzied nationalism was introduced into Argentina's contacts with Britain, and became so controlling that the naturally intimate relations between the complimentary economies of the two countries was deliberately disrupted by the Perón government, at an economic cost from which Argentina seems unlikely to recover. Those who remember when the finest beefsteaks in the world were within the price of every inhabitant of Buenos Aires have seen how, in a period of less than half a dozen years, Argentina was reduced to the rationing of meat as one consequence of her economic nationalism.

The people who formerly constituted the governing classes

of Argentina and England, respectively, had a common education which enabled them to live together in the large world of their common European civilization. They shared a code of manners which enabled them to deal with each other in terms of mutual understanding. Consequently, they could meet each other in friendship, or at least in a sort of friendly rivalry. But bring the *descamisado* of Buenos Aires together with the London cockney and they are as likely as not to fall to blows—if they can find a common language to quarrel in, or if services of interpretation are supplied. There are no common rules to govern their intercourse. Each is a foreigner to the other; each in the presence of the other becomes acutely aware of his own distinctive nationality; each feels the impulse to assert the superiority of that nationality to what the other represents. Much of the new political leadership, today, is representative of the people as the old diplomats were not, but this makes that leadership more rude, quarrelsome, intransigeant, and self-righteous —justifying itself by equating morality with nationalism.

This comes as a disappointment to many of us, because we were brought up on that aspect of Wilsonian idealism which expected the spread of democracy to have the opposite effect. We were told that wars were made by kings, aristocrats, and scheming professional diplomats at the expense of the people (as, in fact, they once were), and that the rule of the people would at last spell peace.[4] But it has not been so. The rule of the people has often spelled, rather, an exacerbated and xenophobic nationalism resulting from the lack of education in a common culture. The people have not wanted war, but they have cheered demagogues who have led them in that direction. They have not wanted war, but they have delighted in that

---

[4] This is a long-lived fallacy. When the French Revolution occurred it was widely believed that the rule of the people meant the end of war. Even when the new regime in France embarked on its course of military aggression "the English Jacobins still refused to admit that a nation which was in charge of its own destinies could be warlike: kings and aristocrats might make war, a people was peaceful in the nature of things" (Alfred Coban, in *The Debate on the French Revolution*, London, 1950, p. 24.) Here we were, still believing the same thing almost a century and a half later.

offensiveness to foreign nations, by their representatives, which leads to war. In the extremes of nationalism, a war against foreigners has even taken on, in the popular mind, the passion of a holy war. And the popular aspiration for peace has been appeased by telling the people that eternal peace would be the outcome of whatever particular war might be in question.

Have I exaggerated? Perhaps. In any case, I have surely oversimplified. This is a complex world in which many factors combine to produce unexpected results. Never trust to one or two factors alone. Switzerland has had popular government for many years, but its people have not fallen victim to demagogues who arouse it to a frenzy of self-righteous and antiforeign zeal. The impact of accumulated experience on the popular mind is one factor that I have left out. Habituation to the requirements of one's own weakness in a dangerous world is another. People learn prudence by bitter experiences, like that of the Thirty Years' War, or they learn it by having to survive in the midst of rival powers stronger than themselves. Often, when they have had their ideological frenzy out and survey the wreckage, moderation and reasonableness have an attraction which had previously been lacking. Or if they have the maturity to see, where such is the case, that they do not have the strength to manage international power politics, but can only be hurt by plunging zealously into them, they form the habit of lying low, of allowing prudence to discipline their behavior. It is among the inexperienced peoples of the world today, those who are new to self-determination, those who still live almost entirely in the realm of legend, that we see the most dangerous and ungoverned extremes of nationalism. There is less of it in the old democracies than among these newcomers. The American people, relatively inexperienced a few years ago, have been learning painfully, perhaps, but at a rate that seems to me extraordinary. We are less nationalistic than a generation ago. It is in this capacity of whole populations to mature that the hope of our day, however slender, resides.

Those who are professionally concerned with international relations are confined to dealing with international problems at their branch ends rather than at their roots. For one thing, they cannot treat those roots that go back into the past and represent the accomplished facts of history. During the period between the two world wars, when the United States was engaged in dispute with its World War I associates as to whether they should pay their war debts, the American isolationist, Will Rogers, proposed a solution for the problem. The solution he proposed was that he wouldn't have lent them the money in the first place! But for the most part retroactivity must remain an unrealizable ideal—as in the case of the man who would solve the population problem by making birth control retroactive. We have to deal with the world as it is, not as it might have been. The professional cannot solve international disputes by abolishing John Dewey and his influence on education, or by making sure that all our populations read Shakespeare and study Gothic architecture. But it will not diminish the essential wisdom with which he approaches the problems at the branch ends if he is aware of the fact that these roots exist.

VIII • In our own day we generally credit the Anglo-Saxon peoples with a special genius in the field of government. The American achievement in establishing one self-governing nation over such a large area is given as an example. British government, in the home islands and abroad, has also been cited. But this Anglo-Saxon genius—in actual practice as distinct from constitutional development—first manifested itself at a late date. One does not find it in the political history of England during the seventeenth century. One hardly finds it in the eighteenth century in England, which presents a record of corruption and misgovernment culminating in the inglorious reign of George III and the loss of the American colonies—although the figures of Burke and the two Pitts at the end relieve the dark picture with gleams of light.

This famous Anglo-Saxon aptitude for government first manifested itself fully in America during the American Revolution. In Washington and Hamilton, in John Adams and his son John Quincy, in Benjamin Franklin, in Thomas Jefferson, and in others America gave the world an example of statesmanship for which, I think, it would be hard to find an equal since the days of Pericles. The weak America of that day would not have become independent of a powerful Britain, or have made good its independence, if Britain, with all her power, had possessed anything like the same quality of statesmanship.

One of the paradoxes in our country's history is that it displayed its greatest maturity in government and policy at the beginning of its national life. We have frequently been called an immature nation, notably during the first third of the present century, but no one could question the maturity of our political conduct and our statesmanship in the generation of our founding. If we have at times shown ourselves less than mature since, it is by decline from the remarkable fullness of our maturity at birth. It is because we became callow with age. The explanation of this paradox lies in a revolution that took place quietly and peaceably—as is often the way with Anglo-Saxon revolutions—in 1829-30. With the election as President of Andrew Jackson of Tennessee to succeed John Quincy Adams of Massachusetts political control was shifted from the eastern seaboard, with its eighteenth-century European culture, to the other side of the Appalachians, where a new and still relatively barbarous America was growing up. With the shift, the United States ceased to be a quasi-aristocratic republic under a highly educated governing class and became instead the first egalitarian democracy—unless an exception is made for the Swiss cantons.

The fact that the Founding Fathers were men who had received an excellent classical education is far from being the whole explanation of America's political maturity in their generation. Behind them lay a century and a half of such experience in self-government as no other people on the face of the earth had had. The rebellion against English rule did not come about, as is so commonly supposed, because the American colonies, after an initial period of development under colonial rule, had reached a point where they were at last ready to make their first flights as independent and self-governing societies. It came about because, having already successfully enjoyed self-government for so many generations, they found themselves faced with an attempt by the mother country to take it away from them. The mother country was foolishly attempting to cage the bird that had all this time been flying free.

84

This fact is important for an understanding of American foreign policy. But it has a greater and more immediate importance. It is significant for the world today. The present revolts of the North Africans and South Asians against colonial rule are commonly likened to the revolt of the North American colonies; just as the revolts of the Spanish Americans against the rule of Spain in the first quarter of the nineteenth century have been likened to the North American revolt. The North American revolt stands in our minds as the prototype of colonial rebellion, the classic original, the revolt that set the pattern for all the others. We Americans, especially, have been prone to see in later revolts a simple re-enactment of our own, with all the promise that implies. But this comparison may lead us to expect too much of the new states that have made good their revolt. It creates an optimistic legend which obscures a bitter and unwelcome reality.

The North American colonies governed themselves with notable sophistication, maturity, and success from the beginning of their independence. From the beginning they established and maintained that balance between freedom and order which is the ultimate achievement in the realm of politics. On the basis of this precedent it might have been expected that the Latin Americans, who all followed the achievement of independence by adopting written constitutions modeled upon that of the United States, would demonstrate a like success in self-government. On the basis of this precedent it is widely expected today that all the North Africans and South Asians will crown the achievement of their independence with the establishment of governments that also maintain political order and freedom at home, and that are able to bear a responsible part in the affairs of the international community.

But the Latin Americans in the nineteenth century and the ex-colonials of our own day have been without one indispensable advantage enjoyed by the American colonists in 1776—the unique previous experience of self-government unmatched by the similar experience of any other people anywhere at the time, whether colonial or otherwise. (I do not count the experience of independence, rather than self-government, formerly enjoyed by the North Africans. Their kingdoms were slave states and the chief role they played in the international community was that of the "Barbary Pirates.") Even the English in England had had no such experience as the Americans at the time of the American Revolution. In England during the seventeenth century no such self-government was known as in England's American colonies. The colonial Englishmen in America enjoyed an independence denied to the Englishmen in England. It was the Americans who, out of that unique experience, could have taught the English the art of government.

In the case of the Latin Americans, not only had they had no experience of self-government, they had not even developed to that point where they were ready to attempt their first trial flights. They became independent, not because they had reached the age of independence, but because while they were still in their childhood the mother country was struck down by the hand of Napoleon. They are to be compared rather to small children orphaned by an accident than to children who leave home because they have grown up. The result was that, for them, the achievement of independence did not bring freedom with order. It did not mean an end to tyranny. It was followed, rather, by generations of chaos, the temporary governments of strong men, utter corruption, and the practice of brutalities against the peoples by barbarous domestic dictators no less harsh than the brutalities previously practiced by representatives of the Spanish crown. According to the legend of nationalism, the grinding heel of a domestic dictator is more tolerable than the touch of a foreign ruler's finger; but to those unhappy mortals who listen for the knock on the door at midnight, for those whose husbands or sons are quietly abducted by the political police and never heard from again, for those who are tortured to death in the prisons to satisfy the lusts of sadists—and all these things are happening every day within domestic jurisdictions—for the innumerable victims of domestic despotism the legend must be scant compensation for the reality, national sovereignty, however beautiful in itself, must seem an inadequate guarantee of human dignity.

While we are bound to hope and to pray that the newly independent ex-colonial peoples of our day will make a better record—and many of them have enjoyed the advantages of a more liberal colonial administration than the Latin Americans ever knew—we must also be prepared for the possibility that, with independence, the practice of irresponsible government among them will become not less but more. We must be prepared for the possibility that international order will become more difficult to maintain.

The legend of the American Revolution and the legend that later colonial revolts merely re-enact it have had a powerful impact on modern history and have especially influenced the foreign policy of the United States. I bring this right down to our own day, when President Nasser's retention of the Suez Canal was facilitated, perhaps was made possible at all, by an unpondered feeling among us Americans that its seizure was something like our "Boston Tea Party." Under the circumstances the weight of the United States was not effectively moved against it.

It is of the essence of the North American success that the English colonies were self-governing from the beginning. This was not a matter of British policy or British desire. On the contrary, until the colonies won their war for independence England always regarded them as mere property to be freely exploited for her own benefit. But right at the start she neglected to provide for their management, and when later she turned her attention to them and sought to repair the neglect she found them already in the habit of managing their own affairs.

The remark has been made that England acquired her empire in a fit of absent-mindedness. It could also be said that it was out of absent-mindedness that she allowed the newly founded colonies in North America to go their own way, governing themselves.

The fact is that England, as a nation, did not set out to establish a colonial empire at all, or even to plant colonies on the North American continent—although there was much talk in government circles of doing so as a means of discomfiting Spain. It was private Englishmen, on their own initiative and with their own financial resources, who established the colonies and the colonial empire. They were attracted by the spectacle of a new and undeveloped land, they got together and raised funds, they acquired ships, and away they sailed to transatlantic shores while the Crown looked on with approbation, perhaps, but took no active hand. "Charles I," says Professor G. M. Trevelyan, "set no bar to these proceedings. . . ."[1] How unlike the Spanish colonization this is! Or how unlike the French colonization in Canada! There were some moves to set up a colonial administration in London but they never came to anything. Soon the English crown found itself preoccupied with rebellion among the Englishmen who had stayed at home and so virtually forgot about the Englishmen who had planted themselves across the Atlantic. They were left to enjoy a salutary neglect, a neglect that is the root of freedom and democracy in America.

The common way in which an English colony was founded, at the beginning of the seventeenth century, was by the formation of a joint stock company for trade and colonization. That is how the first American colony was founded in Virginia. A London company, privately financed and thinking only of trade, was given a royal charter, obtained ships, recruited colonists, and sent them overseas to establish what was in effect a trading outpost of the company at Jamestown, on the shores of that country whose name forever honors what we take to have been the chastity of a great queen. (This suggests how deep in our history are the roots of that private enterprise and private initiative for which we Americans have such respect that we

[1] *History of England* (London, 1926), p. 438.

88

sometimes tremble at the name of socialism, even when we accept the modern necessity of practicing it.)

English fishermen had been establishing themselves without any charters or patents on the shores of Newfoundland and Maine since sometime in the sixteenth century. But that, as far as history goes, is like the discovery of America by the Vikings five hundred years before Columbus. No one made a memorandum of it, and so it was not official. Jamestown was the scene of the first settlement that was both permanent and official. The private London Company dispatched the first official permanent colonizing expedition in December, 1606. Its charter did provide that there should be a Royal Council for Virginia in London, and that this organ of the Crown would have general administrative control. So the British Empire started out not to be self-governing at all. The Royal Council, however, was too far from the scene to deal constructively with unanticipated local difficulties, difficulties which involved the death of more than half the settlers the first year. So it met the situation in what was surely the best possible way, by ceasing to function at all.

At the petition of the interested London merchants, then, a new charter, modeled on those of other trading companies, was issued in 1609. It established the London Company—called "The Treasurer and Company of Adventurers & Planters of the City of London for the First Colony in Virginia"—as proprietor of Virginia. By a third charter in 1612 the general government of this private company was placed in the hands of its shareholders, who would elect a council to carry on executive functions and a supreme executive officer, namely the treasurer. Here, then, is a democratic government of the colony, not by the colonists but by its incorporated owners in London—the shareholders. A lot of big and little people—some lords, some merchants, some shopkeepers—own Virginia, which not only includes the present state of Maryland as well, but presumably a good piece of what is now California. For the charter shows no awareness of mountain barriers, rivers, or deserts. It merely provides that Virginia extends westward to the Pacific Ocean, the charterers not knowing how far west that is.

By 1619 representative government had been established in Virginia. The Virginia Assembly of twenty-two burgesses, representing all the settled districts, held its first meeting on July 30, 1619. From 1619, then, you have the practice of representative government in Virginia, with all the political maneuvering, the debating, and the campaigning that representative government involves, with all the rubbing together of conflicting interests and their mutual accommodation. By the time that the Virginia House of Burgesses took such a decisive role in asserting the independence and achieving the union of the United States it had already accumulated more than a century and a half of experience. Men like Jefferson, Madison, Jay, and Monroe were the product of a long political tradition, a tradition that went back across as many generations of statesmen as there have been generations of statesmen since. Representative government in Virginia was virtually as old, in Jefferson's day, as the United States itself is in our day. Is it any wonder, then, that these people were adept and sophisticated in the arts of government?

True, the London Company was dissolved in 1622 and Virginia then became a crown colony. "But she did not lose the large measure of self-government that she had won. The assembly, the courts of justice, and other organs of local government already being evolved were retained . . . Charles I . . . interfered with the colony less than the company had. . . ."[2]

The Pilgrim Fathers, when they sailed from Holland on the *Mayflower* in 1620, were also headed for Virginia, where they intended to establish their settlement. They had obtained a license for the purpose from the company which owned the territory. But the winds of fortune blew them, instead, to a landfall outside the limits of Virginia, on the shores of what is now New England. After two and a half months at sea it is not surprising that they decided to go no farther, even though this was

[2] Morison and Commager, *op. cit.*, I, pp. 41-42.

not their intended destination. But they were without papers. They had no charter, no license, no *Permis d'Établissement* for this coast. Under the circumstances they anticipated the eighteenth-century theory of the "Contrat Social" by enacting it in practice.

By the so-called "Mayflower Compact," "they agreed to combine themselves into a civil body for their own preservation and to assume such power under the King as was necessary for the framing of just laws and equal ordinances and the appointment of competent officers. [They] thus established a basis for the legal authority of their government in the absence of an express commission from the King. The signatories became in fact the first freemen of a new political community, preserving their allegiance to the English Crown and laws unimpaired, but compelled by reason of distance to govern themselves separately. Such plantation covenants were used in the next twenty years in the founding of many other settlements in New England, and they provided a written fundamental instrument of authority wherever there was no royal grant conferring jurisdiction on a lord proprietor or a chartered company."[3]

Considering this kind of experience, beginning at the very inception of the American colonies, there is evidently an element of absurdity in asking whether the American Revolution did not take place one hundred and fifty years later because the Americans, in the course of their development, had reached the point where they were at last ready for self-government. By 1776, and long before that, there was no people on the face of the earth, colonial or imperial, who had had so much on-the-job training in the art of self-government. The *Mayflower* company showed themselves already up to the responsibility of self-government on the day before they actually landed, in 1620, and they began to practice it forthwith.

Let me now cite another instance of how the British absent-mindedly established their empire in North America and al-

[3] A.P. Newton, *Cambridge History of the British Empire* (Cambridge, 1929), I, pp. 158-59.

lowed it to be self-governing. Another one of these private companies in London, the Massachusetts Bay Company, was chartered by the Crown in 1629. As in the case of the London Company which colonized Virginia, a headquarters organization was established by the company in England to run the settlement which it deposited at Salem, on the shore of Massachusetts Bay. In this case, however, although the organization was the same, the purpose of the company was different from that of the Virginia Company. It was to found a refuge for righteous Puritans across the sea and there, as they put it, "to raise a bulwark against the kingdom of Antichrist. . . ."[4]

The officers of the company in England, pious Puritans all, bethought them of the possibility that they themselves might enjoy the refuge from Antichrist. With the establishment of the Salem colony, therefore, they made a decision which had interesting constitutional implications. They decided to transfer the offices of the company—with its patent, its officers, and all—out of England to Salem. The home office left home and proceeded to make itself at home abroad. By that act the Salem settlement, instead of being governed by an absentee government, in effect found itself under its own independent government, which had joined it. A self-governing dominion had thus been set up by royal charter on the shores of North America—almost as if by sleight of hand.

The descendants of the Massachusetts colonists, a hundred and fifty years later, would complain and rebel at the oppression of the English government. But they themselves had no such cause for complaint. They were quite independent. Colonial oppression, the denial of self-government, would come later. Here, again, one sees how the colonial history of Anglo-America is not a history of gradual growth toward independence but, rather, of mounting attempts against that independence by the metropolitan power, to the point where the colonists would rebel.

Let me give one final example of how complete the inde-

<hr>

[4] *Ibid.*, pp. 147-61.

pendence of the American colonies was, in some instances, at the time of their foundation. I give it in the words of Professor A. P. Newton, writing in the *Cambridge History of the British Empire*.[5] In 1639 settlers along the Connecticut River organized, under the leadership of the Reverend Thomas Hooker, "a formal government on a purely democratic basis. . . . Hooker maintained that the foundation of authority lies in the free consent of the people, and they alone have the power to appoint officers and magistrates and to set bounds and limitations to their authority. The constitution or 'Fundamental Orders' drawn up by the elected representatives of the settlers contained no recognition of any superior authority in England and implied a claim to complete independence. The document remained unknown or unregarded by the English Government which had its hands full elsewhere. It was the first written constitution in the English-speaking world on an ostensibly democratic basis. . . . The Fundamental Orders remained the sole instrument of government in the colony until Governor John Winthrop junior procured a formal charter from Charles II after the Restoration."

Morison and Commager sum up the whole situation in New England. "One thing these New England colonies had in common until 1680," they write: "all were virtually independent commonwealths, acknowledging allegiance to whatever authority had control in England, but making their own laws, trading where they pleased, defending themselves without help from home, and working out their own institutions. Their connection with the mother country was one of sentiment and tradition rather than compulsion; they were every bit as self-reliant and independent as the British dominions of today."[6]

In the next chapter I shall conclude the paradoxical history of how America sprang full-grown from the head of Britannia. I shall then undertake to give an account of the foreign policy which the remarkable generation of the Founding Fathers

[5] Cambridge, 1929, I, p. 163.
[6] *Op. cit.*, I, p. 59.

shaped for the new United States, a policy that enabled it to survive and at last emerge from a tense period in which it was crowded and threatened by powers far greater than itself, a policy that enabled it to open a path through those powers to the West and to the democracy by which it would be transformed when, at last, the man from Tennessee took possession of the executive power which had hitherto belonged to Virginia and Massachusetts. So, by stages, we shall see that foreign policy buffeted, impressed, sometimes reformed and sometimes deformed, by all the internal and external forces that bear upon it, until the twentieth century comes, much too quickly, and our own times, with all the dilemmas and perplexities into which the later chapters will pry.

IX • The American colonies had been self-governing, in practice though not in theory, long before their war for independence. But practice survives only precariously where it lacks the support of theory. For a hundred and fifty years the English in London had one theory about the relation of the colonies to them, the English colonists had another. The Englishmen in England regarded themselves as proprietors. They regarded the colonies as the property of the home country, to be exploited at will for its own wealth and glory. This mercantilistic view made the colonists mere instruments. Benjamin Franklin complained that "every man in England seems to consider himself as a piece of a sovereign over America; seems to jostle himself into the throne with the King, and talks of *our subject in the Colonies.*"[1] But the colonists thought of themselves as Englishmen like any other, with all of an Englishman's rights. All Englishmen, they felt, were created equal. A Massachusetts Englishman stood in precisely the same relationship to the Crown and on the same level as an English Englishman. To the extent that the English Englishmen enjoyed self-government under the Crown, so did the American Englishmen. The theory was succinctly stated by one of the Founding Fathers, James Madison. "The fundamental principle of the Revolution was," he wrote, "that the

[1] Quoted in *Cambridge History of the British Empire,* I, 650.

95

colonies were coordinate members with each other and with Great Britain, of an empire united by a common executive sovereign, but not united by a common legislative sovereign. The legislative power was maintained to be as complete in each American Parliament, as in the British Parliament. . . . A denial of these principles by Great Britain, and the assertion of them by America, produced the Revolution."[2]

The American theory was the same as that on which the present British dominions stand. More than that, it represented the practice, whatever theory the Englishman in England held. In the actual practice of the seventeenth century the New England colonies, at least, were self-governing British dominions, like Canada and Australia today, and they thought of themselves as such. When the Imperial Conference declared in 1926 that Great Britain and the Dominions "are autonomous communities within the British Empire, equal in status, in no way subordinate one to another in any aspect of their domestic or external affairs, though united by a common allegiance to the Crown and freely associated as members of the British Commonwealth of Nations"—when the Imperial Conference made that declaration it was describing the actual situation that had subsisted, widely if not universally, in the seventeenth century. The big difference was that the Crown had more power then over the home-dwelling Englishmen and the overseas Englishmen alike. In fact, the home-dwelling Englishmen enjoyed rather less autonomy under the Crown, were less self-governing, than the overseas Englishmen on the coastal plain of North America. The problem of the seventeenth century, which was not solved without bloodshed, was to win self-government for the Englishmen at home. Thus the Englishmen who remained at home, in rebelling first against Charles I and then against James II, anticipated the American Revolution by more than a century.

When the English people had succeeded in overcoming the

[2] Quoted in "The American Tradition in Foreign Relations," by Frank Tannenbaum, *Foreign Affairs*, October, 1951.

tyranny of the Crown at home, then through their own Parliament they began practicing a new tyranny, political and economic, on those overseas Englishmen who, under the prevailing mercantilistic theory, were proprietary assets of their island kingdom. The Acts of Trade and Navigation, which took away the economic independence of the colonies, coincide with the Restoration in England. For the first time the English in England undertook to give effect to the theory which the whole nation had, in fact, held from the beginning. That is when the trouble began. It broke into the open when Britain's final defeat of Bourbon France, in 1763, allowed her at last to turn her full attention to the care of her neglected children in America.

Since the mercantilistic theory of empire received its death blow at the hands of Adam Smith, in the publication of his *Wealth of Nations,* it is too bad that its publication did not come until 1776, the year of the American Declaration of Independence. Perhaps if it had come in 1763, when the elimination of French colonial rivalry from North America confronted England with the necessity of establishing new working relations with her American subjects, we Americans would today have that dominion status within the British association which we had enjoyed throughout the first generations after our arrival in America. Or, more likely, the day would have come when England, confronting the growing weight of her American partners and the westward displacement of the center of gravity, would have issued her own Declaration of Independence—in which case we Americans might have waged war to put down her rebellion and keep her in the Commonwealth. In any case, the situation might have been different, and I mention this because it again suggests the importance of theory—of the theories that possess men's minds—in the actual practice of international relations.

It is unnecessary to go into the details of the family quarrel which developed after the conclusion of the Seven Years' War and culminated in our Declaration of Independence. American and English historians are agreed, today, that there was a lamentable lack of statesmanship among the ministers of King George III, who tried to impose a mercantilistic servitude on his American subjects. In fact Mr. Edmund Burke and others pointed that out at the time, and in Parliament itself. There was genuine statesmanship in England but, as will sometimes happen anywhere, it was not in office or in power. Mr. Burke played the same enlightened but frustrating role with respect to British policy in that day as Mr. Churchill played with respect to British policy in the 1930's. In the case of both men, the fault was in their being out of power, for which we must not blame them too severely.

Still, there is something to be said for the official British position of the time. The English were not really oppressing us Americans, as we might think, since their exactions were generally inconsequential in their practical effect. The symbolic situation was more important—for example, the imposition of any taxation at all without representation, it mattered not whether the tax was light or heavy. The symbolism of colonial servitude was what counted. You see much the same thing in the colonial revolts of our own day. But the British, too, had their dilemmas, then as now. They had immensely increased their public debt in encompassing the defense of the American colonies against France. Was it not right that the colonists should make their contribution to the continuing problem of meeting a defense budget that applied to them? Benjamin Franklin and other Americans agreed that it was right. But the colonies did not proceed to tax themselves or muster levies of men through their own organs of representation, the colonial assemblies. Where they had representation they still preferred to forgo taxation. Therefore Great Britain undertook to tax them without representation. It was a mistake, as we are all agreed, because events have showed that it was a mistake. The best thing would have been for Britain to console herself with the considerable revenues which the colonial connection afforded her, while continuing to pay for the defense of the colonies by herself. The mistake Britain made, however, was not altogether on the side of injustice. Our American cause was righteous, but not perfectly righteous.

What it amounted to was this. The minute any kind of leash was put on us Americans we strained at it. We strained at it so hard in the 1770's that we broke it, quite without having any original intention of doing so. The War of the American Revolution did not begin as a war for independence, but it ended that way.

On July 6, 1775, two days short of one year before we declared our independence, the Second Continental Congress issued "A Declaration of the Causes and Necessity of Taking up Arms" from which I quote the following: "Lest this declaration should disquiet the minds of our friends and fellow-subjects in any part of the empire, we assure them that we mean not to dissolve that union which has so long and so happily subsisted between us, and which we sincerely wish to see restored. . . . Necessity has not yet driven us into that desperate measure, or induced us to excite any other nation to war against them. . . . We have not raised armies with ambitious designs of separating from Great Britain, and establishing independent states."[3]

It would better fit the theme of these chapters if I could say that what prompted the American Revolution was a determination not to be constantly involved, as had been the case, in the European wars of the mother country. History, however, which is often recalcitrant, will not support me in this. Neutrality with respect to the European balance of power, non-participation, seems to have been an afterthought. But it was a powerful afterthought, just as the movement for complete independence was a powerful afterthought.

The ordinary tendency of humanity everywhere is to accept the *status quo*. The particular world into which each of us is born, however unreasonable it may in fact be, is the world that we grow up to regard as right and normal. Thus those who are born into slavery ordinarily accept their role as implicit in the

[3] Quoted from *Charting Democracy*, A. P. Fernbach and C. J. Bishko (editors) (University of Virginia, 1946), I, p. 93.

order of nature. Those who are born into the governing classes find it easy to assume that nature reserved the function of government for such as they. What seems right, ordinarily, is the world as we have always known it.

This tendency of humanity seems to me indispensable to an essential degree of stability. It expresses itself in the prevalence of custom, or in the sense of legitimacy, and as such is the basis of social order. Without it we should have no civilization at all, or any civilized amenities. Without it there could be no happiness, because an essential element of happiness is basic adjustment to and contentment with one's lot, the assumption one makes that one's own mortal career is part of some larger whole that has the sanction, the dignity, and the glory of something like divine intent.

People are slow and reluctant, therefore, to question the order in which they live. They recognize intuitively that anyone who starts questioning that order is likely to end by upsetting it, perhaps producing chaos in its place. That is why Socrates was given the hemlock to drink. To many of the slaves in the American South, during the years which led to our Civil War, the Abolitionists up North were dangerous radicals to be viewed with alarm.

Nevertheless, the time comes again and again when the old order is questioned by those who cannot fit themselves to it or cannot accept it. Any order of society is continuously obsolescent. New conditions discredit the old order by making it less workable and less sensible than it was under the old conditions. For example, the feudal nobility loses its meaning and its justification when there are no longer Saracens or Norsemen or Turks to fight, or when armies of archers have come into being to fight them more effectively. Eventually it has to be questioned, and once the questioning is begun there is no telling where it will end. The very process of questioning, however limited, tends to destroy the unquestionability of the order which is being questioned. The questioners, in time, come to ask questions that would never have occurred to them, that would even

100

LIBRARY
ST. MARYS SEMINARY JUNIOR COLLEGE

have shocked them, at the beginning of the interrogation. Eventually the whole order may be destroyed by this irreversable and cumulative process. This, in fact, is what is happening in the world around us today—not only in North Africa, but also in Poland and Hungary. This is the meaning of the revolt against colonialism, against class distinctions, against every kind of physical suffering and hardship. It is the explanation of the universal malaise of our time.

The American colonies, right up to the Revolution, accepted without serious question their duty to the English crown and even their support of the Crown in its foreign wars. The umbilical cord, which the government in London was straining, was simply to be loosened, not cut. It was one thing to question the Stamp Tax, to which one had not been brought up, another to question an allegiance to which one had been brought up. One accepted the duty of every Englishman, on both sides of the Atlantic, to render faithful support to the English crown in its foreign wars.

But once the connection had been called into serious question the questioning did not remain confined to particular acts of His Majesty's Government. From questioning the legitimacy of its acts to questioning the legitimacy of the government itself was a logical and all but inevitable step. Here we see the dynamics of revolution, which are like the dynamics of war. The rebellion, begun for some limited objective, gathers its own momentum and, more and more, proceeds to take its own course. It is Frankenstein's monster. Look at France from 1789 to 1793. Look at Russia in 1917. John Adams, Jefferson, Franklin, Washington, and the others began by leading but ended by being compelled.

Once the first blow is struck, once the first blood is drawn, the whole situation changes. It becomes desperate, and what is desperate is also intractable. Desperate necessity becomes the justification for what orthodoxy or morals or good manners or simple prudence would otherwise have forbidden. With the firing of the first shot at Bunker Hill bonds of psychological

101

attachment were broken and total rebellion was loosed. Now the American colonists had to win, all or nothing. But their situation, as I have said, was desperate. Their weakness was no match for the strength of the British. General Washington had next to nothing to fight with.

Under the circumstances the only hope was to bring the French in on our side, which we succeeded in doing after a prolonged and anxious effort of diplomacy. And, to give honor where honor is due, it was the French as much as anyone who won the war. It was His Most Serene Most Christian Majesty Louis XVI, who would later have his own mortal experience of rebellion, who forced his Most Serene fellow King, George III, to let go of us Americans so that we could establish our independent and anti-monarchist republic, a republic which would serve as an example to his own subjects. It is one of the ironies of history that the revolutionary Americans fell into close alliance with the absolutist Bourbon monarchy, fell into warfare with the anti-monarchical French Republic that succeeded it, and then, in 1812, fell onto the same side as the absolutist Emperor Napoleon in that war by which Britain and her allies were undertaking to overthrow his illegitimate tyranny. The ideologies get mixed up here, as often happens under the compelling necessities of war and international relations. A man lying on his back under assault is not likely to be fussy in choosing his allies. He is not likely to require anyone to pass an ideological examination before being allowed to come to his rescue.

We would certainly not have won the war without France. The crucial defeat of General Cornwallis at Yorktown was more the doing of the French fleet under De Grasse and the French army under Rochambeau than of the gallant little band of Americans under Washington—though the two allies did the job together. But France could certainly not have come in on our side if we had not declared an independence which she could recognize. She could not have fought in the cause of Englishmen rebelling against legislative acts of their own acknowledged government, to which they retained their allegiance.

102

Under international law, nations must avert their eyes from quarrels in other families that involve no trespass on their own rights. There is the doctrine of domestic jurisdiction. So the desperate need of bringing France in was one reason why what had not started out as an independence movement had to become so. In war, as Thucydides pointed out, whatever men would do, they do as they must.

So in the American Revolution, once it was started, the issue was all or nothing. It is difficult to fight a serious war on any other basis—as we shall see when we come to deal with such policies as that of "unconditional surrender" in World War II.

Political independence had not been an issue in the civil quarrel that culminated in the American Revolution. Consequently, isolation, non-participation in His Majesty's wars, was not an issue in the quarrel. The two go together. His Majesty's loyal subjects cannot let him fight his wars alone; for if they should do so they would no longer be his loyal subjects. Once His Majesty's subjects began thinking of themselves as independent Americans, however, certain advantages of such a condition presented themselves in a most appealing light. They would no longer have to fight for the Crown in quarrels that concerned them not at all—and they identified such quarrels as those involving the European balance of power. Let me repeat the passage from Dr. Wharton which I quoted in an earlier chapter. The isolationist's ideal "is the non-juridical counterpart of sovereignty and, as regards its parentage, a blood-brother of sovereignty." In the unintended achievement of an independent sovereignty we Americans first grasped the possibility of achieving the isolationist's ideal.

"It remained," writes Professor Bemis, "for a newly arrived English immigrant, Thomas Paine, to point out to the colonists that separation from British sovereignty meant also separation from Britain's wars. The conclusion was immediately irresistible. . . . Colonial experience in being the stakes of European diplomacy, relief at the freedom from that condition which came with American independence, and determination to continue to enjoy it and to profit by it laid the foundation for that persistent policy of the United States which was crystallized in President Washington's Farewell Address and again enunciated in the Monroe Doctrine, public documents not devoid of phraseology resembling certain passages in Thomas Paine's *Common Sense*."[4] One such passage, which Mr. Bemis gives, reads as follows: ". . . any submission to, or dependance [*sic*] on Great Britain, tends directly to involve this continent in European wars and quarrels; and sets us at variance with nations, who would otherwise seek our friendship, and against whom we have neither anger nor complaint. As Europe is our market for trade, we ought to form no partial connection with any part of it. It is the true interest of America to steer clear of European contentions, which she never can do, while by her dependance on Britain, she is made the make-weight in the scale of British politics."

Note that final phrase: "the make-weight in the scale of British politics." This is balance-of-power language. Paine was identifying British politics and European wars alike with the international maneuvers by which a balance of power is maintained. He was identifying them, specifically, with the European balance of power, with respect to which the American colonies of Britain, France, and Spain had been used as helpless "make-weights," with no regard for their own particular interests or their welfare. It was from this balance-of-power system that we were compelled to cut ourselves loose.

This shows, at the very outset of our independent history, that pejorative connotation which has been attached to the balance of power throughout our history. We have never (at least before 1947) regarded the balance of power as anything but nefarious, the enemy of peace, the cause of all wars, the sinister practice by which wicked kings jockey for dynastic advantage at the expense of their helpless subjects. Throughout American history political orators have always been able to stir the American people to indignation by references to the selfish

[4] S. F. Bemis, *A Diplomatic History of the United States* (New York, 1936), p. 12.

104

"power politics" of foreign sovereigns who constantly embroil the world in war for the sake of that vicious political game called balance of power.

As late as March 1, 1945, reporting to the American Congress on the Yalta Conference, President Roosevelt said: "It ought to spell the end of the system of unilateral action, the exclusive alliances, the spheres of influence, the balances of power, and all the other expedients that have been tried for centuries— and have always failed.

"We propose to substitute for all these, a universal organization in which all peace-loving Nations will finally have a chance to join."

President Roosevelt was anxious that the Congress approve American participation in the United Nations. So he offered up, here, the alternatives of the old American Dream and the old American Nightmare. Congress, confronted with this putative choice, voted for the dream. Shortly the United States, having disarmed Germany and Japan, would disarm itself, momentarily leaving the power of the Soviet Union unbalanced. Shortly after that, again, the reality would impinge on the United States, it would wake up from the dream, and it would embark on the most strenuous efforts to re-establish, in the name of "containment," that balance of power which virtually every American statesman from John Adams to Franklin D. Roosevelt had consistently reviled.

X • Sovereignty and isolation were associated in our American minds from the beginning. When we went to war in 1775 we were officially thinking of neither. A year later we were proclaiming both.

We began our national life, then, with a theoretical foreign policy that was clear. In practice, however, we did what circumstances required us to do, even when that was not consistent with the policy of isolation in its absolute theoretical form. This, I think, is the measure of American statesmanship in those days. It kept a bridge between the dream and the reality. Our Founding Fathers had a philosophy or a doctrine of foreign policy by which they were guided. But they also recognized the overriding claims of circumstance. They did not, like pure doctrinnaires, hold workability in contempt or disdain the bounds of possibility.

Of all the great figures Jefferson was, perhaps, the most addicted to theories and dreams. He was the idealist who, if he had lacked experience of responsibility, might have solved the nation's problems on paper, as those who had to solve them in reality could not, thereby establishing before the public his moral and intellectual superiority to those who bore the burden. But he subjected himself, instead, to the discipline of reality— that reality without which there are no problems and all solutions are correspondingly easy.

We do not commonly think of Jefferson as a practitioner of *Realpolitik* or power politics. But he appears to have had no difficulty in reconciling his genuine idealism with the practical politics of survival. While American minister to France from 1784 to 1789, according to Professor Bemis, he "did not fail to measure the sensitive European balance of power. . . . [He] formed while in Europe a settled conviction that sooner or later Europe's quarrels would be sure to be America's advantage, that as long as the European powers were not embarrassed at home, and had energy for aggressive policies in North America, they would never be tender of American independence unless it suited their interests to be so, as it did that of France; but that if the uncertain state of European international relations should involve either Great Britain or Spain, the aggressive colonial back-door neighbours of this country, in war between themselves or in serious diplomatic difficulties they would pay well to secure the friendship of the United States, in order to insure the safety of their adjacent territory in America."[1]

This general principle of foreign policy formed itself in Jefferson's mind at a time when the new United States, unable to govern itself effectively under the Articles of Confederation and without military power for its defense, found itself humiliated, its rights, its interests, and its diplomatic agents treated with contempt in the courts of Europe. But something like this principle proved to be basic to the security of the United States not only in those days but in the twentieth century as well, and even today it is profoundly relevant to our security.

I am not speaking in terms of a narrow interpretation. I do not mean that war in Europe today would be to America's advantage. But a division and dispersion of power among a number of units remaining in some kind of balance, so that they hold one another in check, so that they have cause to value our support or to fear our opposition—this has been and is basic to our security. Twice in this century, when Germany

[1] *The American Secretaries of State and their Diplomacy*, (New York, 1927), II, pp. 9-12.

upset the balance in Europe, we crossed the ocean to restore it. And today, when we have had to take our stand in Europe and Asia with actual armed force to help hold the balance against Russia, the restoration of a division and equilibrium of power outside our own borders seems an indispensable condition of any world order at all in which we can again have that security which we still had at the beginning of the century. This would still be true even if there were an organized world order. I venture to say that it would still be basically true if there were a world government.

Circumstances have forced us to acknowledge this principle in the twentieth century by our actions, but very much against the inclinations of our statesmen and the theories publicly expounded and popularly held. It is a principle that Jefferson understood and accepted, while his successors in the twentieth century found it so repugnant to their ideals that they would not openly acknowledge it even when, in the great emergencies of our times, it determined their actions. Woodrow Wilson and Franklin D. Roosevelt, together with their isolationist opponents, denounced the balance of power—they denounced it even while they took desperate action to preserve or restore it. But on every occasion the action was perilously close to too late and too little because, as was not Jefferson's plight, the vision that these statesmen had of the world as it is was clouded by a view of the world as they or the voters wanted it to be.

Today, when much of the public has been persuaded by the orators that questions of foreign policy are primarily questions of righteousness, to which practical circumstances are secondary, it is interesting to note how Jefferson first applied his principle when he became President Washington's Secretary of State.

In 1789 Spain's dominion over the Pacific coast of North America was implicitly challenged by the action of British fur traders in putting up some shacks on Nootka Sound. Spain returned the challenge by seizing the traders and their two ships. London then delivered an ultimatum in Madrid and, like turkey cocks, the two empires appeared to be advancing toward

108

a clash and a battle. Immediately Jefferson sent instructions to the American minister in London and the American chargé in Madrid, instructions to be acted on only in case the threatened war broke out. The minister in London was then to let the British government know that the granting of various claims which the United States had pending against it would tend to insure United States neutrality in a war with Spain. The chargé in Madrid was to press the Spanish government for the recognition of a putative American right to navigate the Mississippi to the sea. And the American chargé in Paris was instructed to let the French government know that the United States would undoubtedly go to war against its ally, Spain, if Spain did not recognize this right.

I am afraid all this had in it a touch of the disingenuous, even of the Machiavellian. If war between Britain and Spain had broken out, and if both had refused Jefferson's demands, the United States could perhaps have gone to war against both, as Britain's ally against Spain and as Spain's ally against Britain, thereby showing that it meant what it threatened. Professor Bemis assures us, however, that "there is not the slightest reason to believe that Jefferson intended war at this time, even against Spain."[2]

This is the kind of thing that orators of a later day would denounce as power politics. But the legend of Jeffersonian idealism would grow, in time, to obscure the reality of that Jeffersonian statesmanship which was not only a matter of righteousness but also one of survival.

I know of no field that offers so much provocation and so little justification for the sense of moral outrage as that of international politics.

Referring to the United States, Jefferson said: "Were I to indulge my own theory, I should wish them to practise neither commerce nor navigation, but to stand with Europe precisely on the footing of China. We should thus avoid wars, and all our

[2] *Ibid.*, II, p. 42.

citizens would be husbandmen."[3] However, when he heard that
Spain had ceded the mouth of the Mississippi River to Napoleon's France he said: "the day that France takes possession of
New Orleans . . . we must marry ourselves to the British fleet
and nation."[4] What you want is one thing. What circumstances
require is another. Jefferson never failed to make the distinction.

The juxtaposition of these two statements appears to me to
epitomize the dilemma and the paradox of American foreign
policy. The United States was saved by Jefferson's lucky pur-
chase of Louisiana from an open marriage, in church, with the
British fleet and nation. Nevertheless, an unacknowledged liai-
son became necessary in 1823, with the proclamation of the
Monroe Doctrine. Throughout the remainder of the nineteenth
century the United States was an isolationist nation dependent
for its isolation on the British fleet, which gave teeth to the
Doctrine. This association was what made the dissociation possible. It seems unlikely that Jefferson, Washington, Adams, or
Hamilton would have failed, as the generations of their successors did, to recognize this strategic reality.

Jefferson's statement of the isolationist ideal is, characteristically, the most extreme. But his fellow statesmen shared it. Writing retrospectively, old John Adams said: "The principle of
foreign affairs which I then advocated was, that we should make
no treaties of alliance with any European power; that we should
consent to none but treaties of commerce; that we should separate ourselves, as far as possible, from all European politics and
Wars."[5]

Said the Britisher, Mr. Oswald, to Mr. Adams, one day in
November, 1781: "You are afraid of being made the tools of the
powers of Europe."

"Indeed I am," said Mr. Adams. "It is obvious that all the
powers of Europe will be continually manoeuvring with us, to

[8] Quoted in *A History of the Monroe Doctrine* by Dexter Perkins (Boston,
1955), p. 11.
[4] *Ibid.,* p. 19.
[5] *Ibid.,* p. 6.

work us into their real or imaginary balances of power. They will all wish to make us a makeweight candle, while they are weighing out their pounds. . . . But I think it ought to be our rule not to meddle. . . ."[6]

Alexander Hamilton said that we must "prevent our being a ball in the hands of European powers, bandied against each other at their pleasure."[7] And Hamilton had a hand in the classic statement of this policy which George Washington included in his Farewell Address:

"Europe [said Washington] has a set of primary interests, which to us have none, or a very remote relation. Hence, she must be engaged in frequent controversies, the causes of which are essentially foreign to our concerns. Hence, therefore, it must be unwise in us to implicate ourselves, by artificial ties, in the ordinary vicissitudes of her politics, or the ordinary combinations and collisions of her friendships or enmities.

"Our detached and distant situation invites and enables us to pursue a different course. If we remain one people, under an efficient government, the period is not far off, when we may defy material injury from external annoyance; when we may take such an attitude as will cause the neutrality, we may at any time resolve upon, to be scrupulously respected; when belligerent nations, under the impossibility of making acquisitions upon us, will not lightly hazard the giving us provocation; when we may choose peace or war, as our interest, guided by justice, shall counsel.

"Why forego the advantages of so peculiar a situation? Why quit our own to stand upon foreign ground? Why, by interweaving our destiny with that of any part of Europe, entangle our peace and prosperity in the toils of European ambition, rivalship, interest, humor, or caprice?

"It is our true policy to steer clear of permanent alliances with any portion of the foreign world . . ."

Finally, if there is still any doubt that the United States

[6] *Ibid.*, p. 8.
[7] *Ibid.*, p. 11.

was born with a foreign policy, and that this was it, let me refer to the resolution by Congress in 1783 declaring it to be "the fundamental policy" of the United States to remain "as little as possible entangled in the politics and controversies of European nations."[8] Isolation did not begin with the Monroe Doctrine. The Doctrine was merely one of its formulations.

Now, given this clear and compelling policy, this policy on which all sensible men agreed, what was, in fact, our first major action on the international scene? It was to enter into a Treaty of Eternal Alliance with France. One article of that Treaty read as follows:

"The two Parties guarantee mutually from the present time and forever, against all other powers, to wit, the united states to his most Christian Majesty the present Possessions of the Crown of france in America as well as those which it may acquire by the future Treaty of peace: and his most Christian Majesty guarantees on his part to the united states, their liberty, Sovereignty, and Independence absolute, and unlimited, as well in Matters of Government as commerce and also their Possessions . . . ," etc.

Here, again, we see the opposition between the ideal and the real which is our theme in dealing with American foreign policy. All our purpose was to stand aloof from Europe; but our deed was legally to bind ourselves by the most solemn action to France—and to bind ourselves, not just for the duration of the desperate emergency which occasioned the deed, but "forever." This pledge certainly conflicted with the policy of neutrality, just as such an alliance between India and France today would end India's policy of neutrality. It gave a certain poignancy to the phrase "as little as possible" in the Congressional resolution defining our "fundamental policy" as remaining "as little as possible entangled in the . . . controversies of European nations."

In diplomacy as in other human relations no word is so reckless as "forever," because no one knows how rapidly and

[8] *Ibid.*, p. 9.

completely circumstances may change. In 1778 no one foresaw that the historic France of the *ancien régime* was about to suffer an explosion which would leave her unrecognizable and in a badly unsettled condition. No one conceived that Spain, traditionally France's ally and Britain's foe, would shortly be allied with Britain against France, any more than we could conceive today that we would shortly be allied, say, with Communist China against India. Yet the whole course of modern history has been a matter of such reversals and such triumphs of the unexpected.

Our perpetual partnership with France was to face the test of change at the beginning of George Washington's second administration, when Jefferson was Secretary of State. By February, 1793, Louis XVI was dead, France was trying to be something called a republic, and governmental power was being gathered into the hands of the terroristic dictator, Robespierre. The convulsion which had shattered France had shattered Europe. France had broken with her neighbors and was at war with them by a sort of mutual aggression. She had declared war against Britain on February 1. Immediately the American government was confronted with the question of the perpetual alliance embodied in its treaty with France or, in its literal terms, with Louis XVI, now dead. It was confronted with the guarantee to "his most Christian Majesty" of the "Possessions of the Crown of france in America"—against Britain or any other power.

Upon receiving the news of war in Europe, President Washington called a meeting of his Cabinet to consider the question: were we or were we not still bound by this treaty? A debate ensued which should be a source of particular interest for students of international law and international relations. One of the subsidiary questions raised was the identity of the other party to the treaty. Who did we make the treaty with? Certainly we did not make it with the French Republic, because there had been no French Republic at the time. The rough leaders of the National Convention in Paris did not look at all like the elegant courtiers with whom Dr. Benjamin Franklin and his associates had negotiated. If you marry a girl for life and she is suddenly transformed into someone else, can you plead the *clausula rebus sic stantibus?* Were we bound to this strange new France by the ties with which we had bound ourselves to its predecessor?

Washington's Secretary of the Treasury, Alexander Hamilton, thought not. Professor Bemis sums up his argument as follows: "He [Hamilton] was convinced that the accusations made against the King by the Convention, preceding his trial and execution, had been false, that Louis XVI had been overthrown by unfortunate circumstances which did not constitute an act of national justice; that the United States, in repudiating the new regime in France, had a right to free itself from a treaty which by virtue of the violent change in governments in France had become less useful, or materially less advantageous and more dangerous than previously it had been; that the treaty of alliance had been made with the personal monarch Louis XVI, 'a *man* [italics inserted] from whom essential benefits have been received'; that if forced to choose, the grateful and honourable part for the United States would be to join the Coalition and assist the heirs of Louis XVI to get back on the throne rather than to allow our treaty of alliance to bind us to a 'triumphant faction' which had temporarily succeeded the King in power. 'Suppose,' asked Hamilton, 'the call of the actual rulers to be complied with, and the war to have been entered into by the ally [i.e., the United States]. Suppose the expelled monarch to have re-entered his former dominions and to have been joined by one half of his subjects—would the obligation then stand? He will now have added to the title of being the formal party to the contract that of being the actual possessor of one half of the country and of the wishes of one half of the nation.' 'Is it not evident,' he added, 'that there must be an option to consider the operation of the alliance as suspended during the contest concerning the government, that on the one hand there may not be a necessity of taking part with the expelled monarch against the apparent will of the nation, or, on the other, a necessity of joining the ruling powers of the moment against the immediate party with whom the contract was made and from whom the consideration may have flowed?' . . . The military stipulations of the treaties, he argued, were contrary to that neutrality in the quarrels of Europe which it was our true policy to cultivate and maintain."[9]

The Executive Government of the new United States, in the form of President Washington's Cabinet meeting, was faced with a genuine moral dilemma—in fact, a classic moral dilemma, since most governments have, at one time or another, faced something very much like it.

At this point we get a fascinating glimpse into the operations of the human mind in these situations. Hamilton's great opponent Jefferson, as might be expected, dissented from him and took a wholly opposite view of the question. "The treaties between the United States and France," he said, "were not treaties between the United States and Louis Capet, but between the two nations of America and France; and the nations remaining in existence, though both of them since changed their forms of government, the treaties are not annulled by these changes."[10] Only inability to carry out the treaty obligations or the imminent danger of destruction by doing so could justify a default, and neither of these conditions actually obtained. Therefore the treaty was in force and binding upon us.

But did Jefferson therefore propose that the United States gird itself to stand with France against England, as a matter of unquestioned obligation, and in spite of the danger and inevitable damage to the national interest? Did he follow his argument, that our pledge was still binding, with the conclusion that we should therefore be prepared to carry it out? Not at all. He said that if France called on us to carry it out there would then be time enough to consider " 'whether a ten year

[9] *The American Secretaries of State* (New York, 1927), II, pp. 64-65.

[10] Quoted by Bailey, *A Diplomatic History of the American People* (New York, 1950), p. 72.

forebearance in us' " to call on the French for support of our claims against Britain " 'entitles us to some indulgence,' or whether we could be expected to begin a war when not prepared for it, or whether the French West Indies really would be lost if the United States did not save them, or . . . whether England would really venture to involve the United States by attacking those islands."[11] "Jefferson," Professor Bemis tells us, "never had any idea of actually intervening in the war to guarantee French possession of those West India islands. . . ."[12]

We may note, therefore, how this famous battle was fought, how the issue was resolved, and how the national interest was saved. Hamilton, to the detriment of his standing with historians, argued that the treaty was no longer binding on us and so we should not be bound by it. Jefferson, to the enhancement of his historical standing, argued that the treaty was binding on us, but he apparently was equally decided that we should not be bound by it. Those of us who try to understand the real forces which determine international relations should take note, here, however reluctantly, of a certain inevitability that marked our decision on this point. Professor Bemis says that all American statesmen of the period, without exception, were opposed to intervening in the war on the side of France.[13] The real issue, then, seems to have been by which course of agonized reasoning to arrive at this foregone conclusion.

Now let me call attention to something which I find even more significant. I have cited Professor Bemis's authority for the statement that all American statesmen of the period, without exception, were opposed to intervening in the war on the side of France. Everybody in Washington's administration favored a policy of neutrality.[14] There was no issue on this within the government or among the American statesmen of the day.

The case was not at all the same, however, with the American

---

[11] Quoted by Bemis, *The American Secretaries of State, op. cit.,* II, p. 69.
[12] *Ibid.,* II, p. 68.
[13] *Ibid.,* II, p. 67.
[14] *Ibid.,* II, p. 69.

public. Here, according to Bemis, the pro-French republican sympathizers "far outnumbered the conservative members of society."[15] Feeling for France and against Britain ran high. The interventionists, the anti-neutralists, predominated in the population. One of those great ideological storms of public passion which shake the foundations of statecraft was aroused, and it was in the teeth of this storm that President Washington, with a united administration supporting him, issued on April 22, 1793, his so-called "Proclamation of Neutrality."

The immediate consequences for Washington were bitter. He remained standing against the storm, but for the first time in his career he had to sustain within himself that terrible weight of abuse from an outraged public which is, on occasion, among the rewards of statesmanship. The experience strengthened his determination to retire at the end of his term, and it colored the Farewell Address with which he concluded that term. It imparted a personal poignancy to such words as the following: ". . . nothing is more essential than that permanent, inveterate antipathies against particular nations, and passionate attachments for others, should be excluded, and that, in place of them just and amicable feelings toward all should be cultivated. The nation which indulges toward another an habitual hatred, or an habitual fondness, is, in some degree, a slave. It is a slave to its animosity or to its affection, either of which is sufficient to lead it astray from its duty and its interest." These words represented deep experience. They might well have been heeded by all the democratic countries, not least of all our own, not least of all in the twentieth century.

This contest of 1793 between the American government and the American people over the issue of neutrality seems to me to epitomize in classic form the key problem of foreign policy in a democracy, and to anticipate later manifestations of that problem in our own American history.

[15] *Ibid.*, II, p. 79.

XI • Historians of literature, art, and music customarily draw a distinction and a contrast between a classical view of the world, on the one hand, a romantic view on the other. The terms are unsatisfactory, they defy adequate definition, and they imply an excessive categorization. Yet one finds it hard to do without them; for everyone is aware of some broad distinction to which they correspond, a distinction which is real, even though so hard to define or apply. Everyone is aware that there is, in fact, a single generic difference which distinguishes Bach's "Art of the Fugue" from Wagner's *Siegfried,* the frescoes of Michelangelo from the paintings of Delacroix, the works of Racine from the works of Hugo, Melville's *Moby Dick* from the novels of Charles Dickens.

It has not been a custom of political scientists or historians to make a like distinction in describing the policies of states, although the historians sometimes, in a casual way, do use the terms "classical" and "romantic." I care nothing for the terms themselves and propose to drop them at this point. But the distinction itself remains, no less real for being elusive, and certainly as relevant to politics as to poetry. You find it when you put De Tocqueville alongside of Herder, or when you put Cardinal Richelieu alongside Kaiser William II.

Without getting into categorical definition, there may be

some things which can be said to describe and clarify this difference. The one attitude involves a degree of personal detachment which the other rejects. The one cultivates distance and perspective, the other intimacy and involvement. The one is often skeptical, the other is moved by belief. The one is amoral, the other is preoccupied with questions of right or wrong. The one is cold, the other is hot. The one cherishes the processes of the mind, the other is uplifted by noble passions.

We saw the contrast and conflict between these two attitudes vividly exemplified by various reactions to the Soviet brutality in Hungary in the fall of 1956. A friend of mine said to me, at the time, that he agreed in his mind with the Western policy of not intervening forcibly against the Soviet Union in Hungary, since the risk that such intervention would set off a third world war was too great to be accepted. "But emotionally," he said, "I am outraged. I cannot accept it." Here was the conflict of the two attitudes in the breast of a single conscientious man.

Can there be any doubt that of these two attitudes the one dominated by emotion is the more primitive? This, in a sense, is what we are born with; it is native to us; we all have it. The attitude of skeptical intellectual detachment, and the cultivation of cold reason, on the other hand, comes, if it comes at all, with the accumulation of worldly knowledge and experience. To this extent we may say that the one represents youth, the other maturity.

Another form which this opposition takes is the conflict between those who, in advocating foreign policy, appear to be governed by considerations of strategy and those who appear to be governed by ideological considerations. Let me apply the distinction in these terms to a dilemma which, time and again, challenges the policy of states, never more so than it has in our own times: that is, the dilemma of choosing between neutrality and partisanship in the conflicts of others.

Situations arise time and again which, to the strategist, appear to make a policy of impartiality or non-partisanship imperative. Suppose the Netherlands and the Republic of Indonesia to be in conflict over their mutual relations and rights, or over their boundaries of jurisdiction. The United States regards both as its friends. More than that, its own self-interest does not allow it to dispense with the friendship of either. Under the circumstances, the strategic policy for it to adopt is to avoid any situation which would require it to make a choice between the two contestants. This is the kind of dilemma with which the United States is being given ample opportunity to familiarize itself these days. I mentioned the Netherlands and Indonesia; but I might just as well have said Britain and Iran, France and Morocco, Israel and the Arabs, South Africa and India, India and Pakistan, Japan and Korea. In each case, the strategic course for the United States has been to take a non-partisan position, a position of non-alignment.

But to the ideologist this strategic policy is deficient, sometimes even scandalously so, in failing to take account of what is really the crucial question: which side is right and which is wrong. Where Good and Evil do battle can anyone properly proclaim himself neutral and impartial? If the Dutch are brutal imperialistic oppressors and the Indonesians represent the soul of suffering humanity, or if the Dutch represent due process of law while the Indonesians represent grasping corruption and chaos—in either case, can we Americans properly say that this is a conflict in which it is not morally incumbent on us to take sides? The ideologist is honestly outraged at the suggestion.

So the two attitudes conflict with each other, leading to opposed conclusions, to respective recommendations of policy that are mutually incompatible. The strategist says we must remain detached from a foreign quarrel. The ideologist or moralist says we must take sides in it.

These broad generalizations are occasioned by the topic of this chapter, the conflict over foreign policy that arose in 1793 between the Executive Government of President Washington and a dominant part of the American public—a conflict which, as I said, seems to me a political classic, a conflict which is duplicated over and over again throughout the history of American foreign policy.

The impact of the French Revolution, like the impact of the Russian Revolution a century and a quarter later, tended to unsettle the minds of men throughout Europe and America. Conservatives like Edmund Burke and Alexander Hamilton were alarmed by it. They saw it in terms of the threat to legitimacy and the rights of property, or as chaos overthrowing order, or as the disorderly and bestial mob breaking the bonds of civilized rule. But to the most sensitive and humane portion of mankind, those whom we would today call "socially conscious," it was the final downfall of ancient evil. To Thomas Jefferson and many others it seemed like the dawn of a new age for suffering mankind, a sort of millennium in which final judgment would be meted out and the Kingdom of Heaven established, at last, on earth. The long historic ordeal of humanity was over. When that great equalizer, the guillotine, began eliminating the wicked, it was seen as a sort of machine for purging from society the evil which had always oppressed it, the evil which pertained to a particular social class rather than to humanity as a whole. One could not allow oneself to doubt that this evil would now be replaced by good. Very soon, perhaps, there would be only the virtuous left on earth, people like us. In the same way the Soviet Communists undertook to purge "the enemies of the people" a generation ago and are still doing it. Jefferson deplored the fact that some innocent blood was being shed, but rather than that the cause of liberty should fail, he said, "I would have seen half the earth desolated."[1] Today, when we have accumulated an experience of revolutionary dynamics which was not available to him, one would want a guarantee of results before paying such a price. The hopefuls of the time, however, did not then foresee Napoleon and Louis XVIII, just as the hopefuls of 1917 did not foresee Stalin and Khrushchev. They did not foresee that, in a few years, revolutionary France, champion of the rights of man, would be conducting a war of

[1] Bailey, *op. cit.*, p. 58.

extermination against the revolted slaves of Hispaniola, seeking to reimpose servitude upon them. They did not take account of the fact that there is only one species of man, that God did not create two species, one "People" and the other "Enemies of the People," that the common man, too, bears the consequences of Adam's fall.

The French Republic was proclaimed on the 21st of September, 1792. On the 21st of January, four months later, the man who had been Louis XVI was processed by the guillotine. Ten days later the new French Republic declared war on the old England of King George III. This succession of events raised ideological fervor to a high pitch in the United States. The enthusiasts of the new revolutionary dispensation danced in the streets every time there was news of a French victory over the British. They dropped the title "Mister" and began calling one another "Citizen." William Cobbett reported that in Philadelphia, then the capital of the United States, Louis XVI was guillotined in effigy twenty or thirty times every day, and that young women under twenty expressed a willingness to dip their hands in the blood of Marie Antoinette, whose turn beneath the knife had not yet come.[2] "Bliss was it in that dawn to be alive," sang the poet Wordsworth.

Picture, now, the cold, detached minds of old President Washington and his Cabinet, meeting behind closed doors to agree that the nation must remain neutral and impartial between France and Britain, while in the streets the noble passion rages to the strains of "La Marseillaise." This strikes me as immensely poignant and significant—the opposition between the strategic and the ideological, between the classical and the romantic, between the head and the heart, between experienced wisdom and the sense of righteousness, between maturity and youth. That opposition was to precipitate a sort of constitutional crisis, or at least a constitutional issue, the question being whether the government led the people or the people the government in the new nation which had been born on our shores.

[2] Bailey, *op. cit.*, p. 57.

It was into this charged atmosphere of 1793 that a remarkable character, Citizen Genêt, first minister accredited by the new French Republic to the American government, blazed like a comet. Genêt was young, fervent, and more brilliant than judicious. Apparently he thought of himself not only as the emissary of the Girondist administration in Paris but also as the agent of the revolutionary ideology, fraternally bearing salvation to the American people as to all mankind. He might, had he wished, have come directly to Philadelphia to present his credentials to President Washington's government. A house guest usually makes it the first order of his business to say hello to his hostess and shake hands with her. Instead, Genêt landed at Charleston, South Carolina, where he was greeted with wild enthusiasm. He presented his credentials first, so to speak, to the American people. Quite regardless of the fact that the United States had declared its neutrality, a fact of which he had not yet informed himself, he proceeded to organize the conduct of his country's war on American soil, sending out French privateers from Charleston to seize British ships in American waters, setting up prize courts to condemn those ships, preparing a military expedition from American soil against the adjacent provinces of Spain. He presided over the foundation of a local branch of the French Jacobin Clubs. Having done all this, he at last embarked on a long triumphal procession through the back country to Philadelphia. A trip which might have been made in less than a week, says Professor Bailey, "was dragged out over twenty-eight days, to the accompaniment of salvos of artillery, fraternal embraces, and frantic cheering."[3] Philadelphia turned itself out, on his arrival, in a like demonstration of enthusiasm. Now, at last, he was ready to receive the expected embrace of that old man, George Washington, to whose government he had still to present his credentials.

But President Washington stood on cold formality. He was more than twice as old as Citizen Genêt, the fire apparently no longer burned in his breast if it ever had, and Genêt, who did

[3] *Op. cit.*, p. 75.

not find himself received as the bridegroom, quickly concluded that this old man had no right to speak for the young and ardent American people. The President's "Proclamation of Neutrality," which Genêt had just learned about, did not have the authority of the popular will behind it. In the new dawn of freedom Citizen Genêt could not be bound by the usages of a dead past. He had no compunction about disregarding the Proclamation, and he had no compunction about making his appeal from the President to the real sovereign, the people. In fact, he embarked on a political campaign against the government to which he was accredited.

At first this was not done in vain, and President Washington, together with his Cabinet, had the bitter experience (reflected in the Farewell Address) of seeing a great part of the American people, probably a good majority, siding with a foreign envoy against its own government. The authority of the government, its power to govern, was thrown into question, not just by Genêt but by his political following among the American people. Woodcuts appeared of Washington being subjected to the guillotine, just like Louis XVI and the other enemies of the people. He was accused of treason. The *National Gazette* of Philadelphia claimed that the popular reception accorded Citizen Genêt showed that *"sovereignty* still resides with THE PEOPLE, and that neither proclamations nor *royal demeanor and state* can prevent them from exercising it."[4] "In a republican country, it was said," according to Justice Marshall, "the people alone were the basis of government. . . . The doctrine that the sovereignty of the nation resided in the constituted authorities was incompatible with the principles of liberty; . . . if M. Genêt dissented from the interpretation given by the president to existing treaties, he might rightfully appeal to the real sovereign whose agent the president was, and to whom he was responsible for his conduct."[5]

Writing to Jefferson many years later, John Adams said: "You

[4] Bailey, *op. cit.,* p. 76.
[5] John Marshall, *The Life of George Washington,* Philadelphia, 1807, V, p. 452.

certainly never felt the terrorism excited by Genêt, in 1793, when ten thousand people in the streets of Philadelphia, day after day, threatened to drag Washington out of his house, and effect a revolution in the government, or compel it to declare war in favor of the French revolution and against England."[6] During those days, according to Marshall, those who did not share the revolutionary ardor "were calumniated as the tools of Britain and the satellites of despotism. . . . a passion for France . . . was deemed the surest test of patriotism."[7]

All of us who have seen similar surges of popular ideological feeling in our own time, threatening to wise policy and the authority of government alike, can perhaps take courage from the happy ending to this particular tale. President Washington never weakened, Genêt finally went too far, the passion of the day exhausted itself, and the French authorities not only agreed to Genêt's recall but had the guillotine waiting to demonstrate its impartiality upon him. He preferred, however, to take the political asylum in the United States which President Washington offered him. He married the daughter of Governor Clinton of New York and set himself up as a gentleman on the banks of the Hudson River. Who knows but what, with time and reflection, he may at last have gained for himself some of the maturity and wisdom which characterized the old man whom he had held in contempt? In the ultimate appeal from Demos drunk to Demos sober Washington came out well. Before long he was universally honored by us Americans for the wisdom of his policy, his courage, and his firmness. If Washington was vindicated at last, so in a sense was democracy.

I have recounted this old history of Washington's "Neutrality Proclamation" because it illustrates so vividly, at the very outset of our national life, one of the difficulties which attends the prudent conduct of foreign affairs in a democracy. Here we see strategy against ideological partisanship, the mind against

[6] Bailey, op. cit., pp. 76-77.
[7] Marshall, op. cit., V, p. 401.

the heart. Here we see the government unanimous on one side, a dominant part of the people inflamed with noble passion and true belief on the other. Here we see those who, today, are acknowledged to be among the outstanding statesmen of modern history, those who are now held to have been right in 1793, united in the pursuit of a policy that was cold, calculating, selfish in the sense that it took account of the national interest primarily, essentially amoral, not primarily concerned with the treacherous question of righteousness as an issue in international conflicts. On the other side you have what appears to be all nobility, the sword in the hand of the avenging angel, the great cause of human liberation throughout the world, the moral crusade for the salvation of mankind from evil.

Again and again, throughout American history, these forces will contend, even into our own time, even to this very day. Again and again their contention will take the form of a conflict, disguised or not, between government and people, and we may see government resorting to all sorts of devices to carry out what it conceives to be the strategic policy in the face of a public to which strategic thinking is not native and may be repugnant.

But even in the veins of statesmen the blood must sometimes run hot. I think it was General Marshall, a man with something of General Washington's austere self-discipline, who as Secretary of State used to say that the essential for any man in such a position was to keep down his own emotions. In the city of Washington I don't know how many men, remaining outwardly imperturbable all day, go home at night to beat upon the wall with their fists and howl. This is something that many Washington wives know all too well.

Referring to the crisis of 1793, I have pictured the statesmen as cool and calculating strategists, the public as inspired by ideological fervor. That picture requires correction. Just as God did not create two species of humanity, aristocrats and common men, so he did not create as two species government officials and members of the public. It is, in fact, the same blood that runs

126

through the veins of both. If there is a difference it is, perhaps, a difference of information, experience, and responsibility which impels some to discipline the natural ardor of this common blood. But it would be a mistake to think that foreign policy is ever made by mechanical calculators rather than by human beings who are essentially just like us. When I see newspaper commentators, time and again, speculating on what can be the profound and calculated rationale of a particular foreign policy move by Moscow or London or Washington I think to myself that they may well be misleading themselves and their readers. In all likelihood the foreign policy move is to be accounted for by the fact that the men who made it had not been getting enough sleep. If we could see the inside of all these great capitals today, we would find cause to worry because the increasing difficulty of conducting international relations in the modern world has reached a point where it sometimes exceeds the normal tolerance of the human organism. Occasionally this is revealed, as when an Anthony Eden breaks down. More often we, the public, don't see it. I have talked to Washington doctors, however, and many of them could tell a story which none of us would find comforting.

I have referred so far with unqualified admiration to the generation of the American Founding Fathers. But no one can read of the doings of Franklin, Hamilton, Jay, Jefferson, Madison, Monroe, and the rest without being aware that, whatever other qualities they may also have had, they possessed the general weakness of our common nature. It would, for example, be easy to make out a case for behavior that was close to treasonable on the part of Hamilton and of Jay. These men, too, were human beings, though in the long run and collectively they somehow managed to transcend our ordinary bounds.

Citizen Genêt represented impassioned humanity as the men who constituted the American government, apparently, did not. His righteous behavior, as we see it in historical perspective, was not right. But there was nothing unique about it except, perhaps, the degree to which it went. Every government which tries to practice a policy of neutrality or non-partisanship in particular situations faces the problem of making its own warm-blooded diplomats conform, as well as those it receives. It is a daily problem in the State Department. It was a problem for President Washington's second administration, which succeeded hardly better in having its own successive ministers in Paris conform to American neutrality than in having the French minister in Philadelphia conform to it.

While Citizen Genêt was conducting himself so improperly in the United States, Gouverneur Morris, the American minister to France, was openly hostile to the French Revolution and, like Genêt, was working to oppose the domestic policy of the government to which he was accredited. He took an active part in trying to effect the escape of Louis XVI, and he saved those he could from the guillotine by providing asylum for them in his house. Apparently he, too, could not hold himself neutral in a conflict between good and evil, between right and wrong—though his identification of right and wrong happened to be the opposite of that made by Citizen Genêt. When the American government asked for the recall of Citizen Genêt, the French government found that it had the same sort of grounds for demanding the recall of Mr. Morris.

Mr. Morris's successor in Paris was the man who would, thirty years later, give his name to the traditional American doctrine involving non-participation in European quarrels. Nevertheless, the spirit of neutrality was as alien to Mr. James Monroe as to Mr. Morris or Citizen Genêt, and his conduct as the minister to belligerent France of a neutral state showed the same impropriety. He became, quite openly, an ardent supporter of France against Britain. When this partisanship led him into conflict with the policy of his own government (which he assured the French would be overthrown in the election of 1796) it finally became necessary for his government to recall him. Again one sees the difficulty that our ardent human nature makes in the impartial and calculated conduct of foreign relations, as well as the point of Talleyrand's famous

128

advice: *"Surtout, pas trop de zèle."*

I know all too well how painful it is to many among us to be told that foreign relations ought not to be conducted with moral fervor and partisanship, that they ought rather to be calculated in a cold-blooded fashion, weighing advantage and disadvantage. Many of us can find no personal fulfillment in action that does not represent a militant righteousness opposing the powers of darkness. In a world ridden by injustice, a world in which the Kremlin cracks the whip over helpless masses, a world in which the wicked British try to subvert Egypt's newly won sovereignty or a wicked Colonel Nasser commits aggression against the international community, a world in which South Africa oppresses Indians and India oppresses Kashmiris, a world in which power is held by a General Franco or a Marshal Tito, a world that contains such a wicked man as Dulles (or is it Acheson?)—in such a world, how can one be neutral?—how can one refrain from marching in the streets with the forces of righteousness, open hand or fist uplifted as the case may be?—how can one refuse to take one's stand for the good and against the evil? Under such circumstances, to be neutral, to be cold, to be calculating, to think only of oneself, is to stifle one's best instincts, to take away the zest and incentive of life.

To this the mature and skeptical may object that the identification of righteousness is not such a sure thing as this attitude supposes, and that there is even a sin of pride involved in the passionate assurance that one has, in fact, identified it. History gives support to this objection, for what had seemed utterly righteous at the time has generally taken on a different aspect in historical perspective. Is it not a paradox that Washington, the man who was execrated by the righteous in 1793, today seems to represent a greater moral nobility than his opponent, the ideological crusader, Genêt? The skeptic who has read his history well may, in fact, come to fear and distrust the servants of a militant righteousness more than he fears the cool and the calculating. "You shall scarce speak to Cromwell about anything," wrote a contemporary of England's Protector, "but he will lay his hand on his breast, elevate his eyes, and call God to record. He will weep, howl, and repent, even while he doth smite you under the fifth rib."[8] It was in the cause of righteousness that the guillotine drank so much French blood during the period of which I have been speaking. Only righteousness, it appears, can justify the more extreme forms of human brutality.

"While there is battle and hatred," says Professor Butterfield, "men have eyes for nothing save the fact that the enemy is the cause of all the troubles; but long, long afterwards, when all passion has been spent, the historian often sees that it was a conflict between one half-right that was perhaps too wilful, and another half-right that was perhaps too proud. . . ."[9]

In 1793 some Americans saw all righteousness on the side of the British monarchy, but more found it on the side of revolutionary France. A few years later, however, came a revulsion of popular feeling against the French Revolution. There was a sort of panic among many Americans at the subversive ideas which it was spreading. Senator Cabot said that England "is now the only barrier between us and the deathly embraces of our dear Allies—between universal irreligion, immorality and plunder, and what order, probity, virtue and religion is left."[10] With the publication of the famous "X,Y,Z," dispatches in 1798 anti-French feeling rose to a fever pitch which it must have been strange for Gentleman Genêt, now residing on the banks of the Hudson River, to observe. "Loyal addresses poured in on President and Congress, indignation meetings were held, reams of patriotic poetry were produced, and 'millions for defence, but not one cent for tribute' became the toast of the day."[11] The treaty of 1778 with France was, at last, formally abrogated, and the United States found itself engaged in an

[8] John Lilburne, quoted by Dean Acheson in testimony before the House Foreign Affairs Committee, Washington, D.C., Jan. 10, 1957.

[9] Herbert Butterfield, *History and Human Relations* (London, 1951), p. 10.

[10] Morison and Commager, *op. cit.*, I, pp. 371-72.

[11] *Ibid.*, p. 373.

undeclared war with the French Republic. This time the coolness and calculation were shown on the French side, by the unzealous Abbé de Tallyrand, who avoided a declared war and did what he could to appease us. Before we Americans had got over this new access of ideological passion we had gone, under the notorious Alien and Sedition Acts, to unfortunate extremes in suppressing manifestations among us of the dangerous thoughts propagated by the French Revolution.

A couple of years later, however, we had reacted, once more, in the other direction. The anti-French Federalists were voted out of office and Thomas Jefferson became the third President of the United States. The ship of state finally reached, for the time being, an even keel.

XII • After the disciplined statesmanship of the earlier period, the War of 1812 comes as a confused anticlimax. I shall therefore pass quickly by it, pausing just long enough to call attention to the fact that, because it hardly represents any sensible policy, it is merely a disturbing impediment to any account of American policy which seeks to achieve an artistic consistency. No strategic interest prompted us Americans to fight against the side that was fighting Napoleon. Our passions aroused, we simply blundered into the wrong war on the wrong side at the wrong time. In the violation of our neutral rights, which was the cause or the pretext for our going to war, we had roughly equal cause for going to war with either side, the French or the British. Congressman Calhoun suggested that we go to war against them both. But Jefferson thought it would be better to take on the two belligerents successively rather than simultaneously, beginning with Britain. Public indignation was against Britain rather than France, and the prospect of acquiring Canada also exerted an appeal. Some of the passion of the so-called "war hawks" infected President Madison's government, which was not disposed to resist the public pressure. So we found ourselves engaged in a confused war which nobody won, which gained us nothing except a burned capital, and which nobody knew how to end for two long years.

However, the conclusion of the Napoleonic Wars, in which we Americans had played such an anomalous role, marks the true beginning of our American isolation. Through the last quarter of the eighteenth century we had been at war with Britain, allied with France, and then at war with France. In the first fifteen years of the new century Britain had constantly annoyed us in the Ohio territories and on the high seas, and we had finally fallen into war with her again. But after the War of 1812 we settled our immediate boundary difficulties with her, agreed to mutual disarmament on the Great Lakes, and got some of the fisheries problems over which we had been quarreling out of the way. We were now growing big, expanding westward, rising in power, security, and self-confidence. With westward expansion we were becoming more democratic and also more nationalistic. Where we had been Virginians or New Englanders we were all Americans now. We had survived our birth and the hostility of the great powers which had crowded and threatened us for some years after our birth. At last the time had come which Washington foresaw in his Farewell Address, the time when we might "defy material injury from external annoyance."

On the other side, Europe was left exhausted by the Napoleonic Wars. Almost the whole of Spain's empire in the New World had slipped from her grasp and she was about to surrender Florida to us. For the first time in our young history we were encompassed with weakness on all sides. Bursting with our own internal energy, we lived in the midst of what we would today call a "power vacuum." The result was an increasing preoccupation with our "Manifest Destiny," as we came to call it, that of filling up the vacant continent all the way to the Pacific. For the first time we really could do, in fact, what we had so long wanted to do in theory, turn our backs on the Old World, forget about it, and concentrate on our own continent.

We no longer followed European politics in the newspapers. We became narrower even as we expanded. In a word, we now tended to become provincial. Within another generation, when our previous intensive experience of international relations had receded into the past, the sophistication which went with that experience would also fail. Our strength and our security would become a boast, and the young Abraham Lincoln would at last evoke no skepticism when he maintained that "all the armies of Europe, Asia, and Africa combined, with all the treasure of the earth (our own excepted) in their military chest, with a Bonaparte for a commander, could not by force take a drink from the Ohio or make a track on the Blue Ridge in a trial of a thousand years."

By 1823, then, the United States was ready to proclaim the doctrine of the two hemispheres, the doctrine of our own hemisphere's isolation from the other hemisphere, the doctrine that came to be known as the Monroe Doctrine. President Monroe, the once ardent supporter of liberation in Europe, went before the Congress and said: "that the American continents, by the free and independent condition which they have assumed and maintain, are henceforth not to be considered as subjects for future colonization by any European powers. . . . The political system of the allied powers," he said, referring to the members of the Holy Alliance, "is essentially different . . . from that of America. . . . We owe it, therefore, to candor and to the amicable relations existing between the United States and those powers to declare that we should consider any attempt on their part to extend their system to any portion of this hemisphere as dangerous to our peace and safety." At the same time that Mr. Monroe posted this "No Trespassing" sign on the American hemisphere, he made it clear that, with respect to the internal politics of the European Old World, the United States was essentially nothing more than a spectator, that its policy was one of non-interference.

It may seem evident that this policy of keeping a distance between the two hemispheres was based on a solid foundation of strategic thinking. In its most eloquent formulation, that which President Washington had given it in his Farewell Address, it represented the warning of a battered veteran against allowing our partisan passions to draw us into the quarrels and conflicts of the Old World. It represented a triumph of the strategic considerations which called for neutrality over the ideological considerations which summoned us to fight the good fight wherever we saw evil.

In point of fact, however, strategic and ideological considerations were all mixed up together. Look at the circumstances. Europe was in the grip of a conservative reaction against the French Revolution. Counter-revolution dominated it and was symbolized by that sinister or absurd political contraption, the Holy Alliance. The purpose of the Holy Alliance was to stop or reverse history, to undo the work of the late eighteenth century, to re-establish the subjugation of those who had revolted, and, this time, to keep them down.

As long as the Holy Alliance limited the realization of this ideological purpose to Europe it did not touch directly, at least, any of our own strategic interests. It merely provided an argument in favor of our staying clear of Europe and keeping Europe clear of us, an argument in favor of the policy of two separate hemispheres. However, when France, as the agent of the reaction, marched into Spain to re-establish divine right there, a natural alarm was felt that the powers of reaction would also undertake to re-establish divine right in the revolted colonies which Spain had had in the New World. And if, following the undoing of the French Revolution, the Latin American revolutions were to be undone, then would not the logical next step be an attempt to suppress the revolutionary example which the North American republic had been the first to set and which it continued to provide? If this threat was real, and it was certainly vivid, then the warning clauses of the Monroe Doctrine represented a strategic necessity.

But it happened that ideological considerations, here, marched together with strategic considerations. There was no conflict between them, as had been the case in 1793. Ideologically, no less than strategically, we stood opposed to the Holy Alliance. Under the circumstances, can one say that the Monroe

Doctrine was the product of strategic thinking? Might it not have been a product of either or a mixture of both? One would have to enter the private recesses of President Monroe's mind and the minds of his advisers to get an answer to this question of motive; and then one might find things rather mixed up, the human mind being what it is, even with all its glories. And one might find that one mind was moved chiefly by ideological zeal and another chiefly by considerations of strategy.

I shall offer a clue, however. It is in the self-denying clauses of the Monroe Doctrine, those which refer to our policy of not interfering in the political conflicts of the European Old World. For here the case is different from that of the warning or prohibitive clauses. Here strategy and ideology stand mutually opposed. Here ideology is against that neutrality in Europe's quarrels which strategy favors.

At this point the human nature of foreign policy manifests itself and introduces into the cold record a touch of pathos and irony. The first draft of the Monroe Doctrine was the work of James Monroe himself, of that warm-blooded human being whom Washington had recalled from his post as American minister in Paris because his espousal of the French republican cause conflicted with our policy of neutrality.

The Monroe Doctrine, as originally presented by the President to his Cabinet for its consideration, might be regarded as a manifestation of ideological support for popular revolt against monarchy anywhere, in the Old World as well as the New. It not only opposed the reimposition of the Spanish monarchy on the revolted Spanish Americans, it denounced its reimposition by the Holy Alliance on Spain itself. And it announced support for the independence of Greece from Turkish rule. This was not, therefore, a strategic doctrine of two hemispheres at all, but a One World ideological doctrine of support for liberation movements in Europe as well as America. It responded, in particular, to the enthusiasm with which the American people, of whom Mr. Monroe was one, viewed that Greek struggle for independence from the Turkish infidel

136

which had such a romantic appeal for the heirs of ancient Greek civilization, that struggle in which the English poet Byron lost his life. The President, according to Professor Perkins, was willing "to associate the United States with republicanism wherever it showed itself, in Greece no less than in South America."[1] Monroe's original draft of his Doctrine, therefore, did not represent a Washingtonian policy of neutrality at all but, rather, a diametrically opposed policy of taking sides with the right against the wrong in foreign conflicts, whichever the hemisphere in which they occurred. So narrow is the line that sometimes divides opposites!

Secretary of State John Quincy Adams, an heir of the Washingtonian tradition, immediately opposed the President's conception. In his memoirs Adams reports the argument he made. The message, as President Monroe had prepared it, "would be a summons to arms against all Europe, and for objects of policy exclusively European—Greece and Spain. It would be as new, too, in our policy as it would be surprising. For more than thirty years Europe had been in convulsions; every nation of which it had been composed alternately invading and invaded. Empires, kingdoms, principalities, had been over-thrown, revolutionized and counter-revolutionized, and we had looked on, safe in our distance beyond an intervening ocean, and avowing a total forbearance to interfere in any of the combinations of European politics." "The ground that I wish to take," Mr. Adams told Mr. Monroe, "is that of earnest remonstrance against the interference of the European powers by force against South America, but to disclaim all interference on our part with Europe; to make an American cause, and adhere inflexibly to that."[2]

President Monroe saw and came to accept the strategic point which Secretary Adams made. "One of the most striking features of the pronouncement of 1823," says Professor Perkins, "is the sharp dividing line which it draws between the Old World and

[1] Dexter Perkins, *The Monroe Doctrine* (Cambridge, Mass., 1927), I, p. 76.
[2] Quoted by Dexter Perkins, in Bemis, *American Secretaries of State*, IV, pp. 70-71.

the New. The drawing of this line immensely strengthened Monroe's warning against European interference in South America. There is an appealing, if perhaps a specious, logic in the view-point that the United States, in keeping out of European affairs, had a right to demand a like forbearance from Europe with regard to the Americas. As Adams truly remarked, such a position was much more in accord with the traditions of American diplomacy than any other."[3]

Here we see, then, as in 1793, the issue between a strategy of neutrality or isolation and the warm human impulse to take sides everywhere. Neutrality is against human nature. It requires, therefore, a great capacity for detachment or a firm self-discipline among those who would realize it. Switzerland has precisely the same problem, as could be seen in the fall of 1956, when there was cause to wonder whether the depth of popular Swiss sympathy for the oppressed Hungarians might not prejudice the Swiss policy of neutrality. In 1793 we saw the issue resolved between Washington's unanimous Cabinet and an inflamed section of public opinion. In 1823 we see it resolved between the President and his Secretary of State within the bosom of the Cabinet. But the issue itself is perennial. It comes to a climax time and again in our American history and in one form or another is with us, still, today. Who knows but what upon it hangs the future of the world?

This neutrality, represented by the self-denying clauses of the Monroe Doctrine, was our unquestioned policy throughout the remainder of the nineteenth century. The strategic thinking of Washington, summed up in his Farewell Address, remained decisive. It was not up to us to choose sides in the conflicts of another hemisphere not our own, to decide which side was right and which was wrong. As Secretary Adams had had to remind his chief, the issue between monarchy and republicanism in the Balkan or Iberian Peninsula was none of our business.

But if the President of the United States, a man of ample

[3] *Ibid.*, p. 71.

diplomatic experience, a former Secretary of State, the author of the Monroe Doctrine, had had to be reminded of what our true policy was, one can imagine that there were others in the United States who found it no less difficult on particular occasions to remember it. I recall, a few years ago, a long argument over the luncheon table in Washington with one of our career diplomats, an able man but another James Monroe in his ideological zeal. I was trying to convince him that it would not be wise or proper for the United States to pursue an ideological policy designed to overthrow dictatorships in Latin America. It was one of those rare occasions when I have succeeded in convincing anyone of anything. Apparently he was in fact convinced, and he finally acknowledged as much. He agreed that the United States must by no means succumb to the ideological temptation of campaigning against dictatorships in Latin America. But a silence followed, during which he seemed to be engaged in some inner struggle with himself. Finally he burst out, "But I insist on an exception when it comes to that ———— dictator in ————!"

This experience is a parable. To accept a strategic and anti-ideological policy in principle is one thing; to impose on one's ideological sympathies the discipline which the actual realization of such a policy requires is another. The American people accepted the strategic policy of the two hemispheres more easily than they could accept its implementation in situations that aroused their ideological partisanship. This is just as true, still, in our day—when it comes to Arab-Israeli relations, for example. The *New York Times* recently printed a letter, signed by fourteen of the most distinguished men in the United States, pleading the Israeli cause purely on grounds of ideological affinity, and in such terms as to give the impression that strategic considerations would be irrelevant if not indecent under the circumstances. Many of the signatories were professional intellectuals, and professional intellectuals often consider that ideology is their only business, that they need give no heed to strategy and the practical problems of international relations, since these are the business of people in foreign offices who have to do their thinking on a lower level—on the level of George Washington's thinking when he warned that "the nation which indulges toward another an habitual hatred, or an habitual fondness, is, in some degree, a slave."

If President Monroe and a large part of the American people found an attitude of detachment difficult in 1823, when the Greek people were fighting for their independence, our government and people were to find that the revolutionary uprisings of 1848 in Europe made such an attitude no less difficult. And by 1848 the United States had become far more of a democracy than it had been in 1793, when President Washington was able to disregard the popular clamor. Beginning with Andrew Jackson's election to the White House in 1829, a new kind of person came to be associated with the conduct of the executive branch, a Cleon instead of a Pericles, a man who found his justification less in distinctive qualities of character and intellect, or in belonging to a governing class, more in the fact that he was representative of the people. The new type of executive would feel an obligation which Washington and the Adamses, for example, had never felt—which James Monroe had never felt—to carry out the immediate will of the people where that will made itself clearly felt. Washington considered that he had been elected by the people to apply his own judgment to the conduct of the nation's affairs. His later successors have tended more to consider that they were elected, rather, to give expression to the popular judgment. I mention this because it explains why the precedent of 1793, in which the President openly flouted the popular will of the moment, has never been repeated. The popular will has been flouted by later Presidents, as it was in some instances by Franklin D. Roosevelt, as it has been by President Eisenhower, but never openly, always by means of subterfuge in some degree. That subterfuge is an important part of the art of democratic government today—and in more countries than just the United

States. It is sometimes called "public relations." I cannot myself doubt that, in its degree, it is an evil necessity, a necessity which one would hope to see diminish with a growth of public sophistication.

When the European revolutions of 1848 aroused the ideological fervor of the American people the American government of President Zachary Taylor could not disregard that fervor as President Washington had disregarded the pro-French fervor of 1793. Domestic political considerations now imposed themselves on foreign policy, and not for the last time. An articulate part of American public opinion, organized in the so-called "Young America" movement, called for what was in effect a policy of "liberation." The United States should, in particular, make common cause with the Hungarian revolutionaries against the despotisms of Austria and Russia.

Secretary of State Daniel Webster did not resist this clamor, as he logically should have, in the name of our traditional and established policy of the two hemispheres. On the contrary, responding to the clamor, he sent a diplomatic emissary to the Hungarian revolutionaries with authority to promise that the United States would recognize them. The emissary did not get to Hungary before the revolt collapsed and this diplomatic intervention was, therefore, not realized. But the Austrian chargé in Washington nevertheless protested and the American government thereupon embarked on a public quarrel with the Austrian government which strengthened its political standing with the American people—as was the intention. The people were delighted when their Secretary of State, in his official reply to the protest, boasted about the greatness of the United States and referred to the comparative insignificance of Austria in terms that remind one of children quarreling. He said in his note to the Austrian diplomat (for the benefit of his domestic gallery): "The power of this republic at the present moment is spread over a region one of the richest and most fertile on the globe, and of an extent in comparison with which the possessions of the house of Hapsburg are but as a patch on the earth's surface."[4]

When the eloquent and attractive leader of the unsuccessful Hungarian rebellion, Louis Kossuth, came to visit us in 1851, popular enthusiasm went wild. Again the government was carried along with it. The Secretary of State, addressing a banquet in honor of Kossuth, said: "We shall rejoice to see our American model upon the Lower Danube and on the mountains of Hungary. . . . I limit my inspirations for Hungary, for the present, to that single and simple point—Hungarian independence, Hungarian self-government, Hungarian control of Hungarian destinies."[5] One result of these noble remarks was that Austria all but broke off relations with us.

Throughout this whole period the ironclad and established foreign policy of the United States, as set forth in Washington's Farewell Address and the Monroe Doctrine, was non-interference, non-participation, neutrality in the affairs of Europe. Neither Mr. Daniel Webster nor anyone else, as far as I know, proposed that this policy be abandoned. The fact is that Mr. Webster, when he intervened in favor of Hungarian independence, was not concerning himself with foreign policy at all. He was concerning himself with domestic politics. He was not modifying our foreign policy. He was merely allowing it to be overridden by domestic political considerations. The foreign policy remained unchanged and would, presumably, manifest itself again whenever the domestic considerations allowed.

We must not make too much of these episodes. The fact that the ship of state has often wobbled does not mean it has not adhered to a set course. The fact that the Monroe Doctrine took the shape it did is more important and significant than the fact that President Monroe, at one moment, wanted to give it a different shape. The fact that we exchanged diplomatic recriminations with Austria over the issue of Hungarian inde-

[4] Bailey, *op. cit.*, p. 286.
[5] Bailey, *op. cit.*, p. 287.

pendence is insignificant beside the fact that we did not, ultimately, undertake any effective intervention. The American people cheered themselves hoarse when Kossuth visited our shores in the cause of Hungarian independence. But when it became evident that he was summoning us to active intervention in Europe, then, says Professor Bailey: "the enthusiasm evaporated with a suddenness proportionate to its extravagance. The magnetic Hungarian sailed from America a sadder and wiser man, leaving behind him Kossuth beards, Kossuth hats, Kossuth overcoats, and even Kossuth County, Iowa."[6] The fact is that we, the American people, had no intention of departing from our traditional foreign policy in the ultimate test, where it would involve sacrifice as well as shouting.

One can imagine that President Monroe, in 1823, might have aroused a storm of enthusiastic support for himself if he had, in his message, included ringing words on behalf of Greek independence. But if, in addition, he had proposed an American expeditionary force against Turkey he would surely have found the sobriety of the American people wonderful to behold. Perhaps it would have been the same in 1793 if President Washington had called for a general mobilization, conscription, and the doubling of taxes to support the cause which Citizen Genêt represented so appealingly.

I cite these tempests of public opinion and the responses of the politicians because we cannot understand foreign policy in any of our democracies unless we understand what meaning to attach to them. They play an important role, very often a most dangerous role, but generally also a limited role in the democratic conduct of foreign relations. One example is the attitude of a preponderant part of the American public toward Communist China from 1949 to 1954. We Americans were violent in our animus and our professions against Red China. In the summer of 1954 President Syngman Rhee of the Republic of Korea, an outstanding symbol of opposition to the Chinese Communists, was enthusiastically greeted on an official visit

[6] Bailey, *op. cit.*, pp. 287-288.

to the United States. He was paid the rare honor of being invited to address a joint session of Congress in Washington. But when he proposed before that session an all-out attack on Communist China by Korean and Chinese Nationalist armies, with American air and naval support, the sudden silence was startling. You might say that the air all over the United States turned blue with sobriety. There was no more enthusiasm for Mr. Rhee after that. He left the country, precisely as Mr. Kossuth had left it a century earlier, a sadder and a wiser man.

President Rhee failed to understand what should be a first principle for the understanding of these situations. The public, always and everywhere, finds it easy to separate in its mind enthusiasm for a cause from sacrifice for that cause. Shrewd politicians encourage it in this self-deception. When they are riding the wave of one of these accesses of popular ideological passion they call for more dynamic, more militant, more positive policies—but they generally do not couple this with proposals for economic mobilization, for greater manpower conscription, and for higher taxes.

All this has its bearing on the widespread misunderstanding of Secretary Dulles's famous "liberation" policy during the first Eisenhower administration. But this belongs to later chapters.

XIII • I have been giving examples from American history of a conflict that characterizes the development and implementation of foreign policy in any democracy. In intellectual terms the conflict is between the strategical considerations that generally determine foreign policy in its more durable aspects, and the emotional, partisan, or ideological passions which are aroused over particular issues that challenge it. Although this conflict takes place within each of us and within the councils of government, it manifests itself most significantly between government and people in a democracy. Circumstances tend to impress strategical thinking on those who bear the direct responsibility of government, while ideological partisanship remains native to the rank and file of people who are happily free of such responsibility. Where this is the situation a governmental administration is constantly having to weigh foreign policy considerations against domestic political considerations in making the decisions that fall to it.

I have given examples from old history. Let me now give some that are within our memory.

A few years ago President Perón's government in Argentina seized and, in effect, suppressed a famous old newspaper, *La Prensa* of Buenos Aires. This was an action by the Argentine government within the limits of its own domestic jurisdiction.

145

It was wholly outside the jurisdiction of the government of the United States. The United States was a party to treaties by which it had committed itself not to intervene in the internal affairs of any other American republic. This was an internal affair of the Argentine Republic. Consequently, while private Americans, newspaper writers or radio commentators, were quite free to make an issue of the Argentine government's action, the government of the United States was not free to do so.

But our American newspapers, aroused by the fate of a fellow newspaper in Buenos Aires, embarked on a campaign in which they pressed the State Department to do something. It was no use for the officials of the Department to tell the editorial writers that it was not up to the United States government to protect Argentines against their own government, that our foreign policy was not to interfere in the domestic affairs of other American republics, and that we had treaty obligations to this effect. As far as the newspapermen were concerned, this was simply a matter of fighting the good fight against evildoers. Would the State Department stand by and see this innocent newspaper assassinated by a bloodstained tyrant? Would it "appease" Perón? In its addiction to "expediency" was it as callous as all this to moral principle? If our wives and daughters were being assaulted by a monster, would any of us stand idly by because of some legalistic technicality? Were we (in the State Department) men or were we mice?

The answer is that we were men. We were human. The responsible political officials bore the heat for a time, and then succumbed. (I was there and consequently cannot find it in myself to blame them.) A public statement was issued deploring the action of the Argentine government against *La Prensa*, reminding it that in the United States public opinion was paramount, and saying that the action against *La Prensa* might consequently compel a reconsideration of our policy toward Argentina. Our newspapers cheered and the State Department breathed easily once again.

The statement was, in itself, a declaration of national irresponsibility. It said to the world that public opinion in the United States might prevail over our international obligations; and in principle, at least, this was not a good thing to say to other nations. Quite incidentally, it could do *La Prensa* no good and might harm it by arousing nationalistic resentment among the Argentine people at foreign interference in their domestic concerns.

But the incident was unimportant. It counted for nothing in the sweep and range of international affairs. The statement was not a major declaration by the government of the United States. It appeased the American press, had no lasting effect on the situation in Argentina, and was quickly forgotten by everyone. United States policy continued to be, as it is today, that of non-intervention in the internal affairs of the other American republics; just as our policy of non-intervention in European affairs survived, intact, Daniel Webster's support of the Hungarian rebellion. Such incidents represent the ordinary compromises of politics. One must expect them. Whatever may have been true in President Washington's day and in the circumstances of his unique personal prestige, in our day those who do not bend somewhat to the blasts of public opinion end by being broken, and that benefits nobody. These are matters of degree.

Now let me recount another episode that was a few degrees less insignificant than the *La Prensa* intervention. This took place in 1945 and '46. Even the calmest and most disciplined population is liable to an access of uncontrolled emotion in the moment of victory after a war in which it has subjected itself to unwonted discipline and sacrifice. Frustration is released. There is a mood of exaltation and righteousness, a sense of having at last emerged into the millennium, and an insistence on wiping the international slate clean, once and for all, of such villainous elements as still remain, elements which are supposed to have caused all the world's troubles in the past. This is the popular mood that defeated Woodrow Wilson's attempt to bring about, at the end of the First World War, a genuine peace of reconciliation. It was also the mood of the American people in 1945.

In this mood many of us Americans felt a strong indignation at the continued existence, in Argentina, of what was popularly regarded as a fascist regime surviving the defeat of fascism. Our government's recognition of this regime in 1945 therefore aroused the cry of "appeasement," and a storm of popular indignation broke over its head.

At that moment a new American ambassador arrived in Buenos Aires. Spruille Braden's courage and sterling integrity were matched by his fighting spirit. I suspect that international relations presented themselves to him as something not dissimilar to the game of cops and robbers. Fighting the wicked was instinctive with him, and the public clamor stirred his blood. Upon his arrival in Buenos Aires he publicly flung his defiance into the teeth of the government to which he was accredited.

This was the beginning of an extraordinary page in the history of our inter-American relations, a page which reminds one of Citizen Genêt's mission. The American ambassador to Argentina embarked on a deliberate public campaign on Argentine soil to unseat the Argentine government. In speech after speech and interview after interview he denounced a fascist regime—which he said must remain nameless—that trampled on the rights of the people, rode roughshod over women and children, and so forth.

All this made exhilarating reading for our public in the United States, and it went a bit wild in its approval. Here was no "striped-pants" diplomat but a red-blooded two-fisted American whose "shirt-sleeves" diplomacy would make these foreign dictators sit up and take notice. Braden was the hero of the hour. People began talking about him as a possibility for the White House. Under the circumstances, whether he or the government in Washington had made the policy that he was following, the government could not have been expected to

148

challenge him, the more so because it was not itself insensible to the emotions involved.

Nelson Rockefeller, Assistant Secretary for Inter-American Affairs, the advocate of reconciliation with Argentina, had either to bend with the blast or fall. He tried to bend. In an address in Boston he praised Ambassador Braden and supported his actions. But it was too late. Mr. Rockefeller learned, just before delivering his address, what was announced publicly the next day, that "his resignation had been accepted" and that Ambassador Braden had been named to succeed him.

Mr. Braden returned to ,Washington like a Caesar returning from the frontiers for a triumph in Rome. He gave interviews at airports along the way in which he called for an uprising of the Argentine people, and for outside assistance in support of such an uprising.

All this provided a spectacle that satisfied the moral sense of the American people in the mood of 1945. But the quarrel which Mr. Braden had picked with Argentina had practical consequences. It paralyzed the operations of the inter-American system. For example, a conference had already been projected, before the quarrel began, to conclude an inter-American security pact. The importance of such a pact was as a warning to the Soviet Union and a necessary precaution against her possible use of the veto in the Security Council of the United Nations to cover aggression on her part. But when Mr. Braden arrived in Washington he abruptly called the conference off. "In view of recent developments in Argentina," said the announcement, "the United States Government does not feel that it can properly negotiate or sign with the present Argentine regime a treaty of military assistance."

Up to this moment it had not occurred to our people that we must pay a price for our campaign against Argentina, and that the price included postponing indefinitely the prospective hemisphere arrangements for collective defense. Now it appeared that the United States, by picking and prosecuting a quarrel with Argentina, had to forgo action designed to meet

149

the developing threat from the Soviet Union, which was advancing in east Europe and threatening Iran. This realization was instantly sobering in its effect. The tide of opinion began to turn with a rapidity which Mr. Braden could not have expected. He was about to find out now, what General MacArthur was to find out later, that the American people ordinarily prefer their strong men at a distance.

Braden's political demise was the more certain because his policy was having the opposite of the effect it was supposed to have in Argentina. Colonel Perón, the emerging strong man of Argentina, was glad to identify himself in the public eye as the chief target of the foreign interventionist. Now, with elections scheduled, he entered his candidacy for President on the slogan: "Braden or I." Braden campaigned against him in broadcasts from Washington. Perón identified himself with the defense of Argentine sovereignty. When Perón won an overwhelming victory, in what the opposition conceded to have been a fair election, qualified observers agreed that the Braden policy had, in the words of the *New York Times*, "virtually assured Señor Perón's election."[1]

It was only a matter of time, now, before Mr. Braden followed the path of Citizen Genêt—although there was no question, I am glad to say, of guillotining him. He simply retired to the banks of the Hudson River, in the city of New York, where he was forgotten with notable rapidity by the people who had so recently cheered him on.

This episode was of greater consequence than the later episode of *La Prensa* for it confused our inter-American relations and hurt our national prestige. But it represented, essentially, an aberration—the emotional aberration which manifests itself in all peoples at the moment of victory.

Still, the normal tension between a government restrained by prudence and an ideologically impelled people remains, compelling every government to decide how it will reconcile

[1] Article by Milton Bracker from *Buenos Aires*, December 7, 1947.

foreign policy considerations with popular pressures at home.

One of the standard means by which governments meet this dilemma is by a more or less cultivated inconsistency between word and deed. To elicit popular support the spokesmen of government use words freely, proclaiming all sorts of things which, if they are sober and responsible men, they will try to avoid carrying out or will drastically modify in practice.

Students of international affairs ought to understand this, even when others do not. They ought to be able to weigh the extent to which the words of government spokesmen are to be taken at face value as pronouncements of foreign policy, and the extent to which they are to be taken as mere rhetorical devices. Yet I am occasionally surprised at the persons who fail to make this distinction.

I recall listening to an able scholar read a paper on the difference between the foreign policy of President Truman's administration and the foreign policy of the Eisenhower administration. What was the difference? It was that, while the Truman policy had been one of "containment," the Eisenhower policy was one of "liberation." Where the Truman policy was to keep the Soviet Union from adding to the area of its conquests, the Eisenhower policy was to liberate areas already conquered.

I do not doubt that the Eisenhower administration, when it was preparing to assume responsibility for the conduct of our foreign relations, hoped that some means might present itself for the peaceful liberation of the Soviet Union's satellites. I have equally little reason to doubt, however, that the proclamation of its intention to liberate them was based on considerations that were quite outside the realm of foreign affairs. Students of the national political scene in 1952 had persuaded some of the Republican leaders that their party had to have the support of certain minority groups, which ordinarily supported the Democratic party, if it was going to win the national election. These groups represented eastern European stock with affinities for the "old countries" that were languishing in the grip of

151

the Soviet Union. The way to capture their support was to promise to liberate the old countries. No one who knows how single-minded political leaders may become in the course of an election campaign would be surprised to learn that the implications of such a promise for foreign policy may well have been excluded from consideration as irrelevant. When, after the electoral victory, the Eisenhower administration came into power, it may well have considered seriously, for the first time, what means might be available for carrying out a policy of "liberation"; and it may then have faced, for the first time, the fact that such means were not available. Under such circumstances, a situation would have arisen in which "liberation" continued to be proclaimed as the objective of policy, while policy in the sense of what was actually done continued to address itself to the objective of "containment."

There are no grounds for questioning the sincerity of the Republican leaders; for like the Democrats (and like all of us except the Communists) they would have been glad to see the satellites peacefully liberated. But it remains true that the real purpose which "liberation" served was more adequately represented by the results of the 1952 election than by the outcome of the East German riots in 1953 or the Hungarian rebellion in 1956. Here the weight of domestic political considerations was determinative—as when Secretary of State Webster, a century earlier, had called for the liberation of Hungary. Neither in the case of Mr. Webster nor in that of Mr. Dulles was the foreign policy which each had inherited changed or even materially affected by the brave words which he spoke.

During the period in which a political party is out of power its business is with the domestic scene. Except for certain Congressmen who do not represent a general party discipline, the opposition party is not charged with responsibility for foreign policy and the conduct of foreign relations. But its leaders are acutely aware of their responsibility for achieving victory on the domestic scene. This is true of any party which is out of office. One could see it in the Democrats during the

152

national election campaign of 1956. When a party has been out of office for twenty years, as was the plight of the Republicans in 1952, a new generation has grown up through its ranks, a generation that has learned to think only in these domestic terms. The new generation has never had occasion to weigh the reactions of Europeans or Asiatics, since Europeans and Asiatics are not enrolled as voters. Is it not natural that when these new people do finally achieve responsibility, which comes on them abruptly and without effective preparation, they are unable to change their thinking and abandon their preoccupation overnight? We will see the same thing in the Democrats if they remain out of power as long as the Republicans did.

Like "liberation," the doctrine of "massive retaliation," proclaimed by Secretary Dulles in January, 1954, must also be understood, to some extent, in these terms. The Republicans had promised the voters that they would provide more military security for less money, that they would increase the effective military power of the United States while reducing taxes and balancing the budget. Again, I do not question their sincerity, which became manifest to all of us in the government after they achieved the power and responsibility. Whether their belief in what they said during the campaign preceded or followed the saying, the fact is that it had become an article of faith. During the first year or two, especially, the new men were intent on honoring their promise. The country was, after all, waiting to see how they would provide more military security for less money. They had to do something. There was a dilemma. Budget balancing was essentially relevant to the domestic economy, and as such tended to have priority over military considerations, which had to do with external affairs. This thinking was natural to men who hitherto had had a primary concern only with the domestic scene. Inevitably it pushed them in the direction of a greater reliance on big nuclear weapons and the threat of big nuclear weapons—in spite of the fact that the Soviet Union, at that very time, was achieving a nuclear potential of her own which tended to neutralize that threat. It was, therefore, at root a domestic political compulsion which prompted Mr. Dulles to announce, at last, that the United States would rely on its capacity for massive retaliation rather than attempt to couple with that capacity a capacity to fight limited wars with limited means wherever our opponents should see fit to start them. If we were to balance the budget at a reduced level of taxation, then we could not afford to support, at one and the same time, a full-scale nuclear capability and a full-scale capability in what was called "conventional" forces. We would have to make a choice, which meant that we would have to choose the nuclear capability and let the conventional capability go. Again, I do not doubt Mr. Dulles's sincerity, the more so as the full impact of the foreign policy considerations, as distinct from the domestic considerations, may not have struck him until after his announcement of the new policy.

I am sorry that, because my subject is American foreign policy rather than, say, German foreign policy or the foreign policy of India, I have to take my examples so generally from people like Daniel Webster and Secretary Dulles. However, those who serve in diplomatic posts around the world, or at the United Nations in New York, know that response to domestic pressure is not limited to American diplomacy.

A number of years ago the chief of a friendly delegation at the United Nations General Assembly approached one of our American delegates with some embarrassment. He said that he wanted us to know in advance that he was about to make a speech attacking and abusing us. He hoped that we would not take it seriously, that we would try to overlook it. This speech, he said, was strictly "out the window." In other words, while he would ostensibly be addressing the General Assembly, he would really be speaking "out the window" to his own political supporters at home, currying favor with the anti-Americans and the xenophobes among them by bravely attacking us. President Perón of Argentina, too, would sometimes tell our American ambassador in advance when he was going to make a speech heaping insult and abuse on the United States, explaining that

154

the speech should not be regarded as anything except a domestic political tactic. The Communist countries, I note, have carried this tactic to a sort of ultimate extreme.

I shall not pretend that this kind of thing appeals to me or that I regard it as anything except dangerously demoralizing to international relations. It represents a decline in the standards of international conduct which is the price that has been paid for the shift of political power from a cosmopolitan elite to the nationalistic and often xenophobic masses of people. It is dangerous because it impairs that civility on which human relations depend, and also because the verbal excesses to which it leads may go to a point at which there is no longer any possibility of avoiding their implementation by deeds.

In the last chapter I made a distinction between word and deed. The example I gave was Daniel Webster's verbal intervention in the Hungarian rebellion against Austrian rule. This did not, I said, constitute an effective intervention in the Hungarian situation, and it left unaltered our traditional policy of not taking part in European conflicts. The ship of state wobbled and yawed, perhaps, but kept to its course.

But the distinction I made between word and deed was quite misleading. In international affairs words are deeds. If the President of the United States should announce, tomorrow, that he was in favor of having India placed under the rule of the Pakistani government, those mere words of his would upset international relations just as thoroughly as if they had been marching armies. When President Truman, quite inadvertently and mistakenly, told a press conference that the decision as to whether the atom bomb should be used in Korea was up to General MacArthur his words brought Prime Minister Attlee of Great Britain across the Atlantic Ocean on the first plane he could board.

The prime problem of foreign policy is that it has to be made by human beings. This is a dangerous state of affairs—indeed an alarming state of affairs—but I see no way out. We must simply make the best of it. Throughout most of the history of

155

mankind, and in many countries today, foreign policy has been made by one or a few human beings only, and the masses of people have had to bear the consequences. Experience suggests that these consequences were not good. It is a weakness of our human nature to suppose that, when the consequences of adopting one of two alternatives are not good, it has been proved that the other alternative was the right one. This is quite illogical, but it is ingrained in our thinking. Foreign policy by the few having proved defective, we generally drew the conclusion that foreign policy by the many was the solution which would work. But this also involved great dangers, and we shall not cope effectively with those dangers by refusing to recognize that they exist.

What is the conclusion? I think, myself, that we are dealing, here, with matters of degree. Foreign policy ought not to be made by a daily plebiscite or Gallup Poll. Neither should it be made by a few men without reference to the popular will. There must, therefore, be some tension between the few and the many, between government and people, in the conduct of foreign relations. The problem is to achieve the right balance of these elements, and to achieve a maximum stability in that balance. The world's first democracy, Athens, achieved this in the days of Pericles. It lost it when he was succeeded by such demagogues as Cleon and Alcibiades, who in their catering to domestic political popularity led Athens down to disaster—as Thucydides relates in what seems to me the best single book on international politics, his *History of the Peloponnesian War*.

Today as always, whatever the political system we adopt, we live dangerously. This seems to be the nature and the fate of mankind.

XIV • In earlier chapters I have told how, until our own time, the concept of the two hemispheres governed the foreign policy of the United States. We Americans, having a New World in which to make a new start, turned our backs on the Old World.

What about the implications of this concept for our attitude toward the nations that came to share our New World with us? Here the record, down to our own day, is one of ambiguity, involving constant straining to bring a difficult reality into conformity with an insistent legend.

In our own century we have striven to realize the legend of an inter-American community of nations distinguished from the rest of the world and bound together by a common New World ideology. But the Latin American nations, with a different cultural background, have not been able to live up to this legend. Our own attitude toward them, consequently, has been quixotic and unstable, varying back and forth between an eager fraternalism, whenever the legend has dominated our thinking, and an impatient or outraged paternalism whenever the reality has become too vivid for us.

We North Americans have therefore found it hard to determine and fix the basic nature of our relationship with the Latin American nations. We have repeatedly embarrassed ourselves and them by the uncertainty of our own attitude. They have been bewildered by finding themselves in our affectionate embrace one moment, under our stern correction the next. In 1939, at a moment when fraternalism was dominant, we received President Somoza of Nicaragua with the most exaggerated honors in Washington, parading him down Pennsylvania Avenue side by side with President Roosevelt, declaring a government holiday in his honor. Some half dozen years later, in the Braden period, we broke diplomatic relations with him because he was a wicked dictator. And in 1956, when he lay on what proved to be his deathbed, we again went to some lengths to show our solicitude for him. This is what it is to be torn between legend and reality when the disparity becomes too great. General Somoza never changed. He was the same tyrannical dictator in 1939, in 1946, and in 1956. It was we who could not settle in our own minds what our attitude toward him should be.

The element of pretense, associated with legend, has been greater in inter-American relations than it is in the generality of international relations. The Latin Americans are not, as we sometimes pretend, all idealists whose heartbeats spell liberty. Neither are they all gangsters. I daresay that basically they are just people—although people who have suffered from a particularly tragic history and an unfortunate physical environment.

Let me refer to the environment first. Rich as much of the geography of South and Central America is in economic resources, statistically conceived, the distribution of those resources, the climates, and the arrangements of mountain, plain, and river do not lend themselves to the development of civilization in the modern sense. The most habitable and agriculturally productive latitudes in North America correspond to the full breadth of the continent; but the equivalent latitudes in South America correspond to an abrupt narrowing down of the continent. South America is broadest where it is least habitable, where human beings live in a state of enervation and infestation. While our Mississippi River gives access to a vast region which offers health and prosperity to those who inhabit it, the Amazon gives access to an equally large region which is one of the most inhospitable in the world.

Virtually all over the world, with the exception of the area inhabited by the Latin Americans, human population has filled up the lowlands and avoided the steep mountain slopes. In North America, for example, the Mississippi basin is solidly inhabited, but the high Rockies are sparsely populated or not at all. It is only in Central and South America that you find the opposite true. Here the population swarms in the cordillera, while enormous areas of lowland remain largely unpopulated. The reason is not that mountain slopes are less inhospitable here than elsewhere, but that here the lowlands are even worse.

Finally, the physical barriers to communication are such on the mainland of Latin America that it has become divided into seventeen separate nation-states, compared to the two great nation-states which cover the northern part of the hemisphere.

So much for a mere suggestion of why the Latin American geography is, in general, unfortunate. I also said that the Latin Americans were the victims of a tragic history. It begins with a conflict between races which, like all racial conflicts, was degrading to both parties. The English settlers of North America were lucky enough to find a virtually empty continent. But the Spanish conquistadors found lands that were well populated by an alien race of advanced civilization. They therefore had great and established nations to overcome or displace.

Seven hundred years of incessant warfare against the infidel Moors, ending only in the year of Columbus's discovery, had hardened the spirit of the Spaniards, had invested their religious devotion with fanaticism, and had confirmed that hierarchical feudal ordering of their society which the military struggle made necessary. Consequently, the Spanish conquistadors undertook to convert the Indians to Christianity by the sword and to exploit their labor with a ruthlessness which the circumstances of their own peninsular history had made habitual. This led to the extinction, in South and Middle America, of great and ancient civilizations. They were extinguished overnight, almost as Carthage had been extinguished by Rome, and populous nations died because they could not adjust themselves to the new social environment. Those Indians who survived sank to that culturally debased condition in which many of them can still be seen today.

The centralized and hierarchical rule of the Spanish feudal order was imposed on all the Spanish dominions in the New World, so that at a time when the North American colonists were quite self-governing the Creoles and Indians of Spanish America were under the absolutist rule of Madrid and subject to the economic exploitation of an unmoderated mercantilism.

This was still the situation in the first quarter of the nineteenth century, when the Latin Americans suddenly achieved their independence. The legend has it that this independence was their own achievement, under the leadership of such heroic figures as Bolívar, San Martín, and Hidalgo. In point of fact, however, independence came to the Latin Americans long before they were prepared to realize it for themselves. The real liberator, as I mentioned in Chapter VIII, was not Bolívar but Napoleon, who, in striking down the mother country, left them orphans, cast them loose at a time when they were still quite unready to care for themselves. Such struggle as there was took place later, when a restored Spain tried to recapture them.

Take the single case of what is now Argentina, the native land of San Martín, who is today regarded as its heroic liberator. The arrival in Buenos Aires of two English brigantines with the news that Napoleon had conquered Spain led to the prompt disavowal, on May 25, 1810, of allegiance to the captive Crown. A crowd gathered and speeches were made, but not a shot was fired. Independence existed *de facto* and was recognized. That was all. The later campaigns of San Martín and Bolívar, resisting Spanish attempts at reconquest, took place elsewhere in Latin America. According to the Argentine legend, however, the achievement of Argentine independence virtually duplicates the

160

achievement of North American independence, with San Martín corresponding to George Washington.

The combination of these geographical and historical circumstances seems to have prompted an escape from reality as a dominant trait of Latin American culture. Far more than in Europe or North America, a pretense is kept up throughout the gamut of cultural, social, and political life. A North American who refers to the vast areas of reality which Latin Americans do not recognize may be regarded as uncouth and insulting. It is in Latin America, as much as anywhere, that you see the pitiable spectacle of the soiled frock coat and dilapidated wing collar on the householder who lives, privately, in a squalor which he would indignantly deny even to himself. It is such a man who goes in for the endless Latin American oratory that, in the midst of despotism and horrible human suffering, acclaims the New World's achievement of man's highest humanitarian ideals.

This element of pretense is manifested everywhere and in variety. One expression of it, I think, is in the exclusively urban disposition of the socially elite classes. One finds none of that interest in nature and scenery which, in the Western world, is most developed among the English-speaking peoples. When a Latin American thinks about a foreign land he generally means its cities, and he commonly evaluates them according to their night life. How many well-to-do Latin Americans travel back and forth between Guatemala City or Rio de Janeiro and Paris or New York or Los Angeles, year after year, crossing the intervening territory as if it were vacant space between planets! A large proportion of the citizens of Guatemala City, although they know New York and Paris well, are unfamiliar with anything else in their own country beside the ports of embarkation. It cannot be a coincidence that, in the whole modern history of Latin American exploration, one hardly finds a single Latin American name. The names are Von Humboldt, or Darwin, or Bates, or Belt. Exploration has been left entirely to English, North Americans, and Germans because the Latin Americans themselves, so far from being interested in the wild or rural

161

parts of their countries, tend to disdain them as fit only for simple people.

But the land with its people is what supports the cities and their people. Consequently, there is something unhealthy in this avoidance by the urban elite, which generally constitutes the governing class, of any personal relationship to the land, Latin America has been largely governed by cities which regard the country on which they rest with contempt, while the Indians and other peasants who inhabit the country and support the cities suffer the consequent lack of representation or neglect. An extreme example is Buenos Aires, one of the world's greatest and most sophisticated metropolises in the middle of one of the world's backward areas. Or, even more extreme, Manaos with its pretentious opera house in the middle of virgin rain forest two thousand miles up the Amazon. Buenos Aires and Manaos pretend to be Paris; they try to forget the existence of the country that actually surrounds them.

It is undoubtedly apocryphal, but Bolívar is supposed to have said, on his deathbed, "I have plowed the sea—America is ungovernable." Our own John Quincy Adams used words to much the same effect, and these were not apocryphal. "I have never doubted," he said in 1821, "that the final issue of their present struggle [the struggle of the Spanish Americans against Spain] will be their entire independence of Spain . . . but I have not yet seen and do not now see any prospect that they will establish free or liberal institutions of government. They are not likely to promote the spirit either of freedom or order by their example. They have not the first elements of good or free government. Arbitrary power, military and ecclesiastical, is stamped upon their education, upon their habits, and upon all their institutions. Civil dissension is infused into all their seminal principles. War and mutual destruction are in every member of their organization, moral, political, and physical."[1]

These are harsh words, so harsh that one quotes them reluc-

[1] Bemis, *Latin American Policy of the United States* (New York, 1943), p. 44.

tantly. But can anyone say that the history of Latin American efforts at self-government throughout the remainder of the nineteenth century does not bear them out? It is a history of chaos in which a succession of desperadoes play at king-of-the-mountain over the bodies of the people. Shooting in the streets is an ordinary feature of political life.

In 1839 President Van Buren gave John L. Stephens an official mission to Central America to try to find a government with which we could establish relations. Stephens has left a classic account of his long search for such a government in his *Incidents of Travels in Central America, Chiapas, and Yucatán.* He finally came upon a totally illiterate swineherd who had just led a revolt and consequently, to his own bewilderment, found himself occupying the presidential palace in Guatemala City. To him Stephens presented his credentials.

I do not mean to imply that conditions were precisely like this all over Latin America in the nineteenth century. Essentially and generally, however, political chaos did prevail. Large remnants of it may be found, still, in our own day.

I have described this tragic or pathetic situation, not for its own sake, but because the political weakness which it betrays has constituted the prime dilemma for United States foreign policy in Latin America from the beginning. For many decades after the time of John Quincy Adams, however, we did not have to concern ourselves in any active and important way with Latin America—except for Mexico. For all practical purposes, Central and South America were as far away as Antarctica. Most North Americans never had occasion to give this area any thought.

The beginning of a major interest in Latin America does not come until late in the nineteenth century, when we had completed our own expansion to the Pacific and filled up the intervening area with our civilization. For one thing, we now began competing self-consciously for world trade, and so cast a commercial eye on the South American market. For another, the change in our position from an Atlantic coast nation to a continental nation with two ocean fronts to defend suddenly made Central America and the Caribbean an area of vital strategic importance for us. The Isthmus of Panama and the approaches to it represented the main channel through which our power could be moved back and forth between the two oceans at need. We could not, therefore, safely allow it to be dominated by any other power.

But the political chaos among the Caribbean republics was constantly inviting the intervention of European powers in the area. At the beginning of the present century the refusal of the Venezuelan dictator, Castro, to pay debts owed by Venezuela to European investors resulted in a blockade and bombardment of the Venezuelan coast by British, German, and Italian warships. A couple of years later, the same kind of situation in Santo Domingo brought a threat of armed European intervention in that little island republic. The total inability of the Dominicans to govern themselves, the chaos and bloodshed which were the rule among them, had reduced their independent and sovereign state to something like bankruptcy. A receivership was virtually inevitable, whether by the United States, by the European powers, or by a combination of both.

Theodore Roosevelt, who was President of the United States at the time, had positive ideas about the responsibilities of great powers. This was the period in which the concept of "the white man's burden," to use Kipling's unfortunate phrase, was flourishing. According to that concept, the great civilized powers, representing law and order, had a moral obligation to confer or impose the benefits of their civilization on the primitive, immature peoples who could not properly govern themselves. The fact that this lent itself to a pharisaical attitude and to selfish exploitation should not obscure the fact that in the minds of many statesmen it did represent a high and worthy purpose. In some countries, like the Philippines, that purpose was realized. There have been worse forms of imperialism.

Theodore Roosevelt held that the great powers had an obligation to keep order for the peoples who were not yet mature enough to keep it for themselves. At the beginning of this century the concept of an inviolable sovereignty had not yet acquired that sanctity with which an increasingly ardent nationalism has since invested it. If a state failed to meet its international obligations, then the principle of sovereignty should not be allowed to stand in the way of remedial, if not disciplinary action. This was the age of great-power paternalism, of the assumption of the policeman's role by these powers in default of any other agency to assume it.

Under the circumstances, Roosevelt conceived that intervention by European powers in Latin America might, on occasion, be justified. At the time when the Europeans were contemplating their use of naval force against Venezuela he wrote to a friend: "If any South American country misbehaves toward any European country, let the European country spank it."[2] In time, however, Roosevelt came to believe that the Monroe Doctrine could not be securely upheld in the sensitive Caribbean area if European spankings were allowed. If a European power were to take over the Dominican customs in order to collect debts, it might, at last, become permanently ensconced in Santo Domingo. At the same time, however, the Monroe Doctrine must not be used to protect Latin American states against the consequences of misbehavior. Someone had to be responsible for these children. If the United States forbade other powers to spank them, then it would have to do the spanking itself. This, in essence, was the famous "Roosevelt Corollary" to the Monroe Doctrine, under which the United States proceeded to take over and administer the Dominican customs.

While this was a bad thing to do, as we see it in our day, we should note that its consequences were not uniformly bad. Our intervention in Santo Domingo brought, while it lasted, the only period of safety, peace, and prosperity which the Dominican people had so far enjoyed—and some Dominicans doubt

[2] Julius W. Pratt, *A History of United States Foreign Policy* (New York, 1955), p. 416.

whether they have been better off since it ended. While the Dominican state, as such, temporarily lost much of its independence, the Dominican people temporarily gained more independence than they had before or were to have after. The state was worse off, but the human beings within the state were better off. And the history of our intervention under the "Roosevelt Corollary," here and elsewhere in the Caribbean, shows that we were never tempted to remain in permanent possession. We established no protectorates. We were generally eager to get out. When one visits the island of Hispaniola today and sees how many of its institutions like agricultural colleges, hospitals, and waterworks were built by the Americans during their occupation, one can see some point in the view privately expressed by some Haitians and Dominicans that this was a sort of golden age for the island.

However, none of us are good enough to be entrusted with an unchecked police power over others. The temptations to abuse that power are rarely resisted. Certainly the United States, in the period of Roosevelt's successors, did not altogether resist them. The intervention in Nicaragua, which represented the "dollar diplomacy" of the Taft administration, and the moralistic intervention in Mexico, which Woodrow Wilson undertook in the belief that you get good government by overthrowing bad, are less defensible than that practiced by Theodore Roosevelt in the name of international order. The 1915 intervention in Haiti, while it brought notable benefits, also led to the death of more than two thousand Haitians at the hands of the United States Marines.[3] In Nicaragua, too, the Marines found themselves having to fight Nicaraguans under circumstances which went against the grain of American tradition and feeling. When people cannot govern themselves it does not always follow that an outside power can do the job for them. As usual, you have a dilemma. In any case, the people of the United States had no taste for this sort of thing, especially when it was accompanied by mounting alarm and resentment throughout Latin America.

[3] Bailey, *op. cit.*, p. 597.

One trouble with intervention, as this history demonstrates, is that one always tends to get oneself involved deeper than one intended. The dynamics of intervention, in this respect, are like the dynamics of war and of revolution. It is hard to limit it. In any case, we Americans have never been any good at imperialism. We had a small spasm of imperialistic feeling about the turn of the century, but it was not long before we were looking for a way out of the imperialistic commitments which we made at that time. Intervention not only aroused the universal resentment of the Latin Americans, it was generally condemned by our own people.

The era of bad feeling produced by our interventionist policy culminated in 1928 at the Pan American Conference in Havana. There the United States made its last defense of intervention. "What," asked the chief United States delegate, "are we going to do when government breaks down and American citizens are in danger of their lives?" This was a good question—at least, in the absence of effective international organization to impose order and security it was a good question. But the Latin American delegates had no difficulty answering it in a negative sense. Over our dead body they passed a resolution, "That no state has a right to intervene in the internal affairs of another." By its policy the United States had generated the unanimous opposition of the other American republics. It stood alone.

At this point Washington set in motion a major reversal of our interventionist policy in the hemisphere, a reversal which was not devoid of statesmanship and which led to an era of eminently friendly and constructive relations between the United States and the countries which had lined up against it at Havana. The first move was an official finding, embodied in the famous Reuben Clark "Memorandum on the Monroe Doctrine," that the "Roosevelt Corollary" was not "justified by the terms of the Monroe Doctrine. . . ." Then, at the inter-American conferences which followed, in Montevideo and Buenos Aires, the United States entered into a treaty engagement to abstain from intervention in the internal or external affairs of any of the other American republics. In implementation of this new policy, the Platt Amendment allowing us to intervene in Cuba was abrogated and the last intervening American troops in the hemisphere were withdrawn from Haiti in 1934. The era of bad feeling was now quickly followed by a wonderful era of good feeling in inter-American relations.

In the years following 1928, then, we launched upon the stormy seas of our inter-American relations a new something which bore the lovely name of "Good Neighbor" policy. What was this Good Neighbor policy? Basically, I suppose, it could be summed up by the term "equality." Great-power paternalism had implied and reflected a hierarchy in the society of nations. The society of nations consisted of grownups and children. From at least as far back as 1815, responsibility for the maintenance of international law and order had been confined to the great powers—the grownups. The others had to conform to their decisions and behave themselves. Now the United States abandoned this concept, with which it had made play for a few years, and applied to the inter-American community, instead, those principles of democratic egalitarianism which it maintained among its own people. All nation-states were equal under the law, equal in sovereignty, equal in opportunity, equal in dignity, equally worthy of respect. Every nation-state was an inviolable personality, Santo Domingo equally with the United States.

Now I think, myself, that this indiscriminate transfer to nation-states of principles philosophically applicable to individual human souls has some flaws and some dangers. It contributes to that glorification of the state at the expense of the individual which is one of the maladies of our time. But it accorded with the spirit of the twentieth century, and in any case—there it was. We accepted it. It conformed to a language which we held sacred, to the terminology of our Founding Fathers, and so we believed it. We proceeded to give it effect. And, in the event, it worked.

168

If all states were equal, then no state had the right, by itself, to police another. The United States had no more right to intervene in Santo Domingo than Santo Domingo had to intervene in the United States. But suppose government broke down in Santo Domingo, suppose Americans were being massacred, suppose American property was being pillaged. If the individual nation is not allowed to defend its rights and procure justice for itself in the jurisdiction of another, what recourse does it have? The only answer is that the community must be organized to do the job for it. Specifically, you have to have international organization and the right of intervention by the organized community as a whole, unless you accept the only other alternative, which is the anarchy of a world made up of sovereign entities with no effective responsibilities in the unlimited exercise of their respective sovereignties.

Fortunately, our Good Neighbor policy was not tested by anything like the Suez Canal crisis of 1956. The Republic of Panama did not seize the Panama Canal in the name of its sovereign rights. If it had, and if the international community had not prevented it or corrected it, then I feel quite sure that the Good Neighbor policy would have come to a quick end.

As it was, our abjuration of intervention was accompanied by the rapid development of that inter-American system which culminated in the formal establishment of the Organization of American States at Bogotá in 1948. The beginning of the modern inter-American system coincides with the unreserved acceptance by the United States, at the Buenos Aires conference of 1936, of the non-intervention commitment. At that same conference the American Republics also committed themselves to the principle of consultation and co-operative action to preserve the peace of the hemisphere "in the event of an international war outside of America which might menace the peace of the American republics. . . ." By 1940 the entire community of American republics had accepted responsibility for the maintenance of the Monroe Doctrine, hitherto maintained by the United States alone. By 1948, when the Charter of the Organization of American States had been agreed upon at Bogotá, the inter-American system had developed procedures, not just for co-operation to meet aggression, but for the settlement of disputes between member states. I don't know how severe a test this system could bear, but it undoubtedly has had a most constructive effect. It is surely a major factor in the relative tranquillity of inter-American relations since 1941. Today, if we thought the Dominican Republic were misbehaving toward us, we would find at hand procedures for appealing to the organized inter-American community to spank it. How the community would respond to such an appeal is another question.

The concept of "sovereign equality," with non-intervention as its corollary, represents the essence of the Good Neighbor policy. But by itself this is negative. The positive aspect of the Good Neighbor policy manifested itself in something called "inter-American solidarity." In so far as this inter-American solidarity found its expression in close co-operation as a community it had substance and value. Beyond this, however, an enormous amount of verbal energy was lavished on promoting the legend of *ideological* solidarity. Every inter-American conference since the early 1930's has been swamped with oratorical excesses on this theme, and the final acts have been burdened with resolutions expressing in spacious terms the common devotion of all the American republics to those ideals of freedom and democracy which, one gathers, have been realized only in the New World.

In this sense, the doctrine of the two hemispheres takes on a flourishing verbal life in the 1930's, when at last it no longer fits the reality at all. Hemisphere isolationism is implicit in every assertion of ideological solidarity. Ideological solidarity is anti-European. The American hemisphere is conceived of as having a system essentially different from that of the corrupt Old World with its ancient tyrannies. One would think that Philip II still ruled in Spain, and that George III was King of

England, while every Latin American dictator was a Thomas Jefferson or an Abraham Lincoln.

There is, surely, much to be said for lip service. It helps keep ideals alive in the absence of their realization. But to the extreme degree in which inter-American solidarity was identified with ideology the structure had a manifest weakness. It made too great a separation between the legend and the reality. This accounts in part for that repeated revulsion of North American opinion against political corruption and tyranny in Latin America, the revulsion from fraternalism to a stern paternalism, which I mentioned at the outset of this chapter. If the basis of inter-American solidarity was ideological, if the inter-American community represented the liberal Utopia of the New World, then one wondered, all of a sudden, what Colonel Perón was doing in it, or General Somoza, or Generalissimo Trujillo. Having clasped these iron characters to our bosom when overcome by the legend, the sudden perception of reality was at any time liable to produce a revulsion in us. So we would go to the other extreme, still moved by ideology.

There is, perhaps, no logical inconsistency between a policy of non-intervention and a requirement of ideological solidarity. But ideological solidarity implies conformity, and the impulse to enforce conformity leads toward intervention. The American government was under attack by American liberals, up to 1933, for intervening in the affairs of the little Caribbean republics, trying to run their lives for them, telling them how they should govern themselves and how they might not govern themselves. In the period since 1933, many of these same liberals have attacked the government for tolerating dictatorships in these same republics. You see the dilemma. We should respect their right to govern themselves as they see fit, but we should not allow the wrong kind of government among them. The truly difficult decisions, it has been said, are those which raise the problem which of two mutually opposed moral principles we shall choose to govern our policy, knowing that the choice of one means the rejection of the other. It is only the critics of government who,

171

on paper, are free to insist on both—or to insist on whichever of the two alternatives has been rejected.

Basically, then, the Good Neighbor policy represents the substitution of fraternalism for paternalism in our inter-American relations, the practical manifestation of this being the non-intervention commitment. But the ideological solidarity which has been promoted as one feature of the Good Neighbor policy, being at odds with the reality, leads by revulsion to such impulses of paternalistic intervention as were most dramatically manifested in the Braden period. Here you have a tension which makes it hard to stabilize relations between the United States and Latin America.

Furthermore, because inter-American solidarity was so closely identified with the ideological isolation of the hemisphere— the making of a distinction between the ideology of the New World and that of the Old—our abandonment of isolationism in 1947, with the announcement of the Truman Doctrine and the Marshall Plan, was viewed by most Latin Americans as a betrayal or abandonment of the Good Neighbor policy. The Good Neighbor policy meant hemisphere solidarity, and hemisphere solidarity meant that the Latin American republics had first place—indeed, only place—in our affections. The consequence has been bitter Latin American resentment at the Truman Doctrine, the Marshall Plan, and the North Atlantic Treaty Organization (NATO). The United States has proved unfaithful by associating so intimately with the alien powers of the Old World.

Another development which came to be intimately associated with the Good Neighbor policy, although not present at its inception, was economic and technical assistance by the United States to the other American republics. This was virtually absent before 1942, when the Institute of Inter-American Affairs and the Inter-American Educational Foundation were established, under the energetic leadership of Mr. Nelson Rockefeller, as United States government corporations prepared to co-operate with Latin American governments in programs of economic and social development. Such an undertaking, which has since become familiar all over the world as "Point Four," was new and startling in 1942. The programs of the time, however, were only partly eleemosynary. In large part they were regarded as emergency programs connected with the war effort. This was the case, for example, with sanitation programs to make possible the extraction of rubber from the Amazon basin. But the eleemosynary element, associated with winning friendship by generous deeds, was there from the beginning.

As wartime emergency programs it was intended that they should be brought to a close at the end of the war, and Washington actually moved in that direction. Then, however, the development of the conflict with Soviet Russia provided arguments for continuing them—on the valid ground that the defense of the hemisphere required a strengthening of the basic economies of the American republics, and also on the more dubious ground that they would win Latin American good-will and support for our policies generally. Consequently, the scale of this assistance, and of financial assistance through the Export-Import Bank, was greatly increased in the years after the war. There have been good and bad results from this, and I find it hard to strike a balance. But I think that part of the effect has been a demoralization of Latin America and of Latin American relations with the United States. While most Latin American governments were a bit surprised and embarrassed when we first offered this kind of assistance, with the passage of the years they came to take it for granted, and finally they got into the habit of complaining about its inadequacy. As the assistance has increased, so have the accusations of our neglect.

Part of this demoralization, as it seems to me, is represented by an increasing effort on the part of the Latin American governments, in the years since the war, to make almost any kind of political co-operation, including support for our policies at international gatherings, dependent on our meeting their requests for financial and other assistance. At times the effort to engage us in this kind of bargaining has become quite shameful, although it has lately been matched if not surpassed in our relations with some of the Asian countries. I mention this experience in support of my doubt that assistance programs, great as their usefulness may be, are conducive to the improvement of international good feeling in the long run. There is implicit in them an almost inescapable element of degradation, which is perhaps part of the price which must be paid for their very real contribution to the solution of developmental problems when they are successful.

In a sense, this increasingly prominent aspect of the Good Neighbor policy has been contrary to the original conception of that policy. It represents a new kind of paternalism which, like the old, may be adverse to the development of adult independence in its objects. Though the intention has been to provide a kind of economic development that will make the Latin American republics more independent, more able to stand on their own feet, it has seemed to me that these aid programs might be having the opposite effect, that they have in fact been promoting a habit among the Latin Americans to look to the United States for the solution of their problems, and to hold the United States, rather than themselves, responsible. If a Latin American country is in bad shape, its citizens and its officials are likely to ask, today, what the United States is going to do about it. But for the United States the old dilemma remains, that often the political structure of the Latin American country is so little resistant to ineptitude and corruption that our assistance can only be wasted.

I have presented a dark picture of Latin America, and perhaps I should end be relieving that darkness. Nowhere else in the world are population curves, standard-of-living curves, and economic development curves rising as fast as in Latin America. The area is increasing in its basic strength every year. I rather think that its politics, too, are slowly improving. One recalls that the habit of bad government was well entrenched in England before the nineteenth century, when she provided an example of aptitude in government which causes us to assume, now, that it represents a genius which has always been inherent in the Anglo-Saxon peoples. I cannot myself foresee the future of Latin America, but many in Washington and elsewhere see the region as rising to an increasingly important and constructive role in international affairs. I have no doubt that, if good government can be developed by the Latin Americans, these optimists will prove to have been right.

XV • The modern history of American foreign policy, as distinct from its ancient history, begins in 1898. Up to 1898 the United Sates had cultivated and enjoyed the isolation implicit in the geographical concept of two hemispheres. In 1898 it lost or gave up that isolation by assuming commitments overseas. It entered the arena of European rivalries as a newly arrived world power. All this, as we shall see, was implicit in its acquisition of the Philippine Islands as a piece of real estate outside the New World, on the other side of interplanetary space.

This engagement in overseas imperialism was so abrupt and unpremeditated, however, and we were so little prepared for it, that our thinking could not adjust itself. We could not grasp what it meant for our isolation and, consequently, our isolationism. For almost half a century after our isolation was gone we still clung to the isolationist policy. Only a nation with such vast reserves of strength as we had could have survived this failure of understanding to keep up with change. As it was, the price we had to pay was high. We are still paying it today in many ways, including the present weakness of our diplomatic and strategic position in the Far East. But all this will come out in what follows.

One might say that the nineteenth century ends in the 1890's with a period of transition leading to the birth of the twentieth century in 1914. Up through the 1890's the *Pax Britannica* had dominated the world. Britain held the balance of power in Europe. She protected the independence of the American hemisphere. And in the competition for empire around the rim of Asia—a competition that represented an extension of the power contests in Europe—she had the chief role.

But a fundamental change took place in the 1890's with the appearance on the world scene of three new powers: Germany, Japan, and the United States. All three were suddenly realizing their potential strength; all three were being tempted by dreams of what that strength might gain for them; all three were unseasoned, like children who have grown up suddenly to possess an adult strength beyond their wisdom and experience.

Both Germany and Japan, in a sort of ecstasy of power, embarked on a course of empire that was to lead to the crashing collisions of the twentieth century. The United States, in the 1890's, briefly felt the same impulse, tentatively embarked on the same course, made commitments that would plague her, and then subsided again under the overriding sway of her liberal and isolationist traditions alike. After her one brief adventure in empire she retired. She emerged from her retirement and her strength became available to check that of Germany and Japan only when disaster was already upon the world. One might say that Germany and Japan used their newly found strength to disrupt world order, while the United States withheld its newly found strength from the maintenance of world order.

Quite aside from the overseas commitment which we Americans acquired in 1898, the ending of the *Pax Britannica* was bound, in itself, to end our putative isolation. When our surrounding oceans were no longer securely dominated by a power that was well disposed to us we would find ourselves vitally dependent on the outcome of political and military contests across those oceans. Our own security would require us to pursue an active diplomacy designed to prevent any hostile or potentially hostile power on the other side from dominating them.

For the moment, however, I am not concerned with this larger picture. I am concerned with what appears to have been a deliberately assumed commitment on the far side of the Pacific, a commitment which could not have been brought into any logical or practical correspondence with the continuation of an isolationism based on independence of Old World politics. This inconsistency would have been obvious if we had acquired Ireland as a colonial possession which we had to defend. Immediately we would have become, unmistakably, a power in the Old World, deep in its politics. In our acquisition of the Philippines this may have been less obvious, but it was no less true. The Philippines were at the heart of a distant area in which the rival European powers and Japan, greedy for empire, deployed substantially more strength than we did. If we were to defend the Philippines, we would have to muster some military strength of our own in the area and we would have to enter upon the diplomatic game of playing the other powers off against one another. Because we did not see this, the historical record reveals a direct line of causation from our acquisition of the Philippine commitment in 1898 to the Japanese attack on Pearl Harbor in 1941, an attack that coincided with the temporary Japanese capture of the Philippines. Perhaps that same line of causation can be traced even to the Korean War and our conflict with Communist China.

Virtually everyone would agree, today, that it was a mistake to acquire the Philippines and, at the same time, seek to continue our isolationist policy. Most students of the subject, I think, would also agree that, whatever our policy, it was still a mistake to acquire the Philippines. Their possession served no strategic interest but was, rather, a strategic liability, especially as, with the passage of time, it came to represent a challenge to Japan. And what we got from the Philippines in markets and trade was far less than what it cost us to administer and defend them. The Philippines would have been useful to us only if, as a handful of American imperialists in 1898 wanted us to

178

do, we had set out to dominate the world. In fact, however, they were pure burden from start to finish, and we had to recognize them as such. But, once the fateful mistake of acquiring them was made, we were stuck with them, and it is clear that even today, when they have at last become independent, their defense is still a charge upon us. In meeting that charge we have added the defense of Japan, Korea, and Formosa to the burden we already bore.

I am interested in the particular question of how we came, in 1898, to make this strategic misstep. And I mean to explore the question, in this and the following two chapters, not for its own sake but because it seems to me to epitomize the limitations under which statesmen everywhere labor and the compulsion of circumstance that tends to shape the policy of every nation. In other words, such an examination should suggest how history actually is made, and that is its real value.

What I have to say here is the product of an extended investigation of the source materials and the historical interpretations that bear on the question. I started this investigation with the common view that a quite avoidable blunder had been made by the administration of President McKinley in acquiring the Philippines. I wanted to find out at what particular point in the sequence of events the mistake had been made, and by whom, and on the basis of what thinking. I supposed that there was one day and one hour and one place where one man or a group of men had decided that we should take the Philippines, when he or they were quite free to decide that we should not take them. By the time I finished my investigation, however, I had concluded instead that, given the total situation at the time, it would have been virtually impossible for the McKinley administration to have avoided the acquisition of the Philippines. I never did find the single point in the drift of events where its tendency could have been stopped or turned back, where the administration, consequently, really had a choice in the matter—even when it thought that it did have such a choice and was exercising it. If we understand this, in the particular case under scrutiny, we shall understand much better how foreign policy in general develops and is determined—today no less than in the past.

Having presented my conclusion in advance, let me add that it does not necessarily imply historical predestination. I assume, still, that history is made by men who have a certain freedom of choice. But I am impressed by the heavy compulsions that drive them to make one choice rather than another, so that the freedom they enjoy is to oppose forces that are generally too great for them.

Most of us Americans remember, from our history lessons, the Spanish-American War of 1898. This was the first display of that strength which made us a world power. On this occasion we used that strength, as became our liberal tradition, for the liberation of the long-suffering Cubans from the tyranny of Spain. This we all remember. What few of us remember is the Philippine War, which began two days before the formal conclusion of the Spanish-American War, which lasted some four years, and which was substantially more costly in blood and treasure alike. In this second and much heavier war we Americans, to our horror, found ourselves engaged in desperate combat with the distant Filipinos who were resisting our attempt to subjugate them. We have good reason for not wanting to remember this war, in which we became engaged without any intention and essentially against our own will. How was it, then, that we found ourselves fighting to conquer a land off the shores of Asia which, as was widely apparent, we would have done well to refuse as a gift?

When we went to war with Spain on April 25, 1898, virtually no one in the United States had any notion of acquiring an Asiatic empire. It was an exceptional American who knew where the Philippine Islands were, or, perhaps, had even heard of them. Those whom we identify today with their acquisition appear to have had no thought, as yet, of acquiring them. Apparently it was not in the mind of Theodore Roosevelt, then Assistant Secretary of the Navy, when he made the arrangements for Commodore Dewey's attack on the Spanish squadron at Manila;[1] it had not occurred to the Commodore;[2] and Captain Mahan, the philosopher of expansionism, experienced misgivings when it first appeared that we might be committed to their acquisition.[3]

Not only did we have no thought of acquiring the Philippines before we entered upon the course of action by which they became ours, their acquisition, if it had been proposed, would have been regarded as repugnant to our national policy. We believed that a nation like ours, dedicated to representative government with the consent of the governed, could not include within its jurisdiction some seven million distant subjects, unqualified for citizenship, over which it exercised the kind of colonial rule against which it had declared its own independence. Many Americans questioned whether our Constitution, with its guarantees of human rights, would allow it. Even if these bars had not existed, our people had shown before, as they have shown since, their aversion for the kind of empire which the European great powers had been establishing among the "lesser breeds." Yet the fact remains that, early in 1899, we found ourselves already committed to the prosecution of a long and painful war for the subjugation of the Philippines. Our virtually unquestioned policy was one thing; our action was the opposite. How could this be?

The Spanish-American War was not made by statesmen acting with deliberation, weighing their responsibilities, and taking the requirements of national policy as their guide. In 1898 our nation, for the moment, lost its sobriety and abandoned itself to glory. This was a people's war into which our government was swept by public opinion.

[1] *Cf.* Letter of May 25, 1898, Roosevelt to Lodge, *Selections from the Correspondence of Theodore Roosevelt and Henry Cabot Lodge* (New York, 1925), I, 301. Also: S. F. Bemis, *The United States as a World Power* (New York, 1950), p. 6.

[2] George Dewey, *Autobiography* (New York, 1913), p. 185.

[3] Mahan to H. C. Lodge, July 27, 1898; cited by Livesey, *Mahan on Sea Power*, (Oklahoma, 1947), pp. 181-87. Also: A. T. Mahan, *The Problem of Asia* (Boston, 1905), pp. 7-8.

What does it mean to say this? Who were the people? What was public opinion?

Public opinion, as far as governments are concerned, is not the spontaneous expression of the population as a statistical total. It is, rather, the opinion expressed by those who can influence significant parts of that population to a degree which might be politically decisive. In 1898 this meant, most notably, newspaper publishers. The yellow press, competing in sensationalism, deliberately embarked on a campaign against Spanish treatment of the Cubans as a means of increasing its circulation. It elaborated atrocity stories to arouse alike the animal passion and the self-righteousness of its readers. For this and other reasons public pressures were developed, emotional pressures of a nature hard for any government to deal with; since to those who do not share their sobriety the reasons of the sober sound like the counsels of cowardice.

Historians generally recognize today that we had no legitimate *casus belli* against Spain. Her inherited position in Cuba and Puerto Rico, a last remnant of her empire in the New World, had become obsolete and increasingly untenable by the end of the nineteenth century. It would have to be adjusted. But the Spanish government recognized this, and there was no reason to doubt that, given time, patience, and the absence of public excitement in either country, the adjustment could be accomplished without war. It had, in fact, almost been accomplished before the war broke out. The Spanish government, moving as fast as an impassioned public opinion in its own country allowed, was co-operating earnestly with our government to achieve a diplomatic solution. Twenty days before we actually went to war our essential demands had already been met.

By this time, however, the yellow press had another case for incitement to war, in the explosion which had sunk our battleship, *The Maine*, in Havana harbor. This disaster was laid at the door of Spain, even though it had almost surely not been caused by Spain. The press howled for war to avenge the national honor.

The administration of President McKinley bowed, at last, to a basic rule of politics: where you cannot lead you had better follow. It had tried, like its predecessor, to calm public opinion and to achieve a diplomatic settlement with Spain before too late. Now it saw an excited Congress, moved by the mass emotion, preparing to act on its own to have a war. It fell into step and, two days after the Spanish capitulation to our demands, the President sent his war message to Congress.

Historians and statesmen since Thucydides have recognized, as a prime danger inherent in war, that states which embark on it tend to lose control of their own destiny. A typical manifestation of this danger is the repeated inability of states to keep to the limited objectives for which they have gone to war, once victory comes within their reach. Our war with Spain had the sole objective of liberating Cuba. This objective was made explicit in a joint Congressional resolution which disclaimed territorial greed by foreswearing any disposition to acquire Cuba for ourselves.

As we now know, Spain did not have the military means to defend Cuba. We might therefore have confined our military effort to the vicinity of Cuba, making the military objective the same as the political objective, that of pulling Cuba out of the Spanish grasp. There was really no more necessity of attacking Spain's islands in the Pacific than of attacking her islands in the Mediterranean. Military orthodoxy since Clausewitz, however, has held that the prime military objective in warfare (or in warfare at its best) is not the capture of territory but the destruction of the enemy's power and will to fight. Since our military had been brought up on this doctrine it did not occur to them to limit or localize the military effort. It would surely have been hard to show them any reason for doing so.

For many decades we had maintained a small naval squadron in the western Pacific, apparently to support our commerce and "show the flag." Commodore Dewey's predecessor in command of that squadron, seeing the likelihood of war with Spain and knowing that a Spanish naval squadron was roosting in the Philippines, made plans for an attack on that squadron, plans which Commodore Dewey inherited from him.[4] Such action by a naval officer in such a position is less noteworthy, perhaps, than would have been its omission.

In a real sense, no positive decision ever was taken to adopt a policy calling for an attack on the Philippines. The President merely found that this was the naval policy that the navy had in mind, and he seems to have assumed that it must be right. "While we remained at war with Spain," Dewey later wrote, "our purpose must be to strike at the power of Spain wherever possible."[5] This implication of unlimited war, which might have given a Bismarck pause, was unquestioned among us at the time. The *political* objective of the war was to liberate Cuba; but the *military* objective must be to hurt Spain wherever we could until she cried quits. The western Pacific was one of the principal places where we could hurt her. Given these premises, the naval officers were right in assuming that we would strike at the Philippines in case of war. A special policy decision would have been needed rather to exempt them from the area of our military operations than to include them.

The outbreak of war did not, in itself, occasion the dispatch of any orders whatever to Commodore Dewey, who lay in Britain's colony of Hong Kong with our Far Eastern squadron. Action to instruct him on what he should do was taken only in response to an urgent cable from him, reporting that the British declaration of neutrality forced him to leave Hong Kong immediately and requesting instructions. At a meeting in the White House an order to Dewey was drafted and the President approved it. It read: "War has commenced. . . . Proceed at once to Philippine Islands. Commence operations particularly against the Spanish fleet. You must capture vessels or destroy. Use utmost endeavor."[6] No one thought of this

[4] John D. Long, *The New American Navy* (New York, 1903), I, p. 179.
[5] *Autobiography* (New York, 1913), p. 239.
[6] *Appendix to the Report of the Chief of the Bureau of Navigation* (Washington, 1898), p. 67.

order in terms of the significance that it might have for the general position of the United States in the Far East. It represented merely the implementation of a war strategy that had never been questioned.

Dewey carried out his mission with punctilio and daring. He proceeded to the Bay of Manila, where the Spanish squadron lay, and destroyed it at its anchorage without the loss of a single American life.

The American people had been showing increasing frustration at the lack of any heroic military action coincident with the outbreak of war, and the government in Washington had been coming under mounting criticism for timidity. Dewey's departure from Hong Kong and his destination were front-page news on April 25. For five tense days nothing more was heard. Then, on May 2, the news of the victory came. The relief and rejoicing were universal, but no place more so, I suspect, than in the corridors of Washington where the public pressure for action had been so keenly felt. A *New York Times* dispatch reporting this added: "The victory has scarcely been fully reported before the fact flashes upon the Administration, as it has upon the European diplomatic circles, that the United States Government has suddenly acquired a status in the East that was not at all looked for, and that may greatly change the discussion of Eastern problems." This is not the last time, in the course of these chapters, that we shall have occasion to note how implications of an event that become obvious immediately after it takes place remain unforeseen throughout the period in which it is anticipated only.

Until this moment, no one in Washington had concerned himself with the implications and consequences of Dewey's mission. No one had asked: What next? Consequently, when the Spanish squadron had been destroyed Dewey found himself without those landing forces which he would need to carry out the "offensive operations in Philippines" that he had been instructed to undertake after dealing with the squadron. This omission also became obvious to Washington in the moment of victory.

Although Dewey himself was not heard from until May 7, on May 3 the Commanding General of the Army recommended to the Secretary of War that General Thomas M. Anderson be sent "to occupy the Philippine Islands," in command of certain specified troops; and on May 4 the President ordered that these troops be assembled at San Francisco.[7] This represented the decision, made without forethought, to take the Philippines, whether temporarily or permanently.

Still, no one was clear on the mission of these landing forces. The general chosen to command them, having had an interview with the President on May 12, wrote him on the 15th: "I do not yet know whether it is your desire to subdue and hold all of the Spanish territory in the islands, or merely to seize and hold the capital."[8] The President didn't know either. Finally, however, on May 19 he defined the mission of the expeditionary force in a letter to the Secretary of War. He wrote that: "The destruction of the Spanish fleet at Manila, followed by the taking of the naval station at Cavite, the paroling of the garrisons, and acquisition of the control of the bay, have rendered it necessary, in the further prosecution of the measures adopted by this Government for the purpose of bringing about an honorable and durable peace with Spain, to send an army of occupation to the Philippines for the twofold purpose of completing the reduction of the Spanish power in that quarter and of giving order and security to the islands while in the possession of the United States. . . .

"The first effect of the military occupation of the enemy's territory is the severance of the former political relations of the inhabitants and the establishment of a new political power. . . ."[9]

Without looking forward as far as the postwar future, but

[7] Adjutant General's Office, *Correspondence Relating to the War with Spain* . . . (Washington, 1902), II, p. 635.

[8] *Ibid.*, II, pp. 645-46.

[9] *Ibid.*, II, pp. 676-78.

merely trying to stay abreast of the present, the government had concluded that events "rendered it necessary" to take possession of the Philippine Islands.

At this time the American people had shown themselves thoroughly opposed to the acquisition of overseas territory even as close in as the Hawaiian Islands. Consequently, no one, at first, contemplated the possibility that the Philippines might be kept in our possession. To some it seemed that we should hold them as collateral for a Spanish indemnity at the war's end, returning them to Spain upon its payment. To others it seemed logical that we should grant them their independence, as we intended to do with Cuba.

The mental uncertainty and agony which the *New York Times* displayed on its editorial page is representative. On May 3 it found it unthinkable that we should ever return the islands to Spain. Exploring alternatives, it added that "nobody pretends that the natives of the Philippines are fit for self-government, as we believe the Cubans to be. On the other hand, all the arguments against the annexation of Hawaii are available, with even greater force, against our retention of the Philippines for ourselves." It concluded that we had already incurred a responsibility in seizing them which could be discharged only by having Great Britain take them off our hands.

The following day, in one and the same editorial, the *Times* was saying that "we could not in any event take the islands for ourselves," and also that if Britain "declines to take them on reasonable terms we must even retain them for ourselves," since we could neither return them to Spain nor hand them over to their primitive inhabitants. It was thus foreseeing the possibility of a dilemma in which every possible alternative was impossible to contemplate—such a dilemma as is not unique in the conduct of foreign affairs.

Finally, by May 9, the *Times* had at last brought itself to contemplate what could not be contemplated at first. "It is becoming plainer every day," it said, "that paramount necessity will compel us to assume for a time of which we cannot now see the end the duty of governing and controlling the Philippine Islands."

The President, too, was still behind the march of events, trying to catch up with them. Being at a loss to know what we should do with the Philippines, now that they were at our disposal, he postponed decision. One of the conditions that he made for a truce with beaten Spain, on July 30, was that we should continue to occupy "the city, bay and harbor of Manila pending the conclusion of a treaty of peace which shall determine the control, disposition, and the government of the Philippines."[10]

At last, on September 16, in his instructions to the American commissioners appointed to negotiate the peace with Spain, the President wrote: "Without any original thought of complete or even partial acquisition, the presence and success of our arms at Manila imposes upon us obligations which we cannot disregard. The march of events rules and overrules human action. . . . we cannot be unmindful that without any desire or design on our part the war has brought us new duties and responsibilities which we must meet and discharge as becomes a great nation on whose growth and career from the beginning the Ruler of Nations has plainly written the high command and pledge of civilization."[11]

We may not doubt that President McKinley, who sought divine guidance for his decision on the Philippines, wrote this with sincerity. But it confronts us with a paradox that goes to the root of this inquiry. It virtually states, in its first two sentences, that "the presence and success of our arms at Manila" does not belong in the category of "human action" but in some other category that "overrules human action." This other category is identified with "the march of events." Here the government of the United States discounts its own authority over the march of events, conceding the sway of destiny.

[10] Tyler Dennett, *Americans in Eastern Asia* (New York, 1941), p. 620.
[11] *Ibid.*, p. 621.

XVI • President McKinley, unhappily deciding at last that we had no choice but to make the Philippines ours, concluded that destiny must have predetermined an outcome so far from our intentions. This immediately became the view of all who faced the unexpected consequence of Dewey's famous victory at Manila Bay. Captain Alfred Thayer Mahan, who had participated notably in the development of the strategy which led to Dewey's victory, wrote: ". . . the preparation made for us, rather than by us, in the unwilling acquisition of the Philippines, is so obvious as to embolden even the least presumptuous to see in it the hand of Providence."[1]

Surely, however, it was by actions of our own free choice that we at last found ourselves holding the Philippines. Surely we had been free to shape our policy so that we would not acquire them. Surely it was by our own decision that the Philippines came into our hands.

In point of fact, there never was a decision to attach the Philippines to us until it was found that they virtually were attached already. By the time the issue was full-blown, the question which presented itself for decision was not whether we should *take* them. It was whether we should *keep* them. And by this time there was no acceptable alternative to keeping them.

[1] "Effect of Asiatic Conditions," in *The Problem of Asia*, Boston, 1905, p. 175.

What brought us to this point was a succession of particular decisions relating solely to military operations. We ended with a far-reaching commitment that we had not had at the beginning, and the question to which I now address myself is at what point in the succession of decisions we became committed.

The date on which we formally and forcibly deposed the Spanish authority in the Philippines, replacing it with our own, was August 13, 1898. Until then Spain still had a jurisdiction formally unquestioned by any government in the world, including our own, which had made an issue of her jurisdiction in Cuba only. On the preceding day, however, we had concluded in Washington an armistice or peace protocol with Spain whereby we were to occupy Manila pending a later decision on the future of the Philippines. Thus we established ourselves in physical possession while making it clear that we were committed neither to keeping them ourselves nor returning them to Spain.

This left us free, in a formal sense, to decide by leisurely deliberation among ourselves what it was best to do with the islands—whether we should cede them back to Spain, give them to some other power, keep them for ourselves, or grant their independence. In fact, however, our freedom was limited by a moral obligation that had become ours once we had taken physical possession away from Spain. Before we had done that, one might say that the future of the Philippines was no more our concern than the future of the Belgian Congo. After we had taken physical possession, the responsibility for their future became ours. The man who takes an enslaved child from its master is not really free to decide whether he will return it to the old slavery, or whether he will leave it to die of exposure. It would have been one thing to have refrained from disturbing Spain's possession of the islands; it was another to give them back to Spain. In the former case Spain would still have held and exploited them by virtue of Magellan's discovery, with which we had nothing to do; in the latter she would hold and exploit them on our responsibility. No sooner was this alternative thought of than it became morally unthinkable.

The alternative of independence seemed, at first, to make the best sense. The Spanish war had been conceived by our people as a war of liberation. While it was only the Cubans whom we had set out to liberate, by what we call "the fortunes of war" we had now liberated the Filipinos as well. So much the better! It was widely assumed that we would give them their freedom as a matter of course—just as we were to give the Cubans their freedom. As the days passed, however, it began to appear doubtful in Washington that the Filipinos were ready for self-government.

Why? Why should this doubt have arisen? What, after all, is the test of readiness for self-government? Were the Spanish Americans ready for self-government in the first quarter of the nineteenth century, when Napoleon's victory over Spain set them free? Not if one judges by the political chaos that ensued. Was Cuba, herself, ready for self-government in 1898? Judging by the record of her subsequent domestic politics, one might question it. On June 27, 1898, Dewey had cabled Washington: ". . . In my opinion these people [the Filipinos] are far superior in their intelligence and more capable of self-government than the natives of Cuba, and I am familiar with both races."[2]

The situation in the Philippines had been almost exactly parallel to that in Cuba for years. In both places the Spanish authorities had, with inevitable brutality, been resisting a militant insurgent movement supported by the people. Was it up to the United States, newly arrived on the scene, to determine that, in the Philippines as distinct from Cuba, the insurgents could not govern satisfactorily? Was it up to us to take Spain's place in fighting the Filipino insurgents and imposing our rule? It

[2] "Appendix to the Report of the Chief of the Bureau of Navigation," *op. cit.*, p. 103. By the fall of 1899, however, when Dewey wanted to convince the President that we should "never—never" give up the islands, he told him that the Filipinos were not capable of self-government and would not be "for many, many years." [Facsimile of McKinley's memorandum of conversation, in Charles S. Olcott's *The Life of William McKinley*, (Boston, 1916), Vol. II, facing p. 96.] In war and politics it is often more important to be sure than to be right.

seems strange that we should have adopted such contrary policies in Cuba and the Philippines. And if we were going to add one rather than the other to the territory under our jurisdiction, there are obvious reasons why Cuba should have been preferred.

Our discovery that the Filipinos were not ready for self-government appears, in fact, to be based on a rather special test of readiness. Between May 1, 1898, and the fall of the year it became increasingly evident to Washington that the Filipinos, liberated from Spain, would by themselves be unable to keep their independence. If the United States got out, Germany, Japan, France, Russia, or Britain would come in on its heels.

Would-be liberators should keep in mind a lesson that has been repeatedly exemplified since 1898. When you liberate a country, intentionally or otherwise, you almost always find yourself committed to the maintenance of its liberated status. You tend to become the guarantor of your own handiwork. You have to defend its independence. We felt, when the moment of decision came, that we could not separate the Philippines from Spain only to have them fall into the hands of one of the other powers. If, by saving them from the wolf, we allowed them to be torn to pieces by the pack, our role would appear discreditable; we would have failed in our duty as a responsible power. The Philippines were not ready for self-government, in our eyes, primarily because they did not have that capacity for defending themselves which is one of the attributes of a truly independent sovereignty.

After the Battle of Manila Bay various powers sent naval forces to the scene to observe matters and protect the interests of their nationals. Germany maintained in the Bay a naval force greater than Dewey's, and the German commander assumed an arrogance that showed a degree of contempt for Dewey's position. This impressed us. We suspected then what has since been confirmed, that the Kaiser's government was, in fact, moved by a desire to get the Philippines for Germany. If our forces steamed away now, having unseated the Spanish authority, they would leave the forces of Germany and other

192

powers behind them in Manila Bay. This was unthinkable to our people and would have been discreditable in the eyes of other nations. By assuming for ourselves the authority of government, then, we had already become committed to the naval defense of a land far away across the ocean on the coast of Asia —beyond the effective reach of our power as then constituted— and to the maintenance of order among the seven million turbulent people who inhabited that land.

It is true that the price of Cuban liberation was the same, in the sense that we have been committed to the defense of Cuba ever since. But we were already committed, if not under the Monroe Doctrine then by our vital strategic interests, to the defense of the area within which Cuba lay. Here that defense presented no special problem, partly because it was close to our home bases and partly because no other power challenged our hegemony in it. Though chaos should reign inside Cuba, no other power would be at hand to take advantage of it by establishing its rule. The opposite was true in the Philippines, which lay in a distant region that had not been marked off for us, a region in which, until 1945, other powers were to be more strongly established than we were. By assuming a responsibility for the Philippines that could not be discharged without the acquiescence of other powers, we thereby gave the acquiescing powers a hostage. By so much our new position in the far Pacific was one of danger and weakness. Even today, when we have given the Philippines their independence, there is no practicable way by which we could rid ourselves of the continuing responsibility for their defense.

After August 13 we had to decide whether we would give the Philippines back to Spain, allow some other power to have them, leave them to the Filipinos, or keep them for ourselves. In theoretical terms we were free to choose. In practical terms the first two alternatives were foreclosed. The third—that of granting independence—was virtually foreclosed as well, since it would have required us to establish a protectorate and this, in turn, would have entailed, if it was to be effective, such rights of

193

intervention as we retained even in Cuba under the Platt Amendment. We would, in fact, have to be physically present and in command to discharge our obligation to defend the islands.

The only alternative left, then, was for us to continue in possession. It is true that this last alternative might have been regarded as no less unacceptable than the other three. But it represented the existing state of things, which always has the advantage where all alternatives are equally unacceptable. More important, for the moment it seemed far from unacceptable to what was, perhaps, a majority of our interested citizens, and to the administration in Washington. They saw us unexpectedly established by the decree of destiny in a dominating position on the far side of the Pacific, where the cornucopia of commercial opportunities in China was about to be spilled. They tasted by anticipation the glory of our new eminence in the world. And all this was to come to us through no evil machinations on our part, but as the providential reward of our virtue. We were to enjoy what were, for others, the fruits of sin, while retaining our own innocence. No one, at the moment, anticipated the war we were about to fight for the subjugation of the Filipinos, with all the moral confusion that it would entail.

In retrospect one can make a good case for it that by August 13 we were already morally committed to the care and protection of the Philippines for an indefinitely long time. The commitment had already been assumed, and we must look to earlier decisions if we are to find at what point it was assumed.

"If old Dewey had just sailed away when he smashed the Spanish fleet," McKinley is reported to have said later, "what a lot of trouble he would have saved us."[3] Before 1898 was over many of our people were to ask why Dewey did not just sail away, and to this day his failure to do so is widely regarded as

[3] H. H. Kohlsaat, *From McKinley to Harding*, p. 68. (Quoted by F. R. Dulles, *America's Rise to World Power* [New York, 1955], p. 50.)

the fatal omission that left the Philippines on our hands.

To have sailed away, however, would have been a course of action for which Dewey had no authority and which he could not have justified in the circumstances. His governing instructions, in a cable of February 24 from Washington, were to undertake "offensive operations in Philippines" after dealing with the Spanish squadron. However vague this instruction, it clearly did not mean that he might just sail away from the Philippines after dealing with the squadron, and for him to have done so would have been in violation of it.

There were other reasons why just sailing away, after the battle, might have been regarded as a scandal. How would anyone have explained to the American people, in their hour of patriotic exultation, the retirement of their victorious fleet? In the public mind "honor" was as much the issue, now, as anything else. These matters were discussed in terms of alternatives between keeping our flag flying or "hauling it down" in the face of the foe. Was our fleet to come skulking home, leaving Spain in occupation of the field as if the victory had been hers? A question cast in these terms was already as good as answered.

Moreover, there was at least one Spanish gunboat, perhaps more, still at large among the islands. If Dewey had just sailed away, this force, whatever it consisted of, would have remained free to attack our merchant shipping—thereby adding to the scandal.

Finally, by destroying the Spanish squadron Dewey had, to an unknown extent, impaired the governing authority in the islands. That authority had already found itself on the defensive, in the preceding years, against the Filipino insurgents. Was there any assurance that, crippled as it now was, it could still maintain order or protect the lives and property of the people of Manila, including Europeans and Americans? Apparently Dewey, himself, was mindful of a responsibility which had fallen upon him as a result of his blow to Spanish authority. Cabling Washington on May 4, he said: "Much excitement at Manila. Scarcity of provisions on account of not having

195

economized stores. Will protect foreign residents."[4] General Greene of the United States Volunteers in the Philippines reported on August 27: "If the United States evacuate these islands, anarchy and civil war will immediately ensue and lead to foreign intervention."[5] For Dewey to have just sailed away, leaving possible chaos and bloodshed in his wake, would have represented an abdication of humane responsibility for which he might later have been held accountable; and it might have given rise to circumstances in which the forcible intervention of other powers would have been justified and inevitable. Again one must ask how it could have been explained to the American people.

It is hard to avoid the conclusion that it was not politically feasible for Dewey just to sail away. Any administration that had ordered his immediate return would have committed itself to political disaster and would be remembered in infamy to this day. It would, moreover, have been sacrificing itself for a cause of which it was not aware and which was apparent to no one in the first days of May, 1898. After all, men and governments can never act on the basis of knowledge and insights which are not available to them at the time, however much their successors may wish they had.

If, in fact, it was not politically or morally possible for us to hit and run, then our commitment to responsibility for the Philippines was born in the moment when we destroyed the Spanish squadron on May 1. After that we could find no feasible way to rid ourselves of it. In our search, then, for the decision that was responsible for this commitment we ought to look at the decisions that led to the Battle of Manila Bay.

We should put ourselves, now, in the position of any responsible American naval official confronting, in the months before April 24, 1898, the prospect of a war with Spain. The

[4] "Appendix to the Report of the Chief of the Bureau of Navigation," *op. cit.,* p. 68.

[5] Senate Document No. 62, Part 2, 55th Congress, 3rd Session, Washington, 1899, p. 374.

political objective of such a war would be the liberation of Cuba. But the military objective, which concerned the navy, would be to bring Spain to a point where she was willing to submit to our will in the matter. This meant hurting her as hard as possible wherever she could be hurt until she cried out that she was ready to accept our terms. Once that had been done, the political objective of a liberated Cuba would be realized by our civilian negotiators.

If there were political reasons for limiting this effort, for not hurting Spain as much as we could or wherever we could, it was not the navy's business to determine for itself what they might be or, on its own initiative, to be governed by them. This was the business of the President and his principal adviser on foreign policy, the Secretary of State. In the absence of any injunction from the President the Navy's duty was to be prepared with plans for hurting Spain to the utmost. This, after all, is what the Western world has conceived war to be ever since the days of Napoleon and Clausewitz when, after a century and a half, it again became a thoroughly serious business.

The alert naval official who was responsible for plans to meet the contingency of war would naturally look for the points at which Spain was vulnerable, the exposed places. The most conspicuous of these, after Cuba and Puerto Rico, was in the Philippine archipelago, where she maintained a small, antiquated, ineffective squadron of naval vessels, one of which was of wood.

The navy's responsibilities for the defense of American commerce on the high seas would also have to be taken into account by our imaginary naval official. The Spanish ships in the Philippines, unhindered, would be able to raid our merchantmen in the Pacific. The duty of the navy would be to hinder them.

As a matter of routine duty, then, the navy made plans for an attack on the Philippines. The record does not show precisely to what extent these plans were known outside the Navy Department before the outbreak of war. To the extent that they were known, however, say by the President and his Cabinet, they

197

raised an issue in nobody's mind. Consequently, no hard thought was given to their possible political implications.

We should take note of this, because thought and decision in a great bureaucratic government is largely the product of the need to resolve issues. An issue generally has to be made in order to initiate the process. If only one man with a strong enough voice in our councils had raised a question about the political advisability of carrying out these plans, a debate might have ensued and the consequent expenditure of thought might then have revealed the political dangers that, as it was, remained hidden.

As it was, no one thought of any reason for not attacking the Philippines. It occurred to no one that there were dangerous political implications in the projected military operations; and it would have been hard to object to them over the approval of all the competent military authorities. When, on April 24, the President nodded his assent to the dispatch of the order for Dewey to attack, he quite innocently committed the United States to the acquisition of an empire on the shores of Asia. It is this decision, in particular, that we are asked to attribute to destiny.

We have seen that, by displacing the Spanish authority in the Philippines, we made ourselves responsible for them. Going back a bit farther in time, we have seen how Dewey's destruction of the Spanish squadron in Manila Bay could have no other result than that of displacing the Spanish authority— and so making us Americans responsible for the Philippines. The question arises, then, whether it was necessary to have Dewey destroy the Spanish squadron.

Unopposed, the Spanish squadron in Manila Bay would have been free to prey on our merchant shipping in the western Pacific. Could a responsible government in Washington have abstained from doing anything about this? Could it have survived an attempt to explain its abstention to the American people if, in consequence, American lives and property were lost?

What would the effect have been on American prestige abroad? As a practical matter, something surely did have to be done about this threat.[6]

But perhaps it could have been met by less aggressive tactics than those adopted by Dewey when he ran through the entrance of Manila Bay, under the guns of the Spanish forts and without regard for possible mines, to slaughter the Spanish squadron at its anchorage. Perhaps it could have been accomplished with less risk, if also less heroically, by simply blockading Manila Bay. Such a blockade would have involved great technical difficulties in keeping coaled and repaired, since we had no naval base within a radius of several thousand miles, but with determination it might conceivably have been done.

Moreover, it would have been politically feasible. If any of our people had criticized the restraint which it represented, a plausible case could surely have been made for not risking our squadron in a run past the Spanish forts and through a channel that might be mined, only to give the Spaniards the advantage of supplementing the fire of their ships with that of their shore batteries.

A blockade would have adequately served our defensive purpose. But it would have been less effective in the service of that other purpose, which was to force Spain's submission to our will by hurting her and demonstrating her helplessness to resist us. The swift, dramatic victory in Manila Bay was the first blow struck at Spain in the war, and perhaps the most telling. When it was followed by the destruction, off Santiago de Cuba, of the only other naval force which she had committed to battle, she was ready to meet our terms. Without it she might not have given up quite so soon and the war might have been prolonged to some extent, although the outcome could hardly have been in doubt—as we now know in the light of our hindsight.

[6] If it really was a threat. One must keep the question open. After all, we did nothing about the threat of Spanish naval force to our shipping in the Mediterranean.

One can never be sure what might have happened in history had things been otherwise, but we may reasonably suppose that a possible alternative to the destruction of the Spanish power in Manila was to be found in the simple blockade of that power. This might well have left us free just to sail away and come home when the war was over. The islands would have remained, then, a burden and a strategic liability for Spain or for whatever other power succeeded her in their possession.[7]

Dewey, himself, could not have been expected, on political grounds, to make the decision to blockade rather than invade the Bay of Manila. This would have been up to the President. The President, through the Secretary of the Navy, could have ordered him to blockade the Spanish squadron and to avoid putting the power of the United States into any position in which it might find itself responsible for the Philippines. We can see now that this is what he should have done.

Again, however, no one at the time saw the issue, no one weighed the alternatives of blockade and invasion in terms of their political implications. Presumably, if the reader or I had been there we would have shared this universal blindness. Today we are wise after the event.

The crucial decision was the one that dispatched Dewey to the Battle of Manila Bay. As far as external circumstances were concerned the President had freedom of choice in making this decision. He could have made it otherwise than he did and thereby, one supposes, have avoided our acquisition of responsibility for the government of the Philippines. If he had had such foresight, however, he would hardly have been the child of his times which he in fact was. He would have been a prodigy. And one may doubt that such a prodigy, a man so far in advance of the thinking of his countrymen, would have had a better chance of being elected President in 1896 than, say, Henry Adams had.

[7] Germany, especially, with the First World War approaching, might have found that her possession of them confirmed Bismarck's wisdom in warning against the acquisition of a colonial empire.

The decision that sent Dewey to Manila Bay was the President's in a formal sense. It was developed by the more or less routine activity of his subordinates in the Navy Department. Fundamentally, however, it was a product of the culture which predominated in America about the turn of the century. The President in his policy was simply giving expression to the common mind of the day, with all its elements of distinction and all its limitations.

XVII • The human mind is the captive of its time and place. The commonplace conceptions of the age impose themselves upon it. The limitations of the cultural environment hem it in. It accepts the general or fashionable beliefs of the moment as the truth, however little they may have to do with truth.

Above all, the human mind is generally incapable of seeing what lies around the corner ahead. Especially in the field of international affairs, the unexpected is what happens—even though, once it has happened, it takes on an aspect of obvious inevitability which makes us wonder how it ever could have been unexpected.

Isn't it obvious that the American and British governments should have foreseen President Nasser's seizure of the Suez Canal in 1956? I find myself indignant at their failure to do so. Anyone knows that, if you strike at the public prestige of a man like Nasser, he is bound to react drastically, even violently. The manner of withdrawing the proposed assistance for the Aswan Dam, in June of 1956, must have been calculated to strike at his prestige, to humble him. Surely it should have been evident in Washington and London that he would react. The one obvious recourse which he had, by way of reaction, was to seize the Suez Canal. Many experts and commentators later expressed themselves as shocked that Washington and

London failed to foresee this contingency and to be prepared for it. It was so obviously Nasser's next move, his only move. But I don't recall that any of these experts or commentators found it obvious, drew attention to it, or even thought of it as a possibility in the interval between the stroke at Nasser's prestige and the Canal's seizure. It became obvious to them, and to all of us, only the day after it happened.

Before May 1, 1898, when Commodore Dewey destroyed the Spanish squadron in Manila Bay, no one anticipated that this would pose any political problem for us. The American public waited with suspense and excitement for a week before news of Dewey's success reached it. Editorial writers and officials in Washington went around on tiptoe, so to speak, awaiting it. Everybody's mind was on it. It was in the headlines of every newspaper. Yet, before the news of the victory came through on May 2, no one saw what thereupon became obvious to many people, that Dewey's success created grave political problems bearing on the position of the United States in the Far East. It is astonishing, if you look through the newspapers and documents of the period, to note the contrast between our thinking about Dewey's victory before and after. The best minds did not see, on May 1, what was apparent even to ordinary minds on May 2. This is what happens repeatedly in international affairs, especially in connection with war or military adventure.

The illustration of these established limitations has been one reason why I have pried so particularly into the circumstances surrounding our acquisition of the Philippines. Another reason is that this event constitutes the root of our dangerous and difficult embroilment in the Far East ever since. It compelled us to accept a strategic liability which we have not adequately met in the half century that has since elapsed, a liability which has been compounded by our efforts to meet it. In a real sense, the war with Japan from 1941 to 1945, the subsequent Korean War, and the stalemate along the Straits of Formosa are consequences of our commitment to defend the Philippines.

They represent our efforts to meet that commitment with means which have never been sufficient.

There is a primitive notion—more prevalent around the beginning of the century than today—that when a state extends its territory it becomes richer and stronger. The additional territory, however, may be a net liability if the resources required for its administration and defense are in excess of what one might call the revenues. This has been the case with the Philippines, which have been immensely costly to the United States in these statistically measurable terms alone. Far more serious, however, has been the fact that the Philippines have constituted a strategic liability in two senses. *One,* lying so far from our basic national defenses, in another world, they have constituted a hostage which other countries could use and have used in their diplomatic bargaining with us. *Two,* lying in an area of vital interest to Japan in particular, they have, by offering an implicit challenge to Japan, constituted a root of conflict between the United States and Japan.

Let me illustrate the second of these two senses in which the Philippines have been a strategic liability by a brief quotation from Harold and Margaret Sprout's *Rise of American Naval Power:* ". . . an American fleet, strong enough to guarantee security to the Philippines, could destroy the Japanese Navy and blockade Japan. On the other hand, a fleet that could defend the Japanese homeland against the United States would constitute a standing menace to the security of the Philippines."[1]

Now let me illustrate the other sense in which the Philippines have been a strategic liability—as a hostage to be used against us by other powers in their diplomacy. The twentieth century is marked by a series of agreements between the United States and Japan in which the United States agrees to certain things in return for Japan's not worrying us in the Philippines. But I go back to the beginning and quote from an issue of the English *Saturday Review* which appeared during the peace

[1] Princeton, 1939, p. 256.

negotiations between the United States and Spain. In its issue of December 3, 1898, it pointed out that the American peace negotiators who were providing for Spain's cession of the Philippines to us were "making their bargain—whether they realize it or not—under the protecting naval strength of England. And we shall expect, to be quite frank, a material *quid pro quo* for this assistance. We shall expect the States to deal generously with Canada in the matter of tariffs; we shall expect to be remembered when she comes into her kingdom in the Philippines; above all, we shall expect her assistance on the day, quickly approaching, when the future of China shall come up for settlement. For the young imperialist has entered upon a path where she will require a stout friend. . . ."

It is a misfortune that the United States should ever have become responsible for the defense of this archipelago off the coast of Asia. Even such "expansionists" as Theodore Roosevelt and Captain Mahan saw this right away—that is, immediately after it was too late to do anything about it. Once it had happened, however, there was nothing for it but to build up our naval power in the Pacific, acquire the necessary bases, and work out such diplomatic agreements with the other powers in the area as might be necessary or prudent. Our isolation having been lost, we would have to abandon our isolationism.

Look at what the strategic situation was. The naval force which we had mustered to fight Spain in the Pacific consisted of seven ships totaling 20,552 tons. (The modesty of this figure may be appreciated by comparing it with the 85,000 tons which the single British liner, *Queen Elizabeth,* weighs.) We could now provide bases for this or an enlarged fleet in the Philippines themselves. But how about our line of communications? In the entire stretch of five thousand miles that separated the Philippines from Hawaii our ships had no place to roost. They might, however, have had places to roost. Paralleling the line of communication from Hawaii to the Philippines for two thousand miles were the Caroline and Palau Islands. And cutting across this line in a barrier reaching from the western Carolines toward Japan were the Ladrone (or Mariana) Islands. Anyone conversant with naval strategy, one supposes, would have seen that, if we were going to defend the Philippines across such a distance, we had to have at least a potentially dominating position in these intervening islands. And whom did these islands belong to? They all belonged to Spain, to our about-to-be defeated enemy. Moreover, they were undefended. While the war lasted they were ours for the taking, to be had without firing a shot. Why, then, did we not acquire them during the war or at the peace table, as essential to the defense of the Philippines, at the same time that we acquired the Philippines? I suppose the answer is that we did not acquire them because we were not empire-minded, because we found it uncongenial to think of seizing foreign real estate.

The seat of government for the Ladrones was the island of Guam, the one bit of land in this whole stretch of five thousand miles that we did acquire. Before the end of 1898 the Navy Department had published the documents relating to this acquisition of Guam under the heading: "Seizure of the Ladrone Islands."[2] Now this was a strange heading, for the fact is that we had not seized the Ladrone Islands. The navy officials must simply have assumed, quite wrongly, that their acquisition was implicit in our capture of Guam, the seat of their government.

The order to capture Guam was incidental to those plans for the dispatch of troops to Manila which were made so hurriedly when news of Dewey's victory reached Washington on May 2. For some reason it was thought necessary to convoy the first troop transports, even though the Spanish fleet had been destroyed. The cruiser *Charleston*, Captain Glass, was ordered to rendezvous with them at Honolulu. Glass was given a sealed order, dated May 10, which he opened at sea on June 4. It told him to proceed with the transports to Manila, adding:

[2] "Appendix to the Report of the Chief of the Bureau of Navigation," *op. cit.*, p. 151.

"On your way, you are hereby directed to stop at the Spanish Island of Guam. You will use such force as may be necessary to capture the port of Guam, making prisoners of the governor and other officials and any armed force that may be there. You will also destroy any fortifications on said island and any Spanish naval vessels that may be there, or in the immediate vicinity. These operations at the Island of Guam should be very brief, and should not occupy more than one or two days."[3]

Captain Glass arrived at Guam June 20, fired some shots over an abandoned fort merely to get the range, and was thereupon visited by two Spanish officers who were astonished to learn that Spain and the United States were at war (although they had been at war for some two months by then). Glass's mission was simplified by the fact that the island's defenses were not in operating order. A courteous exchange of letters took place that same day between him and the Governor. The Governor wrote to say that he had been informed by the captain of the port "that you have advised him that war has been declared between our respective nations, and that you have come for the purpose of occupying these Spanish islands." But Glass had no instructions to occupy the islands. His instructions were merely to capture "the port of Guam." Therefore, by way of reply, he demanded, "in compliance with the orders of my Government, . . . the immediate surrender of the defenses of the Island of Guam, with arms of all kinds, all officials and persons in the military service of Spain now in this island." So the Governor, instead of surrendering the Ladrones as he had expected to do, simply surrendered himself, his staff on the island, his arms, and the island's defenses. Captain Glass had, in effect, refused the Ladrones. The convoy continued on to Manila, there to deposit the troops that would fight a long and bloody war in order to take the Philippines— after the Ladrones had been refused as a gift.

So it is that the United States, having acquired the Philippines, did not acquire the Spanish islands that intervened,

[3] *Ibid.*, p. 151.

between her and the Philippines, along her line of communication. So it is that Spain, having lost the Philippines, was left, still, with most of the Micronesian Islands on her hands. She promptly began to negotiate with Germany for their sale and, two days before the formal conclusion of the Spanish-American War, on the very day that we found ourselves plunged into a new war against the Filipinos, Germany agreed to pay twenty-five million pesetas for the Palaus, the Carolines, and all the Ladrones except Guam.

And now I bring this story up to more recent times.

At the end of World War I these same islands, together with the Marshall group, were taken from Germany and mandated to Japan. Japan fortified them and, in 1941, availed itself of their protection to launch the surprise attack on Pearl Harbor. We found ourselves cut off from the Philippines, which we promptly lost, regaining them only after three and a half years, when we had fought our way back through these same islands in the campaign that ended at Hiroshima and Nagasaki.

See how blind are the men who make history! Two orders issued by the Navy Department in 1898 had an importance that was not appreciated at the time. The character of the order for Dewey to attack Manila was determined by our national and human nature. It has an aspect of inevitability. But the character of the order to Captain Glass was shaped more casually, representing, perhaps, simply the carelessness of busy men who had no thoughts of empire. Our failure to take Saipan, Truk, and the rest of Spanish Oceania in 1898, rather than in the 1940's, was an oversight.

By the acquisition of the Philippines the United States had put itself in a distressing moral position. We could not possibly reconcile the forcible subjugation of seven millions of people to our government with the principles upon which we had established and developed our own nation. What we were doing violated every syllable of the passage of our Declaration of Independence which read: "We hold these truths to be self-evident, that all men are created equal; that they are endowed by their Creator with certain unalienable rights; that among these are life, liberty, and the pursuit of happiness. That, to secure these rights, governments are instituted among men, deriving their just powers from the consent of the governed; that, whenever any form of government becomes destructive of these ends, it is the right of the people to alter or to abolish it, . . ." If this meant anything, it meant that we had no right to impose our government on the Filipinos, and they had every right to refuse submission.

Nothing in our history as a nation, before or since, has caused such distress to moral men as this imposition of our rule on the Philippines. Even the issue of slavery had no such shocking effect, since it had been with us from the beginning. Here the question was not of continuing a morally unjustifiable practice of long standing, but of instituting a new practice that was morally unjustifiable. Many good and wise Americans despaired of our future as a nation when they saw us embarking on that imperialism against which we had ourselves rebelled in the very foundation and constitution of our own national society. They were heartsick at the spectacle. They saw us as a morally ruined nation, flouting the very principles on which our own freedom depended. The printed pages of the day are full of their genuine anguish at what was happening.

The events of 1898 set off a debate among us that lasted through the election campaign of 1900, a debate in which the moral issue was paramount. On one side were the "expansionists," as they called themselves—preferring that title to the term "imperialists." Most of them were men who had, in greater or less degree, been infected with the spirit of imperialism which was dominant at the turn of the century—in England, in Germany, and in Japan, as well as in America. This spirit was based partly on England's experience of imperial greatness, which aroused a desire of emulation in others. It was based partly on the missionary impulse, the impulse to bring the light of our civilization to the heathen. It was based partly on visions of commercial profit. It was also based partly on Darwinism, the concept of a struggle for survival among the races. Finally, it got much of its strength among us from the sense of destiny with which our own rapid growth as a nation had filled us. It seemed to have been a "manifest destiny" that we should expand across the American continent. Now, at one bound, we had projected that expansion clear across the Pacific as well—and by what seemed the intention of Providence rather than any of our own. The greatness of empire appeared to be thrust upon us by our destiny, and piety itself demanded that we accept it.

Opposed to the expansionists were the "anti-imperialists," a group which attracted to it the more intellectual and idealistic elements of the population. Men like Senator Hoar, Carl Schurz, and William Graham Sumner represented what we might call the enlightened elements. They represented conscience. It was the people like this who felt most deeply the sense of moral distress occasioned by our departure from the path of freedom, our setting out on the path of military empire.

As we look back on this debate, as we follow it in the press of the time, which side ought we to identify ourselves with? Which side was right? It seems to me that, in this respect, the appeal of the anti-imperialists is distinctly the greater. History has proved that those expansionists were wrong who believed that it was our destiny to rule the world, or to rule great tracts of colonial empire across the seas. Those expansionists were wrong, in fact, who thought that such an empire would be an asset in the twentieth century. Such an undertaking surely would have been foreign to our national character, repugnant to everything we had ever stood for, and corrupting to our institutions. Moreover, as I have noted, there is no doubt today that our acquisition of the Philippines was a misfortune.

Surely, then, the anti-imperialists were right. We should not have taken the Philippines. Imperialism was indeed repugnant to our national character and our institutions. Yet, as one reads the arguments of the anti-imperialists today one cannot quite accord them the measure of respect which, on the face of it, they ought to have. These men were essentially armchair statesmen, right in an abstract and theoretical way. Their morality was more easily applicable in the classroom than at the seat of authority. They did not understand the limits of possible action. They did not sufficiently take into consideration the tyranny of circumstance or the necessity of evil. If we often find them being right, then, it is generally for the wrong reasons.[4]

I will not raise, at this point, the question whether the solicitude of the anti-imperialists for the oppressed Filipinos was a wrong reason. Let me examine, first, another reason which was dominant in their arguments and which I find theoretically unassailable. Pointing out that the forcible imposition of our rule on the Filipinos was tyrannical, they argued that if we practiced tyranny abroad we would end by practicing it at home. If we abandoned the principles for which we stood in our dealings abroad, we would end by losing those principles at home.

This seems to me an altogether logical and plausible argument. I find no fault with it. I would certainly include it as a basic general rule in any book of political philosophy which I ever had occasion to compose. The only reason why it cannot be accepted in the present case is that history failed to bear it out. This is history's way, to confound time and again the anticipations of the best and most logical minds, to introduce some unexpected element that produces an entirely different result from what had been so plausibly foreseen. The anti-imperialists would have been right except for one thing. None of them foresaw that our authority in the Philippines, imposed by the most tyrannical means, would in its continuance be lacking in tyranny. They fell into the error of expecting, in the world of reality, such consistency as gave distinction to the microcosms of their own minds. Once we had pacified the Philip-

[4] *Cf.* Fred. H. Harrington, "The Anti-Imperialist Movement in the United States, 1898-1900," in *Mississippi Valley Historical Review*, Vol. XXII (Sept., 1935), pp. 211-12.

pines by brute force, however, we applied ourselves to the task of governing them in the spirit of our own institutions. Instead of our imperialism altering the character of our institutions, our institutions determined the character of our imperialism. We devoted ourselves to good works in the Philippines, to the establishment of human rights and the preparation of the natives for that self-government which they now enjoy. Our record in the Philippines is, today, a source of pride and moral self-confidence to all Americans. The anti-imperialists were wholly wrong in their wholly plausible apprehensions.

The retrospective argument against our acquisition of the Philippines, unlike the argument of the anti-imperialists, is made entirely on grounds of strategic self-interest. It has no morality in it at all. If Dewey had just sailed away, supposing that had been possible, the cause of tyranny would have been served; the fate of the Filipinos would presumably have been worse, but ours would presumably have been better. The natives of the Philippines would have been subjugated by Germany or one of the other powers that lacked our liberal traditions. We, on the other hand, would not have become strategically overextended. We would not have given a hostage to the rising sun of Japan or established ourselves in a position where our commitments could hardly be reconciled with her own requirements for defense in the circumstances of the twentieth century.

Because reality is more various and changeable than our verbal categories the historian is constantly confronted with verbal paradoxes. Theodore Roosevelt, at the turn of the century, was chief of the expansionists. But in the longer view of his career we find him on the other side. The realistic strategic thinking that today identifies our acquisition of the Philippines as the "Great Aberration of 1898" was native to him. Watching the sun of Japan rising in the East, he wanted to see us relieved, if that could be decently managed, of any responsibility for the Philippines. Even the romantic Roosevelt of the first days seems to have had some reservations about the advantage to us of the role which circumstance and duty, in his view, imposed on us. These reservations had become anxieties of the realistic Roosevelt by 1905, with the Japanese defeat of Russia. By 1914 he was clear in his desire to see us depart entirely from "the Asiatic coast." "I hope," he wrote, ". . . that the Filipinos will be given their independence at an early date and without any guarantee from us which might in any way hamper our future action or commit us to staying on the Asiatic coast. . . . Any kind of position by us in the Philippines merely results in making them our heel of Achilles if we are attacked by a foreign power. . . . If we were to retain complete control over them and to continue the course of action which in the past sixteen years has resulted in such immeasurable benefit for them, then I should feel that it was our duty to stay and work for them in spite of the expense incurred by us and the risk we thereby ran. . . . If the Filipinos are entitled to independence, then we are entitled to be freed from all the responsibility and risk which our presence in the islands entails upon us."[5]

In terms of our present morality, even in terms of the morality that predominated at the time, we did a good deed when we liberated the Cubans from Spain and gave them their independence; but we did an evil and a wicked thing when we fought the Filipinos for four long years to establish our empire over them. Yet the passage of the subsequent years, and the concurrent unfolding of circumstances unforeseen, have altered the perspective in which these matters are viewed and have rendered obsolete the old judgments. We liberated the Cubans and they found themselves securely included in the area of our national defenses. We not only liberated the Filipinos but we made ourselves indefinitely responsible for defending their independence far outside the area of our national defenses. The Filipinos have benefited at least as much from the policy of the expansionists as they would have been likely to benefit from the policy of the anti-imperialists.

All these things considered, and all the matters covered

[5] *New York Times*, Nov. 22, 1914.

in this and the last two chapters, I find it hard to come to any sure moral judgment of these events. I think of the words once spoken by Winston Churchill out of his considerable experience. "It is not given to human beings, happily for them, for otherwise life would be intolerable, to foresee or to predict to any large extent the unfolding course of events. In one phase men seem to have been right, in another they seem to have been wrong. Then again, a few years later, when the perspective of time has lengthened, all stands in a different setting. There is a new proportion. There is another scale of values. History with its flickering lamp stumbles along the trail of the past, trying to reconstruct its scenes, to revive its echoes, and kindle with pale gleams the passion of former days."[6]

Beginning in 1898, the United States had a new problem. That problem was to form a Far Eastern policy, for it was now established irrevocably at the very center of all the tangled international politics of the Far East. Unfortunately, nothing in our previous history told us how we should deal with this problem. Washington's Farewell Address gave no help. The Monroe Doctrine gave no help. What we had been taught in school gave no help. In the chapters that follow I shall consider how we have dealt with this fateful problem over the three score years that now separate us from its birth.

[6] Speech to House of Commons, Nov. 12, 1940.

XVIII • In a world of independent but interdependent nation-states, each must have a foreign policy to guide its conduct. I use the term "foreign policy" in its basic sense, signifying broad and established principles of conduct.

Swiss neutrality, for example, is a principle of conduct which has become so established that it is not, itself, seriously in question. It is axiomatic in Swiss thinking. Questions of what Switzerland's conduct should be in any particular situation, then, can be answered by reference to the principle. Suppose that France requested Berne's permission to fly its bombers over Switzerland on their way to attack Ruritania. The only question which Berne would have to ask itself would be whether the granting of such permission would or would not be compatible with its policy of neutrality. It would see no occasion to ask itself the larger question, whether neutrality itself was a good idea. The nation long ago made up its mind about that and for generations, now, the question has been closed. If it were not closed, if it had to be reconsidered and redebated every time you had something like the French request, you would simply have chaos or paralysis in the conduct of Swiss foreign affairs.

By its very nature, then, foreign policy has to be dogma, rooted in tradition and therefore not easily reconsidered or abandoned. But suppose that the course of history renders a foreign policy obsolete. The world has moved on and the old dogma no longer applies. Now its unquestionability becomes an obstacle to what has to be done. You can no more jettison old dogmas overnight and substitute new ones than you can abolish or create old traditions overnight, no matter how great the need. It is bound to take at least a generation for the reorientation of traditional thinking. New people have to grow up and replace the old. Meanwhile, the nation's foreign policy will be in disorder and many things will go wrong in the conduct of its external affairs. When a foreign policy becomes obsolete, then, there is almost sure to be at least a generation of chaos and near-disaster before a new foreign policy can be formed and established in its place.

When I have said this I have characterized the period with which I am about to deal—the half century from 1898 to 1947 in the evolution of American foreign policy. It is that intellectually chaotic period of transition between two dogmas, marked by the disasters of two world wars. The acquisition of the Philippines made Washington's Farewell Address and the Monroe Doctrine inapplicable to the chief problems of our foreign affairs. They would, in any case, have become obsolete in the years that followed, with the passing of the *Pax Britannica* and the technological development of war and communications. Our acquisition of the Philippines, however, had the effect of making them obsolete overnight rather than gradually. The situation is summed up in a single sentence from the Sprouts' *Rise of American Naval Power:* The annexation of the Philippines transformed the United States "from a geographically isolated continental Power into a scattered empire with a strategic problem virtually insoluble without recourse to alliances absolutely incompatible with the traditions of American foreign policy."[1]

Until 1898 the United States had an established foreign policy, rooted in tradition, enshrined in the sacred writings of the Founding Fathers, and accepted as dogma. With Dewey's

[1] *Op cit.,* p. 230.

stroke at the Philippines that policy became irrelevant overnight. But it took us fifty years to accept this fact and to do the rethinking which it required. As humanity goes, fifty years is not bad, especially for a people altogether inexperienced in the intricate and deceptive field of foreign policy. But during those fifty years, inevitably, we floundered.

Our unexpected acquisition of the Philippines embroiled us permanently in the Far East. It required us to maintain power overseas, in alien territory, or to ally ourselves with power overseas, in order to meet our new commitment.

In actual fact, however, our commitment to defend the Philippines does not play the dominant role in our Far Eastern affairs which one might expect from all that I have written. Our great disputes of the twentieth century in this area do not revolve around the Philippines at all, so that one might think I had been exaggerating the importance of the commitment. But the only reason why this particular commitment does not loom larger in the subsequent record is that, almost immediately after assuming it, we embarked on a course of policy by which we gradually assumed a still larger commitment in the Far East—a commitment that at first was vague and rather rhetorical, but that hardened with the passage of time. Our commitment to defend the Philippines was dwarfed by our subsequent commitment to defend the administrative and territorial integrity of China itself, that vast and crumbling empire which reached into the remotest parts of Asia. It was this commitment that was the direct cause of our long quarrel with Japan.

I wish I could offer a simple strategic explanation of such a staggering undertaking, pointing out that the integrity of China had, for us, some such strategic significance as the integrity of Belgium had for the British in 1914. But there is no such explanation, and one may as well say at the start that this can hardly be explained except as the impulsive commitment of a Don Quixote. We saw China as a lovely lady by the wayside beset by bullies, and we gallantly interfered. We didn't draw

217

our sword, because we had none to draw, but we said we would defend her against the bullies who did have swords. The consequences of this gallantry, undertaken so casually and with so little thought of where it would lead, have been far-reaching. For half a century the lady looked to us for a protection which we were hardly prepared to give her.

The most significant thing about our position in the Far East, then, has been the fact that throughout the present century we have looked upon half of Asia as something approaching an American protectorate. All of us Americans were brought up assuming that of course it was the duty of the United States to defend the integrity of China. If anyone had asked why, I suppose we would have said that China was our special friend. But this would simply have begged the question. Once a man has committed matrimony he has no choice but to defend his wife, but the decision to marry her was presumably taken freely. The fact is, however, that none of us appear ever to have asked why we got ourselves into this position. We have simply accepted, as in the nature of things, our moral obligation to defend China from those who wanted to exploit her. Most of us have been proud of the idealism which this represents in our conduct.

But this moral obligation still seems strange to me, because we never felt obliged to protect the Sudan, say, from the British, or the Congo from the Belgians. Perhaps the explanation is, in part at least, that we had so many missionary societies operating in China. Their own paternalistic attitude toward the Chinese communicated itself to our whole nation. We came to cherish the Chinese as our pupils. Whatever the explanation, the fact is that this relationship of ours to China became dogma in our American thinking. Entanglement with China, just like non-entanglement with Europe, came to be traditional. By what course of events did this happen?

One of the most dangerous of the standard situations which occur again and again in history is that created by the disintegration of great empires. The disintegration of the Turkish Empire produced a whole series of conflicts from the Crimean War to World War I. The disintegration of the Spanish Empire brought about the Spanish-American War and that rivalry for possession of the Philippines which forced us to take them for ourselves. The disintegration of the ancient Chinese Empire produced great disorder in the Far East, beginning with the Opium War of 1840 and continuing to the victory of the Chinese Communists in 1949.

It seems to me a standard mistake, in these situations, to attribute the disintegration primarily to external rather than to internal forces—to suppose, for example, that Turkey would be all right if Russia were not bullying her, that the Spanish Empire would be sound if the United States left it alone, that the Middle Kingdom of China would go on as it has been for another couple of thousand years if only the greedy imperialistic powers were restrained, or that the Nationalist regime of China is suffering from nothing except Communist aggression. The failure to realize that the basic weakness is internal, and perhaps incurable, may lead to the mistake of guaranteeing what cannot be guaranteed, the survival and integrity of the crumbling structure.

China at the turn of the century was disintegrating of its own internal weakness. The incursions of the powers were secondary. A vacuum of effective authority had developed in an area in which the powers had nationals in residence and large interests, so that they were drawn almost irresistibly to set up their own authority. The danger of committing oneself to maintain the territorial and administrative integrity of China was that, even though one was able to hold back the vultures, the sick empire would continue to disintegrate. If the Chinese were unable to maintain their own integrity, no outsider would be able to do it for them.

Everyone judges the world by his own experience. He reads his experience into what is happening to others. Accordingly, it has been the tendency of us Americans to equate imperialistic conflicts in other parts of the world with our own heroic struggle for independence against King George and his redcoats. There could be no doubt, under the circumstances, where American sympathies would be when the European powers moved to partition China among themselves. As early as the 1850's, when the Taiping rebellion threatened anarchy in China, Mr. Humphrey Marshall, our American commissioner on the scene, reported to Washington his opinion of what our policy should be. Referring to "the avarice or the ambitions of Russia or Great Britain," he said that the fate of Asia would be sealed "unless *now* the United States shall foil the untoward result by adopting a sound policy." And what was Mr. Marshall's notion of "a sound policy"? "It is my opinion," he wrote, "that the highest interests of the United States are involved in sustaining China—maintaining order here and engrafting on this worn out stock the healthy principles which give life and health to governments, rather than to see China become the theater of widespread anarchy, and ultimately the prey of European ambitions.[2]

Here, at the outset of the contest among the great powers for influence in China, Mr. Marshall proposed that the United States, which was still fighting Indians and seeking to establish order on its own continent, intervene to sustain the integrity of China and halt any aggression by Britain or Russia. I call attention not only to his total disregard of the power factors involved, but also to that optimism which is native to us and which makes it seem a casual undertaking to maintain order in China and to engraft on the Chinese nation "the healthy principles which give life and health to governments." When we were still struggling to dominate our own continent, we were to undertake the establishment of order among hundreds of millions of alien people on the other side of the globe—and to re-educate them.

The policy advocated by Mr. Marshall was the one that we actually adopted, and with the same insouciance, at the turn of

[2] Foster Rhea Dulles, *China and America* (Princeton, 1946), p. 51.

the century. The innocence in which we undertook the commitment to defend and support China is represented by the way
we went about it. Because we had been an isolationist nation for
so long, our government was not organized, at the turn of the
century, for the responsible formulation of foreign policy by
men with professional knowledge. Our best statesmen were
amateurs recruited from the fields of belles-lettres, scholarship,
or domestic politics. Our policy toward China in the twentieth
century was initially the creation of two Sinologists without
official position in our government, one an Englishman who
happened to be passing through Baltimore, the other an American who had been brought up in France, who had been an officer
in the French Foreign Legion, and who, in the entire span of
his life, spent only thirteen years in the United States. Both
were moved by a nostalgic regard for the old Chinese civilization, which they wanted to save as one might wish to save a Ming
porcelain.

W. W. Rockhill, the former French officer, was of misanthro-
pic disposition. All his life he tried to escape from the ordinary
society of men either in his study or in expeditions through
Mongolia and Tibet. His avocation was the study of oriental
languages and religions. He was already known through his
books and lectures on the Far East, and a certain glamour must
have attached itself to him in the eyes of Washington society.
It is not always that one can produce in one's own drawing room
an explorer of Tibet—a man, moreover, with a mandarin mous-
tache, a foreign accent, and an air of eccentricity.

When Rockhill's friend John Hay, an American poet and
essayist, become Secretary of State, at a time when it appeared
that we had suddenly become a Far Eastern power, he seems to
have seen the usefulness of having close by an authority on the
Far East. After an effort to have Rockhill appointed Librarian
of Congress failed, he was given instead the post of director general of the Pan American Union (then called the Bureau of
American Republics). Though this was an international office,
Rockhill found himself serving as a confidential private con-

sultant to the Secretary of State, a rather informal arrangement by which he became the key figure in the shaping of our new Far Eastern policy.

This was at a time when the final partitioning of China appeared about to take place. Since mid-century the United States had had a policy which seemed well adapted to this situation and which President McKinley saw no reason to change. By that policy the United States disclaimed all ambition for territory, spheres of influence, or any special privileges in China. It asked only that its citizens be allowed to share on a basis of equality any privileges accorded to the citizens of other foreign powers in China. If other foreign powers got trading privileges for their nationals, then America should have them too. In other words, we asked for most-favored-nation treatment.

The imminent establishment of the spheres of influence by which China would be partitioned required that we assure ourselves that the rights of our nationals would be preserved under the new dispensation. There was the danger that the partitioning powers would establish commercial monopolies from which American traders would be excluded. What, if anything, ought we to be doing about this? Hay relied on Rockhill to answer the question.

At this time there was considerable expansionist sentiment in the United States that, flushed by our acquisition of the Philippines, saw the American flag advancing around the world. It was also a common belief that commercial opportunities in China were boundless, although our actual commerce with China was insignificant. But Rockhill had nothing to do with commerce, as a Sinologist he tended to be hostile to missionaries, and he was not a flag-waving patriot. He had in his mind no clear motive for an American policy except his scholar's desire to see a precious ruin preserved.[3]

The picture of Rockhill's mind comes out in the memoranda he wrote. It was an earnest mind, full of information in disarray.

[3] For an excellent discussion of Rockhill's life and character see Paul A. Varg, *Open Door Diplomat: The Life of W. W. Rockhill* (Urbana, Ill., 1952). Rockhill's motives are discussed on p. 30.

It had trouble when it tried to put things together, or follow a line of thought, or grasp a general idea. His memoranda are full of sentences that get nowhere, of paragraphs that wander from the path and meet other paragraphs coming back along the line of argument. They are too long, and one keeps on reading them only in the hope that eventually they will find a way of revealing what it is they want to say.

Rockhill was saved from the fate of having to depend on his own mind, in this contingency, by the fortuitous advent of an English acquaintance whose mind had all the clarity which his own lacked. Alfred E. Hippisley, an Englishman resident in China, had stopped over in Baltimore to visit his wife's family on his way back to England for home leave. With Washington only forty miles away, he thought he would drop in on his old friend Rockhill, too, the more so because he wanted to talk about what was happening in China.

Hippisley was a commissioner of the imperial maritime customs service in China and an authority on Chinese ceramics.[4] He was able to bring Rockhill up to date on developments across the Pacific. Matters had already gone so far, he reported, that the division of China had to be accepted as an accomplished fact. The thing to do now was somehow to persuade the powers involved not to close the door against the commerce of others in their respective spheres of influence. This was perfectly in keeping with our American policy of seeking most-favored-nation treatment. The only real novelty was in generalizing it, in proposing equal treatment for all comers rather than for American interests alone. This, however, was a fateful novelty because of the effect it would have on public opinion in the United States. By virtue of it, what had been a selfish interest became the general moral principle of the "Open Door."

The proposal was that the United States address notes to the powers that were dividing China asking them to agree to the "Open Door." How casually this was approached is indicated

---

[4] Cf. Hippisley, A sketch of the History of Ceramic Art in China, with a catalogue of the Hippisley Collection of Chinese Porcelains (Washington, 1902).

by the form of Secretary Hay's assignment of the matter to Rockhill. Hay was spending the summer of 1899, as he spent every
summer, at his country estate in New Hampshire. From there
he wrote to Rockhill: "If you have time between now and next
Wednesday to set down your views on this question—in the
form of a draft instruction to Mr. Choate, Mr. White, Mr.
Tower and General Porter—I would be greatly obliged. . . .
But if it should not be convenient, all right."[5] One may judge
from this that the Secretary of State did not yet regard the proposed "Open Door" notes as having historic significance for the
development of American foreign policy.

On the face of it, one may well ask, even today, why they
should be regarded as a turning point in the history of our
policy. They represented no radical departure from our position, merely the generalizing of it in the form of the "Open
Door" proposal to the partitioning powers. However, once the
"Open Door" notes had been sent, and replies to them received,
they were publicized as an achievement of our diplomacy, they
were theatrically identified with American morality in opposition to Old World chicanery, and the American electorate was
encouraged to take a magnified view of them in connection with
the 1900 elections. The McKinley administration was tempted
to present itself to the voters as one that had, in the name of a
newly arisen America, brought the slinking dogs of European
imperialism to heel in Asia. It did not resist the temptation.

Here was a demonstration, to be repeated at every crisis in
the following half century, of the disposition among our people
to support foreign policies only when they are presented in the
guise of great principles. Defense merely of our own commercial
rights in China had no such appeal as the "Open Door" for
all nations (semanticists and politicians should note the special
magic in the word "open"); protection of our shipping, in 1914-
17, had no such appeal as "Freedom of the Seas." "Don't tread
on me!" has never aroused us as have "self-determination,"
"open covenants openly arrived at," or universal "freedom from

[5] Quoted by A. Whitney Griswold, *The Far Eastern Policy of the United
States* (New York, 1938,) p. 73.

224

want and freedom from fear." Policies given such names as "containment," however creditable, have been regarded as being, somehow, wicked. In this sense the Eisenhower administration was well advised when it undertook to continue the Truman administration's policy of "containment" under the new name of "liberation."

The fact is that Hippisley's "Open Door" policy, so far from frustrating the imperialistic designs of the powers on China, represented the acceptance of China's partitioning. It did not seek guarantees from the government of China but, rather, from the governments of the powers that were replacing Chinese authority with their own. It recognized the new authority and acquiesced in it. If the purpose had been to forbid encroachment by the powers, then it would have made strange sense to seek guarantees from those powers for the treatment of others in the areas in which they encroached.

All this was made explicit for Rockhill's understanding by Hippisley. "Spheres of interest," he wrote, " . . . must be treated as existing facts. . . . I venture therefore to suggest that the U. S. loses [sic] no time in calling the attention of all the Powers to the changes now taking place in China, and—while disclaiming any desire on her own part to annex territory—in expressing her determination not to sacrifice for her annually increasing trade any of the rights or privileges she has secured by treaty with China. . . ." But Rockhill had difficulty in grasping the idea. He told Hippisley, in reply, that he would like to see the United States "make a declaration in some form or other, which would be understood by China as a pledge on our part to assist in maintaining the integrity of the Empire."[6] In addition to telling the powers to leave the door open behind them when they trespassed, Rockhill wanted to put up a "No Trespassing" sign.

Rockhill's intellectual confusion, combined with the administration's desire to appear before the voters as the slayer of the dragon of imperialism, ultimately determined our policy and so became enshrined in history. This is why the original "Open Door Notes" are regarded to this day as the notes by which we

[6] For this correspondence see *ibid.*, pp. 66-67.

undertook to slam the door to China shut in the face of the great imperialistic powers.

Hay and McKinley, finding themselves publicly regarded by the American people as knights in shining armor, and that on the eve of a presidential election, can hardly be blamed for failing to insist on a more modest view. Instead, they seized the next occasion to send out a second round of "Open Door Notes" —this time, and for the first time, explicitly identifying the United States with the preservation of China's "territorial and administrative entity." The United States, unwittingly, had set its foot on the path that would lead, step by step, to the disaster at Pearl Harbor in 1941.

The original "Open Door Notes," as we have seen, were Hippisley's conception. He virtually wrote them, since Rockhill largely accepted his language and Hay—who was, as usual, spending the summer in New Hampshire—signed substantially what Rockhill put before him.

What was Hippisley's interest in all this? The evidence indicates that he was not serving and, in some instances, was even opposing British policy. The point of departure for his thinking was acceptance of China's partitioning. This does not mean that he did not, like Rockhill, have the welfare of China at heart. He simply did not think Rockhill was being realistic in his suggestion that the United States pledge itself to maintain the integrity of an empire which had already lost its integrity.

Hippisley did, however, contribute one rather odd item to the original Notes, in response to Rockhill's desire to support the integrity of China. The Notes asked the powers to agree not only that the Chinese tariff of the time should apply in any treaty port, but also "that duties so leviable shall be collected by the Chinese Government." And what was the agency of "the Chinese Government" responsible for collecting duties in the ports? It was the Chinese Maritime Customs Service, a foreign board of customs inspectors established in 1854 to collect customs on behalf of the Chinese government. One of its officers was Mr. Hippisley, who by including this provision in the Notes

226

of the United States government contributed to keeping his agency in business.

So the policy of the United States was made. The Notes were sent out, and the powers, momentarily glancing aside from their struggles to maintain or upset the balance of power, made polite replies that were chiefly designed to prevent any appearance that they were not on the side of the angels. The administration, in its public treatment of these replies, gave the impression that the powers would not have been on the side of the angels had it not been for its action in recalling them to the paths of moral duty. Hay appears to have had few illusions about what the replies really meant. Living in a world of his own, however, Rockhill was moved to see in them evidence that, as he put it in a private letter, "this country holds the balance of power in China."[7] If a feather could have held the balance of power in China Rockhill might have been right.

In point of fact, it is hard to see any effect that our publicized exchange of notes had on the foreign situation to which it was addressed. When, exhilarated by the domestic success of the Notes, the administration in June of that election year, 1900, sent out the second round of "Open Door Notes," this time calling upon the powers to respect China's "territorial and administrative" integrity, the foreign effect appears to have been no greater. If the final partitioning of China was not carried through at this time, it was, as Professor Griswold has pointed out, "a case of political stalemate rather than conversion to principle."[8]

Only a few months after we had announced to the great powers our policy of supporting the integrity of China the Russians virtually grabbed China's richest province, Manchuria, and made it their own. "I take it for granted," Secretary Hay wrote to President Theodore Roosevelt, "that Russia knows as we do that we will not fight over Manchuria, for the simple reason that we cannot." When Russia refused to get out of Man-

[7] *Ibid.*, pp. 76-77.
[8] *Ibid.*, p. 82.

churia in deference to our policy, Hay wrote the President: "I am sure you will think it is out of the question that we should adopt any scheme of concerted action with England and Japan. Public opinion in this country would not support such a course, nor do I think it would be to our permanent advantage . . ."[9] Here we see the persistence of the dogma of "no entangling alliances" in an altered situation to which it no longer had any relevance.

A few years later, when Japan ousted Russia from Manchuria, we again placed that province under the nominal protection which we extended to all the territory of China; and when again it was taken from China, this time by Japan, we found it more embarrassing to do nothing about it. Finally, almost a century after Mr. Marshall first proposed that the United States protect China against aggression, his policy involved us in the war which, surely, had been implicit in it from the beginning.

I have said that this vast commitment was assumed gradually. Let me, in conclusion, again quote Mr. Griswold on the subject.[10] "Legally the United States was no more bound to pursue the policy of the notes than the powers which had, in varying degrees, evaded their demands. It was the style of the notes, the fact that they were promulgated in a manner deliberately contrived to mobilize public opinion and create the impression of an international commitment, and most important of all, the way Hay's successors practiced what he preached that molded American policy. It may be conceded that the Secretaries of State who followed John Hay did not adhere to the principles of the open door and the preservation of China's territorial integrity solely because he had done so, and at the same time, that tradition and precedent exert a powerful influence on foreign policy."

What Hay did elicited public praise. Therefore, he and his successors were tempted to do it again and again, each time to the applause of the electorate. So we embarked and continued on the road to Pearl Harbor.

[9] *Ibid.*, p. 88.
[10] *Ibid.*, p. 86.

XIX • In the last chapter I related the tragic tale of how, at the turn of the century, the United States so ingenuously embarked on that policy of protecting the integrity of China which led to the Pacific war of the 1940's. I was writing about dead men—McKinley, Hay, and Rockhill—from the superior vantage point of the living who come after. I had the knowledge of subsequent events which was denied to them, and I took advantage of it to show how foolish they were in the light of that knowledge.

But their folly is in part a function of what came after them. The mistakes they made were small at the time. They grew and became magnified by the course which their successors followed. If their successors had followed a different course, or if fate had been more generous in its distribution of that undeserved good luck on which we all depend, then they might not have looked so foolish half a century later.

In point of fact, until World War II John Hay, with his "Open Door" policy, was quite generally regarded as one of our great Secretaries of State. He represented in our minds an early assertion, in the international field, of that American idealism by which the world was to be saved. Since Pearl Harbor, however—that end of the road on which he first set our feet—there has been occasion to revise this estimate. But one should not take advantage of this occasion to sneer at those whom history has deprived, *ex post facto,* of credit. The men who are dead are now judged. Our advantage is that we still await judgment.

When the twentieth century opened the United States was not conscious of any need for a comprehensive re-examination of its foreign policy. No committees were appointed to make recommendations, no studies were instituted.

At that very time the British government had just been engaged in a systematic re-examination of British policy in its entirety, that re-examination which led to England's abandonment of "splendid isolation," to her quest for allies, to her conclusion of the Japanese alliance in 1902 and of the Entente Cordiale with France in 1904. England was moving deliberately from an old policy to a new. But it was a consciousness of the fact that her position in the World was weakening that made her do this.

The United States was conscious of the opposite development, of the fact that her position in the world was growing stronger. What had happened in the Philippines, for example, while it brought new dangers for us, increased our confidence rather than arousing our apprehension. Our interventions to maintain China's integrity, while they were wasted, did not seem so to us. On the contrary, this spectacle of the United States standing for international morality on the other side of the world was entirely favorable to a growth of satisfaction with our policy.

The conscious, professional study and consideration of foreign policy, moreover, was not a habit with us. From 1776 to 1823, the generation of our Founding Fathers, intensive thought had been given to foreign policy by men of long professional experience. But in the seventy-seven years that had since elapsed there had been no need for this kind of thinking. Now there was no one trained in it. We had no professionals who understood it because, for two generations, we had had nothing for such professionals to do, if we had had them. We had one brilliant amateur in Theodore Roosevelt; but he was erratic, and more a man of action, perhaps, than a student and questioner.

Consequently, our international conduct at the beginning of the new century was more natural and spontaneous, let us say, less crafty and self-conscious, than that of England. We might have learned something from our inability to protect Manchuria. But this produced in us no sense of failure to bring us up short, to inhibit us from repeating our interventions and repeating them until a tradition and a hard commitment to maintain China's integrity had been established.

For example: in 1904 the British, countering Russian intrigues north of the Indian border, sent an armed expedition into Tibet which occupied its capital, Lhasa. We immediately delivered a vigorous protest in London, reminding the English government that our policy was to promote the "absolute integrity and independence" of the Chinese Empire, in which we included Tibet.[1]

Only half a dozen years earlier, the United States had been in a state of shocked astonishment at finding itself involved as far away as the Philippines. Now it was asserting its policy of protecting Tibet against encroachment by its powerful next-door neighbors. If we had been in an introspective state of mind, we might well have pondered the question whether our intervention in Tibet, even if it had borne any relationship to international realities, did not render obsolete President Monroe's dictum that we confined ourselves to the role of spectators in the world of European rivalries across the seas.

I do not say that what we did in Tibet was necessarily inconsistent with the self-denying provisions of the Monroe Doctrine, which could be interpreted to apply only to events in Europe. One could even say that what we did merely extended the protection of the Monroe Doctrine to Tibet. But what we did in Tibet might have occasioned a re-examination of the whole traditional complex of isolationist thinking which had come down to us from the Monroe Doctrine and Washington's Farewell Address. The question we might have asked ouselves

[1] Griswold, *op. cit.*, p. 101.

was whether our position in the Philippines and our undertaking on behalf of China imposed requirements to which we would have to adjust our thinking and policy alike. But after our one hard spasm of introspection in the late 1890's we had subsided and were no longer tempted to think anxiously about these matters. In all our history, before and since, we never reached such a peak of self-confidence as in these opening years of the twentieth century.

But the old habits of thought persisted, the isolationist habits that belonged to the concept of two hemispheres separated by interplanetary space.

Let me give an example. President Theodore Roosevelt, who understood the realities of international relations better than his fellow Americans, pressed hard for a big navy to support our more active policy overseas. His successor, President Taft, continued that pressure against mounting resistance from the Congress and people. As late as 1913 a minority report of the Naval Committee of the House of Representatives had this to say: "For the purpose of defending our country against attacks from any nation on earth we confidently believe that our Navy is amply sufficient and fully adequate, and for any other purpose we need no navy at all." Here is a statement by responsible men, men who for years had been debating the question of our naval requirements, which is quite oblivious to any commitments or vital interests beyond our own shores. It is oblivious to our obligation to defend the Philippines. It is oblivious of our undertaking to preserve the integrity of China. The Sprouts, quoting this statement in their *Rise of American Naval Power*,[2] suggest that it "well summed up the prevailing state of opinion."

This obliviousness to the implications of our new positions overseas applied no less to diplomatic than to naval policy. No American in an official position would have dared to suggest, in 1913, that we should enter into entangling alliances with other powers in order to secure the defense of the Philippines or the integrity of China. This was the beginning of that pass-

[2] *Op. cit.*, p. 290.

232

ing era in which the writing of diplomatic notes seemed to most of us all that was comprised or required in the conduct of diplomacy. The notion that diplomacy calls for an equation of means with objectives, which had been vivid to our Founding Fathers, did not enter our minds. Part of the reason that it did not enter our minds was that, as the century advanced, we came to think of our own self-contained strength as practically unlimited, while hardly appreciating the weight of the charges against that strength which we had been incurring in the world overseas.

What could one expect, after all? If the National City Bank were suddenly put into the hands of people like me, with no banking experience at all, and they had to run it by themselves, they would commit follies which would seem inexcusable to any seasoned banker. The conduct of foreign relations is not a less subtle and complex business than banking. It calls for sophisticated skill and knowledge based on long experience. This in turn requires such a professional corps and such professional thinking as can be built up only over the generations. We emerged from our isolation in 1898 without this indispensable equipment for playing an active and responsible role in the world, and it took us half a century to develop it.

I do not mean to set forth here the diplomatic history of this period. Let me, however, point to certain incidents in that history.

Assume, for the moment, that the maintenance of China's integrity was a valid objective of American foreign policy. Our acquisition of the Philippines, it was commonly believed, gave us a strong position for dealing with Far Eastern matters and thus advancing this objective. I daresay that might have been true if we had mounted overwhelming force in the Philippines. In actual fact, however, it was the opposite of true. The Philippines were a hostage to Japan for the sake of which we had to compromise on the integrity of China—and that as early as 1905, when Japan showed her strength in the area by defeating Russia. In 1905 Secretary of War Taft went out to Tokyo and came back with a secret agreement in which we paid for Japan's disavowal of aggressive intentions toward the Philippines by acquiescing in "the establishment by Japanese troops of a suzerainty over Korea . . ." Korea was, perhaps, only ambiguously a part of China, but this was also the case with Manchuria and with Tibet, which we had explicitly included within the area of China's territorial integrity. We were forced to give way on Korea by our possession of the Philippines, for which we paid this price.

Since these matters are relevant to the problems of diplomacy in a democracy, I call attention to the fact that our "Open Door" enterprises on behalf of China's integrity were widely publicized by Washington and earned the approval of our people for their idealism. But here, when we dealt with a real problem in terms of its necessities, we felt constrained to keep the matter secret. The publicizing of our rhetorical diplomacy, combined with secrecy for our real diplomacy, was not conducive to the education of the American people in the realities of international relations.

With the conclusion of the Russo-Japanese War, President Roosevelt became increasingly anxious about the Philippines. "Instead of affording him a weapon," Professor Griswold writes, "the Philippines preyed on the President's mind and inhibited his diplomacy." By 1906 he would have been glad to be rid of them. In 1907 he referred to them as America's "Achilles heel."[3] In 1908 he entered into an arrangement with Japan whereby, according to the interpretation accepted by Professor Griswold,[4] in return for a Japanese pledge to respect the security of the Philippines, the United States gave Japan a free hand in Manchuria. Roosevelt, in effect, was dropping the Rockhill-Hay policy.

By 1909 Roosevelt was an older and wiser man than he had been ten years earlier. Manchuria, he wrote, was so vital to Japan that she simply could not "submit to much outside interference therein." We could not stop her in Manchuria, he

[3] Griswold, *op. cit.*, p. 123.
[4] *Ibid.*, p. 129.

234

said, unless we were prepared to go to war, "and a successful war about Manchuria would require a fleet as good as that of England, plus an army as good as that of Germany." The Open Door policy, he wrote, "completely disappears as soon as a powerful nation determines to disregard it, and is willing to run the risk of war rather than forego its intention."[5] In other words, as far as President Roosevelt was concerned, the Open Door policy had disappeared.

This wisdom of Roosevelt's seems to me to make the better sense when one recalls that the United States had no real national interest in Manchuria or, for that matter, on the Asiatic mainland. By 1909 we were stuck with the Philippines. Fortunately, however, the rising might of Japan was not moving in their direction. Instead, it was moving in the other direction, north and west, onto the illimitable Asiatic mainland where it came into conflict with Russia. Surely it was as well for us not to attempt to bar Japan's passage in this direction, not to deflect her expanding power away from northeast Asia, perhaps southward toward the Philippines. In 1909 the thing to do was to forget the venture embarked on so innocently by Mr. Rockhill and Secretary Hay, to abandon it quietly as a diplomatic vagary of no lasting importance. And this, in effect, is what Roosevelt was doing when he authorized the Taft-Katsura and the Root-Takahira agreements, agreements bowing ourselves out of Japan's way in Korea and Manchuria.

But this retreat was not followed through by the Taft administration. There is an element in our American character that must be understood if we are to understand American foreign policy. Our behavior, on more than one occasion, has been that of a person who has more vital energy than he knows what to do with. We like to plunge into new things, and to plunge in all the way, and to keep on going to the end. We do nothing by halves or halfheartedly. We either abstain from intervention or we intervene hard. We don't retreat, tactically or strategically, and it is always hard for us even to wait and see, to play a pas-

[5] Roosevelt to Taft, 22/XII/10. Quoted by Griswold, *op. cit.*, p. 132.

sive role of any sort. If we are going to be involved at all, in whatever the adventure is, then we are determined that we shall seize the initiative and hold it. It is this psychology—a common psychology of the young—which explains much of the animus that has arisen among our people against the passive concept of "containment." It explains the effectiveness of the Republican electoral promise in 1952 that the Eisenhower administration would "seize the initiative" in foreign affairs, and would substitute "liberation" for "containment." It explains the difficulty we had in holding ourselves to a limited war in Korea.

But the fact is that in diplomacy, as in love, it is often better to have the other side take the initiative while you sit back and wait, to have the other party come to you and be the suitor to you, to have it be anxious about your attitude while betraying its own. And also, in diplomacy, the best of alternatives is often to do nothing in a situation in which one does not have to be involved. The best of alternatives, often, is simply to be lazy, not to go out of one's way in search of trouble.

This trait of character has often been good in its consequences. At other times it has done us harm. In the Spanish-American War, Spain did the absolute minimum that she had to do if she was to fight the war at all. We did a great deal more than it was necessary for us to do and finished by finding the Philippines on our hands.

If Theodore Roosevelt's view had prevailed in 1909, history might still have taken a course in which the Rockhill-Hay initiative would have been remembered only as a passing and aberrant incident in the development of American foreign policy. But at this moment our Far Eastern policy fell into the hands of a dynamic lad of twenty-eight, Willard Straight, who had been in Korea when the Japanese occupied it, whose militant anti-Japanese behavior as American consul general in Manchuria had made it advisable to recall him, and who was disgusted with Roosevelt's policy of giving way to Japan in Korea and Manchuria. Willard Straight joined with Secretary of State Philander Knox, in the Taft administration, to institute the famous policy of "dollar diplomacy."

We sometimes think of "dollar diplomacy" as meaning dollars first, followed by diplomats. Wall Street decides to invest in a foreign land and then calls in the State Department to support its enterprise by diplomacy. The government is the servant of the private capitalists. But it was the other way around, at least in the classic case of China. Wall Street was not interested in China. However, the State Department felt that the objective of preserving China's integrity could be realized only if there were heavy American capital investment in China, which there was not at the time. Consequently, the State Department took the initiative with a reluctant Wall Street. It was not a case of saving China for American business enterprise but of prodding American business enterprise in order to save China.

"Dollar diplomacy" in the Far East finally came to an end in 1913 when the New York bankers refused to play the game any longer. The stake of American business, as had been the case all along, continued greater in Japanese trade than in Chinese. But Washington's Far Eastern policy was seriously antagonizing the Japanese, who were already sufficiently antagonized by racial discrimination in California and the exclusion of Japanese immigration.[6] Increasingly, during the second decade of this century, there was talk of war between the United States and Japan, those two powers which had hitherto marched together in a friendship that no conflict of national interests had risen to disturb. There was anxiety that England, bound to Japan by the treaty of alliance, would be under obligation to side with Japan in such a war. And England, like Russia and France, had been irritated by our energetic intervention in matters in which we apparently had no stake.

When Theodore Roosevelt had pointed out in a letter that it was against our national interest to challenge and oppose Japanese policy toward China, Secretary Knox had answered with the argument that our policy was a matter of principle rather than of selfish considerations. But our policy of saving

6 Griswold, *op. cit.*, pp. 172-74.

China was having, if anything, the opposite of its intended effect. It merely prompted the encroaching powers to realize their imperialistic ambitions sooner and more firmly. American proposals for loans to China, forced on the Chinese government, weakened it because of the suspicion they aroused among the Chinese people. The Manchu regime, which Rockhill had set out to save, fell. Russia virtually annexed Mongolia, England assumed control of Tibet, while Japan took Korea and consolidated her position in Manchuria.

By now, however, it was almost too late to ask whether it was our job to undertake the salvation of China even if we could succeed in it. Secretary Knox and Mr. Straight tacitly took the position that the policy was established beyond questioning. For the first time, now, one finds references to our "traditional" policy of promoting the territorial and administrative integrity of China. Over the span of only nine years, what had sprouted so casually in the mind of Mr. Rockhill had become a national tradition. To the dogma of "no entangling alliances," and to the dogma of hemisphere isolation, there had now been added the traditional American dogma of defending the independence and integrity of China.

I am reminded of a Foreign Service Officer who, in such moments of cynicism as come to all that labor in government vineyards, used to say, "There's no reason for this. It's just our policy."

Now that we have seen how this policy became irremediably established it remains only to refer briefly to the successive developments by which it finally led to a war with Japan which its authors had never contemplated.

Upon the outbreak of World War I Japan, taking advantage of the preoccupation of all her rivals, set out to make herself dominant in China. This was a time when the realities of power politics tended to make themselves vivid everywhere. In response to a Chinese appeal for help against Japan, Acting Secretary of State Lansing noted that "it would be quixotic in the extreme to allow the question of China's territorial integrity to entangle the United States in international difficulties.[7]"

Nevertheless, when it came to the enunciation of general principles we again fell into the language of tradition. In connection with a compromise settlement between Tokyo and Peking in 1915, Secretary of State Bryan informed the Japanese government that we could not "recognize any agreement or undertaking which has been entered into or which may be entered into between the Governments of Japan and China, impairing . . . . the political or territorial integrity of the Republic of China . . ."[8] Here we have the birth of the famous Doctrine of Non-Recognition. Though it was probably not the intention, Japan was again given notice that she might eventually have to choose between abandoning the foreign policy to which she was committed or overcoming the United States, since the United States seemed to have planted itself squarely in the path of that policy's realization.

At the Paris Peace Conference, President Wilson fought hard, fought alone, and fought unsuccessfully to get Japan out of China. When Japan, following the joint intervention of the powers in Russian Siberia, kept her forces there, Wilson and his successor, President Harding, successively set themselves to get her out of there as well. Secretary of State Hughes told the British ambassador that America's Far Eastern policy "now in view of existing conditions also embraced the integrity of Russia."[9]

In 1921 and 1922, at the Washington Conference, Secretary Hughes engaged in strenuous and remarkably effective diplomacy to put a leash on Japan. In the Nine Power Agreement he obtained the signatures of all the conferees, including Japan, to a pledge of support for the territorial integrity of China. But at this same conference, in return for undertakings conducive

[7] *Ibid.*, p. 184.
[8] *Ibid.*, pp. 194-95.
[9] *Ibid.*, p. 280.

to the security of the Philippines, the United States agreed to Japanese naval supremacy in the western Pacific. By our agreement not to fortify our own Pacific possessions west of Hawaii we left Japan in a position in which she could expand on the Chinese mainland with substantial impunity.

The reason why this concession of naval supremacy to Japan did not seem to us incompatible with our policy of trying to contain Japan was that, as had been the case from the beginning, we never associated considerations of military power, in our minds, with the objectives of our policy in the area. "Hay and Roosevelt," says Professor Griswold, "had come eventually to the conclusion that the American people would neither fight for the open door and the territorial integrity of China nor support a Far Eastern policy based on the use of force. The reason for this attitude was . . . that the Far East was a relatively unimportant market for American commerce and investment and an area in which no vital American interests of any kind were at stake. Hughes had evidently reached the same conclusion as his predecessors. That did not prevent him, however, from making the most vigorous effort to defend China's integrity and the open door—in the traditional manner—yet on record."[10]

This, it seems to me, is a classic example of a mistake to which democracies (especially inexperienced democracies) are prone, the mistake of insisting on the pursuit of bold objectives, but only by cautious means which involve no risk or sacrifice. Year by year, as we pursued our Far Eastern objectives by the safe and easy devices to which we meant to confine ourselves, we were steadily approaching a point at which we would at last confront the choice of either fighting or backing down—since Japan, which was convinced that her vital interests were at stake as ours were not, would not back down. We were, in fact, approaching a point at which we would have little choice but to fight because, morally or politically, we would find that it was virtually too late for us to back down.

One of the factors that certainly bound us more firmly to the

10 *Ibid.*, p. 321.

containment of Japan was our own successful effort to generalize the particular, and to gain international agreement upon the consequent generalizations. This is the normal tendency of those who wish to identify their special objectives with universal morality. We had generalized the policy of seeking equal access for ourselves to the trade of China, transforming it into the principle of the Open Door for all nations. Now, in our own brain child, the League of Nations Covenant, not just the integrity of China but the integrity of nations in general was affirmed. In the Pact of Paris of 1928 war was universally outlawed as an instrument of national policy. These agreements, together with the Nine Power Pact, had the advantage of identifying the international community, however considerable its reservations, with the objectives of American policy. They had the disadvantage of burning the bridges behind us, if they had not already been burned.

The mortal flaw in the international legal system as it thus developed after 1918 was that, in effect, it undertook by paper bonds to fix the international *status quo* of the moment for all time to come. If a nation, through internal weakness, disintegrated into a heap of dust, still its integrity and independence were inviolable; and its neighbors, however hard-pressed by the dynamics of their own internal growth, would have to contain themselves.

The first real break in this rigid international system came in 1931, when Japan sent her troops into Manchuria and made it a puppet state. The United States was now deeply committed to oppose this, though it had consistently abjured the means of opposing it effectively. There was nothing for it but to pull out of the files the old verbal formulas which had failed at every previous use, and which would now fail again. Secretary of State Stimson reiterated the non-recognition doctrine of 1915, informing Japan that the United States would not recognize a situation that violated agreements relating to "the territorial and administrative integrity of the Republic of China, or to the international policy relative to China, commonly known as the open-door policy."[11] England, France, and the other signatories of the Nine Power Pact prudently refrained from taking any parallel action. Then, when Japan extended her operations by an attack on Shanghai, the American fleet was transferred to permanent station at Pearl Harbor, where the Japanese would find it on December 7, 1941. Having for years considered it unthinkable that we should ever resort to war for the integrity of China, the train of accumulated circumstances was now, at last, forcing us down the path to war. We were at the close of the third act in a Shakespearian tragedy.

[11] Identical note to China and Japan, *ibid.*, p. 424.

XX • Up to the First World War we had enjoyed a considerable freedom of choice in the determination of our Far Eastern policy. After the settlement of the war, however, our course of cumulative commitment to the east Asian *status quo* was already so far advanced that it becomes increasingly hard to find clear or easy alternatives. We had first dogmatized our policy, making it an American tradition. Then we had universalized it, making it part of an excessively rigid system of international law which would have kept peace by freezing the *status quo* everywhere. An abandonment of our policy in China would now have meant a defeat for those forces of law and order with which we had identified ourselves.

Opposed to this consideration was the fact that now the catastrophic end of the road was clearly in view for the public as well as the government to see. While the American people were becoming more aroused in opposition to Japan's course of empire, they were also determined not to get into war. This contradiction, which had been inherent in our policy from the beginning, now closed in upon the government and imprisoned it.

The administration of Franklin D. Roosevelt had, at first, tried to avoid provoking Japan. But history was in a groove now. On the other side of the Pacific the indignities to which the body of China had so long been subjected were at last arousing it. The Chinese people were being wakened to life again by the spirit of nationalism. The corpse was reviving, as the corpse of Turkey had revived. Japan found that its virtual annexation of Manchuria, instead of being accepted by a passive China, was being resisted by measures of hostility that included effective trade boycotts. The eternal dynamics of conquest now confronted Japan with the eternal doom of the conqueror. To make her conquest good she had to keep on extending it, until at last she had overextended it. She could not stop with Manchuria because of the retaliatory spirit which its seizure had provoked in the Chinese. So she was impelled to turn south, as she did in 1937, to subdue and discipline China itself. This action, in turn, provoked increasingly formidable resistance by the Chinese, impelling the Japanese to extend still farther the area of their operations.

Quite aside from our commitment to the defense of China, this southward movement of the Japanese was bound to concern us as something more than a spectator. American missionaries, American traders, American concessions were in the path of the advancing Japanese. The consequent incidents were bound to be more serious because the Japanese had less occasion for restraint than they would have had if hostility had not already grown up between them and us, or if we had made our naval position in the Far East formidable. But increasingly the Japanese armies, stretched to the limit, would be acting out of that desperation which knows no restraint. And when, in 1939, Japan occupied the island of Hainan, she put herself in a position directly threatening both to the Philippines and to America's chief sources of rubber and tin in southeast Asia. This was not the same as the occupation of Manchuria, of eastern Mongolia, or of Siberia.

In 1937, when Japan invaded China proper, President Roosevelt delivered the Chicago address in which he proposed collective action to "quarantine" aggressors. But he thereby impaled himself on the other horn of our dilemma. The public reaction in the United States to the implication of warlike action was so bad that he felt compelled immediately to disavow the plain meaning of his own words.

So the contradiction of our policy still held us in its grip. We clung to isolation, to non-involvement, to a neutrality which Congress had now written into law. The complexion of our thinking was pacifist. At the same time we would not give way in China. By 1939 Britain and France, their lives threatened in Europe, were willing to stand out of Japan's way. But Acting Secretary of State Welles told the British ambassador that "the American government . . . would not depart from the position and principles which it had been defending since first Japan began its conquest of Asia."[1]

Nevertheless, all this time Japan had been buying basic raw materials for the conquest of China in our American markets. Now, as the crisis deepened, we were about to close those markets to her. Our ambassador to Tokyo, Mr. Grew, had an interview with President Roosevelt which he reported in his diary. He told the President "that if we cut off Japanese supplies of oil and that if Japan then finds that she cannot obtain sufficient oil from other commercial sources to ensure her national security, she will in all probability send her fleet down to take the Dutch East Indies. The President replied significantly, 'Then we could easily intercept her fleet.' "[2]

It is around this corner, then, that the end of the long road at last comes into view. Mr. Rockhill's policy, so casual and innocent at birth, had at last developed to the point where our navy would be obliged to move out of Pearl Harbor for the interception of the Japanese navy on its way to fresh conquests. But the Japanese navy did not wait for our turn, now that the game had reached its climax. At the same instant that it sailed south to conquer, it wrecked our navy by the surprise stroke upon Pearl Harbor.

This is how the contradiction and dilemma that American

[1] Herbert Feis, *Road to Pearl Harbor* (Princeton, 1950), p. 43.
[2] *Ibid.*, p. 41.

policy faced for forty-one years was at last resolved. This, too, is how Japan's increasing dilemma was resolved. Both countries were stricken by the disaster upon which their respective policies had impelled them. Both had miscalculated from the start.

But at the end the greater miscalculation was Japan's. On December 6, 1941, our American government was still paralyzed by a profound and intractable division among our people. Probably a majority were passionately against involvement in war unless the country was itself directly attacked. Under the circumstances, think how great would have been the weakness, the confusion, and the embarrassment of the government if Japan had struck only at British and Dutch possessions. Could the President have sent our navy to the defense of imperialistic Europe's colonies? It seems unlikely that Congress would have voted a declaration of war, or that the American people would have been willing to shed their blood in defense of the British and Dutch empires. But our consequent inaction or halfheartedness might have led, at last, to true American isolation in a world dominated by the marauders of the tripartite Axis.

All this was averted from us by the fact that Japan's first stroke was at American territory, her first bombs fell on American ships and American boys. By the close of December 7, the United States was united behind its government as never before in history, grimly determined to beat the Japanese into the ground. The defeat of the Axis in World War II had now been prepared by Japan's miscalculation. All that remained was to pay the terrible price.

Our Far Eastern policy from 1900 to 1941 was high-minded and disastrous. Under the circumstances I cannot help but wonder whether, if it had been lower-minded, the outcome might have been better. Speculation is irresistible. Suppose we had thought only in terms of strategic self-interest. We would have seen how vital it was that, if Japan was going to expand, she should not expand southward toward the Philippines and the southeast Asian area in which we had vital economic

246

interests. While it would, perhaps, have been too Machiavellian (or Bismarckian) actively to encourage her to look away from the south, toward the limitless mainland of northeast Asia where we had no interests, we might have refrained with some complacency from actively discouraging her. And we might reasonably have considered that such northward expansion was Soviet Russia's problem before it was our own. For here in northeast Asia, Japan came into conflict with the Soviet Union, a power which had constituted itself a recognized threat to our civilization. An intense preoccupation of the Soviet Union with her southeastern borders might have seemed not altogether a bad thing to us. Meanwhile, the Philippines and the East Indies would have been more secure if Japan, facing in the opposite direction, dissipated her strength punching the Chinese pillow and standing against the Soviet Union. We might, under such circumstances, have seen no reason for any effort which would relieve the Russians and draw the fire of the Japanese imperialists upon ourselves.

However, no one knows what would have been encountered along the paths which were not taken. Perhaps disasters equal to those which did occur.

I have already given my opinion that international relations are governed as much by legend as by truth. Foreign policy is built on myth. This principle has special relevance in time of war, when fear is a prime driving force and whole populations are called upon to make extraordinary efforts. Under the circumstances, utility may not have less weight than truth in testing the value of what we believe. It becomes important to survival for us to make ourselves believe whatever will move us to fight, to sacrifice, and to endure.

This has its sinister as well as its pitiful aspects, but they seem to me quite secondary. Government propaganda is not the main factor, and even it is generally as much an expression of self-deception as of objective deceit. When we are afraid we find relief in anger, and angry people cultivate hate. It makes

247

it easier to be angry. We do this to ourselves without waiting for others to practice upon us.

The prime requirement is to dehumanize the enemy. The enemy population is not a population of pitiable people like our own, made up of men and women who are moved at the sight of their children as we are at the sight of ours, who are often afraid or bewildered as we are, who enjoy lingering sunsets on peaceful evenings, who cherish old family jokes, and who are prone to succumb, just as we are, to the basic human passions. The enemy population is not composed of little men who want to be more esteemed in the world or ordinary women who dream of being admired. Instead, these creatures are essentially monsters, human shapes into which devils have entered. The devils have inspired these shapes with a demoniac purpose to destroy the good and peaceful peoples and establish their own rule over the earth. Whatever they do shows this purpose and the lack of common humanity, for even when they had appeared warm and friendly they were practicing a satanic guile, a deceit that had made them the more dangerous. All the time they had been plotting the ruthless subjugation of the world. "Premeditation and deep design," Professor Coolidge once wrote, "are qualities which nations are prompt to attribute to one another, and slow to acknowledge in themselves. Each is conscious of its own hesitations, fears, changes of mind, but it judges the intentions of others by results only. This is especially true when the results take the form of territorial gains. The rest of the world will never believe them to be accidental: it will always find proof to its own satisfaction that they are the fruit of long-matured plans."[3]

The American people have always had two images of the Japanese, just as they have had two images of the Germans. In one image they are "the greatest little people on earth," enterprising and progressive businessmen, wonderful tennis players, charming hosts, lovers of nature and of art who have combined the two exquisitely in their miniature gardens and

[3] A. C. Coolidge, *The United States as a World Power* (New York, 1908), p. 148.

248

flower arrangements. In the other image they are apelike "grinning devils." By the manner of their attack on Pearl Harbor the benign image was erased from the American mind overnight. Only the "grinning devils" were left. Experts on Japanese psychology arose among us to explain the terrible fanaticism of these people, when the devil gets into them, their cruelty, their toughness, their endurance, and the preference of every last one of them for death rather than surrender. Of their utter deceitfulness we had Pearl Harbor to witness.

There were, surely, elements of truth in this distortion, for the Japanese have their share of the evil that lies at the core of our being too, and not always dormant in us either. Our soldiers experienced Japanese cruelty, Japanese fanaticism, and the preference for death to surrender. But the image was carried too far, and its essential dehumanization was without basis.

It has seemed to me necessary to say all these things because I want to explain, as much to myself as to others, why we ended the Japanese war as badly as I think we did. I do not refer, now, to the moral factors, though I acknowledge their greatness. Let me confine myself to the surer ground of strategic advantage. It seems to me that, albeit under different circumstances, we made the same strategic error in 1945 that we had made in 1898, and with essentially the same result. Fighting an unlimited war for unlimited objectives, we ended in occupation of the Japanese islands, saddled with responsibility for their administration and defense. I shall come to the strategic consequences of this, but first I want to ask what necessity there may have been for it.

There was never any difference of opinion within the allied councils on how to end the war with Japan. The Japanese must be made to surrender unconditionally, their homeland must be occupied, their power must be utterly destroyed. How could the allies do less if they were dealing, not with ordinary human beings, but with demons who harbored the fanatical purpose of making themselves lords of the earth? One cannot make a real peace with such beings; one can only bear them down by force and, having done so, render them helpless for the future.

What, after all, was the cause of war in the Far East, as far back as anyone could remember? The cause of war was always Japanese aggression—in 1895, in 1904, in 1931, in 1937, and in 1941. See how plausible this is. And the reason why Japan always aggressed was simply that she was an "aggressor nation." Presumably there always would be war in the Far East as long as Japan retained the power to make it. The way to establish the reign of peace, then, was to deprive her of that power in perpetuity.

If this view seems too simple, remember that the premises of policy must have just such simplicity if a wide range of more or less simple people are to join in accepting them. It was the very simplicity of this view which enabled it to become—for soldiers, for civilians, for politicians and voters alike—the premise of policy. Its dogmatic sway is indicated by the fact that one of the most intelligent and thoughtful men involved in these events, Ambassador Joseph Grew, was able to say, in October 1942: ". . . once Japan is destroyed as an aggressive force, we know of no other challenging power that can appear in the Pacific. . . . Once militant Japan is out of the picture, there should remain no threat of further war in the Pacific area. I say this advisedly. Japan is the one enemy, and the only enemy, of the peaceful peoples whose shores overlook the Pacific Ocean."[4]

Anything short of total victory, any negotiated compromise with Japan, was therefore out of the question. Our military objective had to be unconditional surrender. All the documents I have seen, defining this objective, include two requirements: first, the surrender must be complete; second, it must be brought about at the earliest possible date. We know the reason why the surrender had to be complete. "Only the complete destruction of [Japan's] military power," Secretary of

[4] Address of Oct. 10, 1942.

War Stimson later wrote, "could open the way to lasting peace."[5] But I can only speculate on the reason for making the earliest possible date of surrender a prime requirement. The desire to get the suffering over with is understandable. But as one looks back on these times one wonders that our leaders did not ask themselves whether they had to make a choice between a prompt victory at great expense in casualties and resources, or a slower victory at less expense. I find no evidence, however, that such a choice was ever considered. On the contrary, the leaders seem to have assumed that the casualties and other expenses would be proportionate to the length of the war, that they would be greater the longer it lasted, and that the reason for bringing it to the earliest possible conclusion was precisely that of saving lives and resources.

I have some difficulty in reconciling this assumption with what, in retrospect, appears to have been a willingness to pay a terrible price in casualties and resources for the sake of shortening the war. In the spring of 1945 Japan was quite evidently a beaten nation. Her navy was virtually gone. Her air force was gone except for what could serve to make suicidal attacks on landing forces. Allied warships ranged her coastal waters, allied planes flew back and forth over her homeland, and all met with "little opposition."[6] Japan could no longer defend the integrity of her homeland against us and, dependent as she was on overseas supplies of food and fuel, she would not much longer be able to eat. The allies were now free, one supposes, to withdraw most of their troops, leaving naval forces for a sea blockade and air forces for an internal blockade of communications. It would simply be a matter of waiting until the Japanese had made the inevitable choice between starvation and surrender.

But this was incompatible with the requirement for promptness, and it was apparently to meet this requirement, which

[5] Stimson and Bundy, *On Active Service in Peace and War* (New York, 1948), p. 617.

[6] General Marshall's Third Report, *The War Reports* (Philadelphia, 1947), p. 243 See also Stimson and Bundy, *op. cit.*, p. 621.

no one questioned, that the allies had decided on an invasion of Japan's home islands by ground forces at an estimated possible expense of a million American lives plus a large number of British lives. This was a ghastly prospect, enough to keep even the most hardened military commanders awake nights. It justified paying a price to get Russia into the fight against Japan. But no one seems to have seen any alternative until, at the last moment, the atomic bomb came like a godsend to show us a way out.[7] There is no doubt that the decision to use the atomic bomb on Japan was based primarily on humanitarian considerations.[8] Given the overriding requirement of unconditional surrender at the earliest possible date, the alternative to the atomic bomb appeared distinctly worse on humanitarian grounds alone.

During the winter of 1944 to '45, while these terrible prospects were brewing, an already defeated Japan was preparing to seek terms of surrender. The government in Tokyo was divided between those who recognized the defeat and wanted to end the war on whatever terms they might still be able to get, and the fanatics who preferred annihilation. But the government was moving toward surrender and, by July, was seeking the mediation of Moscow for that purpose. From the Potsdam Conference the allies issued a warning to Japan to surrender unconditionally on pain of a heavy increase in the blows upon her (although the atomic bomb was not mentioned). But the warning also made it plain that the consequences of unconditional surrender would be harsh indeed, stopping short only of genocide or permanent enslavement. And the failure to give any assurance that the sacred person of the Emperor would be spared put the Japanese in the position of presumably being accessories to a sacrilege or a deep dishonor if they surrendered.

The wartime legend that governed our thinking had tended to equate the Emperor Hirohito with Mussolini and Hitler as

[7] For a possible exception see Leahy, *I Was There*, (New York, 1950), p. 414.
[8] See Stimson and Bundy, *op. cit.*, pp. 630-33; and Churchill, *The Second World War*, VI, London, 1954, pp. 552-53.

the symbol or personal embodiment of all the evil which we associated with our enemies. This was absurd, as legend sometimes is, but it was simple, it was appealing, and it was convenient for the political cartoonists. Men like Ambassador Grew, who had the courage to argue for a concession to the Japanese with respect to their Emperor, were called "appeasers," and at first their view could not prevail. In the end, however, after two atomic bombs had fallen and the Japanese had made the safety of their Emperor their only condition for surrender, their view did at last prevail. In the midst of so much unwisdom we should not refrain from acknowledging this gleam of statesmanship.

So, having smashed Japan, we occupied her homeland, disbanded her remaining armed forces, dismantled her heavy industries, and established our rule over her. The consequences of this second formal war which we had ever fought in the Pacific were not unlike those of the first. We ended with a commitment for the government and defense of eighty million alien people inhabiting a group of islands off the coast of Asia. This has been and continues to be a heavy strategic burden, for while we have restored self-government to Japan, as we have also granted it to the Philippines, we have not been able to rid ourselves of the responsibility for her defense.

When the government of the United States became the government of Japan (as it did in effect), when the American armed forces took over the basic responsibilities that Japanese armed forces had hitherto borne, then the strategic problem of our Far Eastern policy became at once more extensive and less manageable. The security requirements of every great nation involve it in heavy obligations and liabilities. At one stroke we removed the historic Japanese obligations and liabilities from the backs of the Japanese and set them on our own. When, as now happened, it became a matter of our concern that the Japanese economy function to feed the Japanese people, then we ourselves inherited from Japan that interest in having access to the industrial raw materials of Manchuria which had hitherto prompted us to clash with her. We also acquired her economic interest in that region which she had euphemistically called the "Greater East Asia Co-prosperity Sphere." We inherited, at heavy cost to us, the strategic interest in the Korean Peninsula and the consequent conflict over that peninsula with China that had been going on, intermittently, for centuries, ever since there had been a Japan. For Korea is the Rhineland between these two nations, strategically important to both. As successor to the Japanese government, then, we fell into a continuation of the old warfare with China, with that vast and reviving nation which until this moment of history had always been our special friend, which now became our deadly enemy as it had been Japan's. And by coming into conflict with China we now, as had been the case with the Japanese before us, had to establish ourselves on the island of Formosa. Instead of returning Formosa to China, as we had thought it would be right to do, we now newly perceived the strategic necessity of withholding it from her.

These consequences of unconditional surrender were not foreseen before it took place, nor was their reality grasped in the days that followed. We ruled out the participation of Japanese manpower in the support of these commitments by a provision of the new Japanese constitution forbidding in perpetuity the re-creation of Japanese armed forces. American armed forces had to take their place. Not appreciating the strategic importance that the Korean Peninsula had suddenly acquired for us, with our assumption of responsibility for Japan's defense, we withdrew our armed forces from it, and our Far Eastern commander (rather than, as commonly supposed, our Secretary of State) first revealed that we considered it outside the perimeter of our defense.[9] Again, not appreciating what vast new commitments we had assumed, we disbanded the bulk of our armed forces, leaving the power on the other side of the

[9] Interview with General MacArthur, reported in *The New York Times,* March 2, 1949.

Korean boundary line unbalanced and therefore unchecked. A great deal of discussion has taken place as to who was responsible among us for these failures. But the whole nation, plainly, was responsible. Republicans were not divided from Democrats on these matters, and it is hardly conceivable that any political elements in the country could have prevailed against the overwhelming tide of opinion which wanted a return to prewar normalcy. It seems to me not impossible that, except for what happened in Korea, relations between the United States and the Communist succession government in China might have been normalized. The ideological difference would have constituted a barrier to such a development, but not an insuperable barrier. If one can generalize at all from historical experience, then I think one can say that, given time, strategical considerations tend to override ideological considerations when the two come into conflict. We have seen this demonstrated in Yugoslavia, and there are reasons why it might have been demonstrated in China as well, if we had not had to take Japan's place in Korea and Formosa.

In the three to five years after the Second World War we saw the last stand of several illusions traditionally cherished by the American people. One was what Professor Denis Brogan has called "the illusion of American omnipotence." Recall that, as early as the 1850's, our American commissioner in China proposed that we adopt a policy of "maintaining order" in China, engrafting on its stock "the healthy principles which give life and health to governments." Our people have always tacitly assumed that our own government was in a position to determine the character of political processes and governments, not only throughout Latin America, but in China as well. Therefore, when the Chinese Nationalist regime crumbled and the Chinese Communist regime took its place it was natural for many Americans to suspect something like treason in Washington. The momentary loss of confidence and the confusion were great, though passing.

Still, the main reason for delay in officially recognizing the fact of the Communist succession was that the new regime, while exercising restraint in its treatment of Englishmen and others, treated our own nationals and even our official representatives with a lawless barbarity that, in earlier times, would have been cause enough for war, and that would in our day have justified outlawing the new regime by international action if we were living in a world in which law prevailed. Nevertheless, the eventual normalization remained an expectation to which Mr. John Foster Dulles gave expression in his book, *War or Peace,* saying: "If the Communist government of China in fact proves its ability to govern China without serious domestic resistance, then it, too, should be admitted to the United Nations. However, a regime that claims to have become the government of a country through civil war should not be recognized until it has been tested over a reasonable period of time."[10]

Before the "reasonable period of time" was up we had, vice Japan, fallen into war with China. When our retirement from Korea was followed by a Communist advance we woke up overnight to the true strategic situation, turned around, and went back in. (Here is another example of the way the implications of a situation, not grasped by anyone when it is merely anticipated, become clear to everyone when it turns into a reality.)

The irony of history has full play at this point. Our blunder in Korea led to the most notable Communist defeat since the Cold War began. Under the aegis of the United Nations, we moved our raw, unprepared occupation forces from Japan into Korea to stop the Communist advance. Against all the odds, these non-combat troops, with air and naval support, did stop it and they defeated it.

But here, as in 1898, Clausewitz may have been our undoing. The object of war, he said, is not to capture territory but to destroy the enemy's will and capacity to fight. Our military, raised on this doctrine, were not brought up to fight limited

[10] New York, 1950, p. 190.

256

wars. Even if they had been, it would have been hard enough to stop and dig in at the narrow waist of the Korean peninsula. What looked like a God-given opportunity to unite Korea by force presented itself. Who, under such circumstances, would accept the responsibility and take the blame for calling the pursuing troops to a halt? The Chinese threatened to come in, and many wise heads in Washington believed they would. But our Far Eastern commander reported that they would not. So his troops continued their march toward the Chinese border, and the Chinese hordes did pour into Korea across that border to repel them. Our victory was nullified, transformed into what was at best a stalemate, leaving Communist China in control of North Korea and free to mount her strength there.

XXI • The self-denying clauses of the Monroe Doctrine, in which we proclaimed our abstention from Old World politics, had no reference to Asia. In 1823 the United States was still a nation occupying a strip of the eastern seaboard of North America, facing across the Atlantic toward old Europe, from which its people had escaped. Behind it stretched a blank on the map, a continental wilderness, unconquered and largely unknown. The Pacific Ocean could hardly have been more remote, for one sailed around the southern tip of South America or across the Indian Ocean, or one toiled through the jungles of Panama, to get to it. And far away across the Pacific were the unknown empires of Cathay and Nippon, their borders sealed to Western curiosity. We had no foreign relations in this area and as much occasion for making foreign policy with respect to it as for making foreign policy with respect to Mars. The Monroe Doctrine related to Europe—to the known world, not to the unknown.

As our nation expanded across the Appalachian barrier and the western plains it increased its distance and its detachment from Europe. It began to face the other way. Our people got the habit of looking westward, away from Europe, for their future. It was in this anti-European direction that they saw their destiny. And this tendency to look westward for the realization of their dreams did not expire when the impulse which it represented brought the nation out, at last, upon the shores of the Pacific. Westward across the Pacific was still away from Europe, toward unspoiled lands of romance and infinite possibilities. It was easy to conceive that those lands were waiting for us, that we had a special claim or position with respect to them.

Perhaps it was some such dreamlike attitude which caused us to take our quixotic stand against European encroachment across the Pacific at the turn of the century. Escaping westward from Europe, we found ourselves again facing Europe, which had, in its imperialistic course, come around the globe in the opposite direction. Our reaction was to intervene actively in this situation across the Pacific in order to hold her back. Perhaps it was an impulse of this nature, never consciously realized, that accounts for the initiation of that interventionist policy in Asia which contrasted so sharply with our policy of abstention in Europe. Otherwise, perhaps, Rockhill's whimsey would not have proved so enduring. For there must have been more than the vagary of one man to account for a policy so quickly and firmly rooted among our traditions.

This speculation is consistent with the fact that our anti-European isolationists have been (and those that remain still are) our most militant advocates of intervention in the Far East. Isolationists are "Asia-firsters"; "Asia-firsters" are, almost by definition, isolationists in relation to Europe. Perhaps one can say that typical American isolationists regard not only the Western Hemisphere, but the Far East as well, as our own preserve. Their hope of China has been the hope of its Americanization.

Our twentieth-century policy of intervening in Asia, then, represented the confirmation rather than the abandonment of our isolationist policy. The extraordinary figure of Theodore Roosevelt, who dominated our national scene during the first decade of this century, should not lead us astray on this point. He loved power politics and could no more keep out of them than some of us can keep from running to a fire. Intervening in a Franco-German quarrel, he stage-managed the Algeciras

Conference of 1906 and took an active hand in settling the future of Morocco. And the Hague Peace Conference of 1907 was called at his original suggestion. These acts were hardly isolationist in character; but at the same time as he was thus abandoning or compromising isolationism in his transatlantic policy, Roosevelt was trying to abandon our transpacific interventionism. He retreated as much as possible from the commitment to uphold China's integrity and he advocated complete withdrawal from the Philippines if that could ever be done honorably. Just as the isolationists were interventionists in Asia, so this opponent of interventionism in Asia followed an anti-isolationist course of intervention in Europe. Roosevelt, more and more, faced east, toward Europe, while the tendency of the country was still to face west. Therefore he proves the rule.

"The suggestion occurs," wrote Simeon Strunsky, "that Roosevelt, at the height of his power, imposed himself on his countrymen rather than convinced them; that all along he was out of tune with the basic sentiment in the country, and that this sentiment asserted itself once he had stepped from the scene at Washington."[1]

Historians find it hard to decide whether Theodore Roosevelt was a romantic and irresponsible child or a statesman whose mature insight into world affairs was unmatched among his countrymen. Perhaps one should never ask these either/or questions in trying to assess human beings; for all complex individuals, at least, are several persons in one. Surely Roosevelt was both an ungoverned child who should not have been entrusted with a toy pistol, and a statesman whose vision might have averted much of the grief that has come upon us in this century.

Roosevelt's complete opposite, the man for whom he reserved his bitterest contempt, was another such compound figure.

[1] "Theodore Roosevelt and the Prelude to 1914," *Foreign Affairs*, Vol. IV, No. 1, Oct., 1925, p. 146.

Woodrow Wilson, the only political scientist ever to become President, in some respects was a child when it came to grasping the nature of the international world through which he had to guide our nation. But he also had a vision of how the First World War must end, if peace was to ensue, that lifts him to the first rank among statesmen.

Few men have ever equaled Wilson's capacity for being blind and brilliantly wrong in the field which he had made his profession. In his magisterial book on *Congressional Government* he foresaw that the authority of the presidential office was at an end, a plausible thesis which no one disproved so completely as he did himself when he came, at last, to occupy that office. His understanding of international relations was flawed by his failure to understand their most elementary feature, the essential role of power.

Woodrow Wilson's first administration may be summed up as a case of the blind leading the blind. We, with our retrospective vision, are now able to see what the situation was. For half a century our experience of foreign relations had been, in great part, that of relations with Great Britain. Here the role of military force was quite subordinate or insignificant because the nature of those relations tended to rule out war as a means of resolving the frequent quarrels between us—just as war is ruled out in our relations with Canada today. At the same time, the British navy, as master of the Atlantic, insulated us from any other threat of military power. We saw ourselves secure and prosperous without any great military force to make us so—for we did not recognize the role of the British navy. Why, then, could not all countries follow our example and conduct their relations likewise by a diplomacy that did not rely on warships and guns?

But the shield which we did not recognize was about to fail us. With the opening of the twentieth century, German ambitions "engaged the energies of Great Britain," as Professor Buehrig puts it. "Absorbed in the compelling necessities of European politics, Britain . . . ceased to serve effectively as a buffer between Europe and the United States.

"Had it been accustomed to acting on power considerations, the United States might have based a policy forthrightly on Germany's attempt to supplant Great Britain. But the United States was not habituated to viewing international politics in such harsh terms. . . . There was, consequently, no head-on collision with Germany. Rather German-American relations entered a legalistic maze in the perplexing intricacies of which the two countries came to blows." What "the probing of the [German] submarine revealed" was the benevolent character, for us, of Britain's hitherto unchallenged control of the Atlantic. "Unwittingly, it was the instrument which laid bare the political connection with Europe which most Americans had ceased to believe existed, and which they [still] were disposed to act on instinctively, rather than face the full implications of what was disclosed."[2]

The greatest issue of World War I, at least in terms of its entire scope, was Germany's challenge to Great Britain's world-wide position, which included her control of the Atlantic. Germany had undertaken to cast down the barrier of the British navy, which stood between us and Europe, protecting our isolation. Germany had attacked our partner, behind whose shield we stood. If our minds had been trained so that we were able to grasp this, we would have realized that, for our own sake, we could not stand aside and allow the shield to be beaten down. We would have realized that we could not really be neutral because we had a vital strategic stake in the frustration of Germany.

But the American people were blind to this implication of power politics, and their leader was as blind as they. What seemed of the most vital importance was that the United States not be snagged and dragged into this foreign war. American mothers said they had not raised their sons to be soldiers. Mr. Wilson had a more sophisticated reason for wanting us to stay

[2] Edward H. Buehrig, *Woodrow Wilson and the Balance of Power* (Indiana, 1955), p. ix.

out. He appreciated the fact that the war was a major disaster for civilization. The longer it continued and the wider it spread, the more profound would be the damage that civilization must suffer—damage from which it might not recover. If the United States stayed out it could keep burning, within its own wide confines, the light with which to rekindle the lamps of Europe when the war was over. Of more immediate importance, by remaining detached and impartial with respect to the combatants, it might by its diplomacy be able to stop the war before the damage and the destruction had gone much further. Note that this latter consideration, looking to the exercise of decisive influence by the United States in bringing peace to the world, is not isolationist. To this extent Wilson's neutrality represented a strategy for influencing the situation rather than a belief that the situation was not our business.

It was the contribution which physical power makes to national influence that Wilson did not understand. He was opposed to having us arm ourselves or make any other preparation for the possibility that we would become involved in the war. He seems to have shared the then prevalent view that to prepare for war was to make it more likely that we would get it. Theodore Roosevelt's formula had been: "Walk softly but carry a big stick." Wilson's belief was that, if you really mean to have peace, then don't carry any stick at all.

One morning, as late as the fall of 1915, President Wilson summoned Mr. Breckenridge, the Acting Secretary of War, to the White House. Breckenridge "found him holding a copy of the *Baltimore Sun* in his hand, 'trembling and white with passion.' The President pointed to a little paragraph of two lines in an out-of-the-way part of a sheet, evidently put in just to fill space. It read something like this: 'It is understood that the General Staff is preparing a plan in the event of war with Germany.'" The President thereupon directed Breckenridge to investigate immediately and, if the paragraph proved to be true, "to relieve at once every officer of the General Staff and order him out of Washington."[3] I don't suppose that Mr. Wilson's outrage would have been less if he had known that our military at the time not only had plans for the contingency of a war with Germany, but had them also for the several contingencies of war with England, France, Italy, Japan, Mexico, and other countries.

This attitude of refusing to countenance our potential weight in the balance of military power was not likely to make for an increase in that influence by means of which Wilson hoped to bring about a negotiated discontinuance of the war.

Today we can see that the threat offered by an aggressive and imperialistic German regime to Britain's control of the Atlantic was a threat to us. If the German submarine had won the success which it seemed about to win at one point, we would have found no space intervening between Germany's advancing military power and our own shores. One can imagine the belated alarm among the American people if Britain had suddenly acknowledged defeat and surrendered her navy to the Kaiser; for then the danger would have forced itself upon our consciousness as an unpleasant surprise.

But it was not our habit to think of international affairs primarily in terms of strategic self-interest. It had, rather, become our habit to think of them in terms of abstract moral principles and legal rules. Therefore we did not allow ourselves to see that the problem which the German submarine posed for us was that of preserving our outer line of defense. Instead, we persuaded ourselves that the problem was simply a problem of right or wrong in terms of universal law and morality. We clung to the fiction that we had no self-interest in which side won, and we expressed our concern with the German submarine rather in terms of our devotion to a set of fairly abstruse rules of warfare, rules which the invention of the submarine had itself, in some instances, rendered virtually impossible of appli-

[3] Frederick Palmer, *Newton D. Baker* (New York, 1931), I, 40. See also Buehrig, *op. cit.*, pp. 110-11.

cation. Consequently, the Wilson administration allowed itself to become more and more enmeshed in a fine-spun public dispute with Germany over difficult issues of international law which were summed up for the public by the phrase "Freedom of the Seas." This dispute over technicalities of procedure, dubious legal rights, and uncertain moral principles served to obscure the massive strategic realities.

However, the intellectual dilemmas into which Wilson fell during the first two years of the war, suspended as he was between legend and reality, constituted a process of forced education from which he profited. The contradictions in which he had allowed himself to become entangled began to present themselves quite clearly to him. For example, we find him telling a Pittsburgh audience at the beginning of 1916: "There are two things which practically everybody who comes to the Executive Office in Washington tells me. They tell me, 'The people are counting upon you to keep us out of this war.' And in the next breath what do they tell, 'The people are equally counting upon you to maintain the honor of the United States.' Have you reflected that a time might come when I could not do both? And have you made yourselves ready to stand behind your Government for the maintenance of the peace of the country? If I am to maintain the honor of the United States and it should be necessary to exert the force of the United States in order to do it, have you made the force ready?"[4] In another speech that same month Wilson said: "We live in a world which we did not make, which we can not alter, which we can not think into a different condition from that which actually exists."[5]

As the legalistic disputes with Germany over such issues as the rights of American nationals on armed merchantmen of belligerent powers between belligerent and neutral ports on the high seas—as disputes over such refined and doubtful issues brought us to the brink of war, Wilson began to see the need

[4] *The Record of American Diplomacy* (New York, 1954), p. 449.
[5] Buehrig, *op. cit.*, p. 117.

for a broader and surer basis on which to fight if the nation should have to go over the brink. He told Secretary of State Lansing "that he did not believe the people of the United States were willing to go to war because a few Americans had been killed."[6]

Wilson, under Lansing's coaxing, at last solved his dilemma by broadening the legal issue into an ideological issue. The German Empire's violation of technical maritime rights was made secondary by equating it with an autocratic form of government hostile to democracy. The issue of the war was the challenge to democracy; the cause in which it was being fought by Britain and her allies was "to make the world safe for democracy." And by making the world safe for democracy, this would be the war to end war. It was on this platform that Wilson rose to the full majesty of his power and authority as the moral leader of the American people—almost, one might say, of the world's people. For a moment, before he fell, he was to tower above the international horizon, against the lightning and the storm clouds of war, as no other figure in the twentieth century has towered.

It seems to me that this shift from an emphasis on legal technicalities to ideology might well be interpreted as the movement of Wilson's mind, compelled by intractable circumstance, in the direction of reality. The reason why German control of the Atlantic would be a danger to us, where British control was not, had some relationship to differences in ideology. The autocratic form of the German state was congenial to a policy of aggression; its processes lent themselves to secrecy and surprise. What it represented—ideologically as well as in structure —did render the world less safe for democracy.

However, all this was obscured for the public by being cast in terms of general principles without specific reference to the national interest. We see here what we saw in our Far Eastern policy, where the general principle of the Open Door—open to all comers—was preferred over a claim advanced on behalf

[6] *Ibid.*, p. 56.

of Americans only. We did not say that a German victory would make the United States unsafe. We said that autocracy had to be put down to make the world safe for democracy. We did not limit ourselves to the defense of the United States, but proclaimed unlimited Utopian objectives: a final end to wars and a world in which democracy was, at last, safe. This was the hope that was held out to the men who went overseas and the women who stayed at home, sacrificing their happiness.

This, then, was the evolution of our thinking during the course of World War I. We began in isolationism: the war, we said, was a war in the Old World with which the New World had nothing to do. Being disinterested in its outcome, we proclaimed our neutrality. But our neutral rights were repeatedly violated—violated, as a matter of fact, by both sides. Perhaps partly because of subconscious elements in our thinking, we allowed this to draw us into serious quarrels with Germany while we did not allow it to draw us into serious quarrels with Britain.[7] Finding our neutrality and our noninvolvement thus increasingly compromised, we finally abandoned them altogether and, leaping into the fray against Germany, went to the opposite extreme. We had begun by assuming or pretending that our national safety was not at issue. When circumstances discredited this, showing in the menacing attitude of the submarine that our safety was at issue, we proclaimed war, not for the selfish reason of that safety, but for the salvation of democracy and the final establishment of peace all over the world. The test of success, then, would not be the modest one of whether we had averted the immediate danger to our state, but whether we had averted all dangers forever.

The consequence of this indulgence in Utopian promises for the postwar attitude of the American people was radical. By applying the more modest and realistic test of the national safety we would have concluded, at the end of the war, that we had successfully achieved the objective of our participation

[7] A heavy investment in loans to Britain may also have made its contribution.

in it. We had warded off the danger. But by applying, instead, a test which overlooked the limits of possibility it appeared to us that the objective of our participation had not been gained, and that our participation, consequently, had not been justified. We had not brought into being a world in which democracy was safe and future wars unthinkable.

Without any attack having taken place on our territory, and without any direct threat to our well-being having arisen, we had nevertheless abandoned our isolation and gone to war. Our men had subjected themselves to the horrors of trench warfare to save democracy elsewhere and on the promise that a world-wide Utopia would be their payment. But when it was all over the payment was not forthcoming. The world manifestly remained the wicked old world that it had always been, a world that contrasted more than ever with the virtue we had shown. A wave of cynical disillusionment among us was the consequence. Since we had never been told that there were selfish national reasons for going to war, we supposed that we might have abstained with impunity. We believed that we had failed to abstain because we had been swayed by our idealism and generosity to abandon that self-interested detachment from the quarrels of others which George Washington had urged us to preserve. Like Orpheus, we had succumbed to the temptation of looking back toward that underworld from which our nation had escaped. Allowing our heart to prevail over our head, we had gone back across the sea to save others. We had, as we put it, pulled the British chestnuts out of the fire. We had rescued France. And what was the result? With the war over, with the British and French saved by our generosity, we did not even have their gratitude. They refused to pay their war debts to us, and when we asked for our money back they called us "Uncle Shylock." That was what we got for thinking of others instead of ourselves. Our preponderant reaction was: Never again! Never again would we make the mistake of abandoning our isolation to save the rest of the world!

This was the consequence of the legend that our wartime

leaders had created to justify our participation in the war. I know too well the dilemmas that democratic governments face in these situations to be willing to blame those leaders. Very likely they had no choice. The immediate need was to summon up the energies of our people for the winning of a war that might otherwise have been lost. What counted was that the nation do the job that had to be done, whether it did it for the right reasons or for the wrong reasons. But if the reality, that what we had to deal with was a threat to ourselves, had not been obscured by the legend that we were saving the rest of the world, then we might have learned the right lesson instead of the wrong lesson from our experience. We might have learned that the decline in Britain's relative power had put an end to that security which had for so long enabled us to abstain from the power politics of the Old World, that our security now required us to share with Britain the burden, which she could no longer bear alone, of guarding the Atlantic and preserving the balance of power on the Continent. The lesson we would have learned was that our isolationism was obsolete. Instead, the lesson that we read into our experience was precisely the opposite—that our safety lay in returning to our traditional policy of isolation, in not abandoning it again.

In this stern world men and nations learn their lessons only at the price of bitter experience. It seems to me particularly tragic that we paid the price of the lesson, here, and yet did not learn it. What did this mean but that we would have to pay the price all over again, that we would have to go through a Second World War before we finally learned what, if we had faced the truth, we might have learned by the First World War, thereby averting a second?

Not having understood the real reason for our participation in World War I, we reverted, during the two decades that followed, to our isolationist policy, determined not to lapse from it again. But the experience of one lapse suggested the possibility that, in spite of our determination, the same thing might happen all over again. We did not trust ourselves. After all, we had been just as determined to stay out of the First World War as we were now determined to stay out of any future war. If we could learn the specific causes of our first lapse, then we might prevent a second lapse by doing away with those causes. So we asked ourselves, and for two decades we debated, the question why we got into the world war.

When we try to understand the world in which we live, right answers are important. But what is even more important is to begin by asking the right questions. We should have been asking ourselves whether it had been necessary for us to get into the war—and, if so, why. Instead, we assumed that it had not been necessary and asked ourselves why, in the absence of necessity, we had allowed ourselves to be drawn into it anyway. Because this question was based on a false premise, any answer to it was bound to contribute to our self-delusion and thereby reduce our ability to deal with the realities of the world.

Historians, journalists, and Congressional committees set to work on the record of how we got drawn, and needlessly drawn, into the world war. What the record showed, on its face, was that our insistence on a technical freedom of the seas brought us into increasing conflict with Germany. A principal issue, for example, had been our insistence that Americans had the right to travel in the ships of Germany's enemies without having their lives jeopardized by German submarine attack upon those ships. Here was a right so tenuous and so remote from any real national interest that one could hardly justify going to war to uphold it. President Wilson had realized this with increasing embarrassment at the time when he was prosecuting the quarrel with Germany over it. In the 1930's the Senate realized it too, and produced legislation authorizing the President to forbid American citizens to travel on belligerent vessels in time of war except at their own risk.

The Senate Munitions Investigating Committee ("Nye Committee") held public hearings in which it was tempted to charge

270

American financiers and munitions makers with having pushed us into the war for the sake of their own profits. It came to be widely believed that our entrance into the war was the result of a conspiracy by the Morgan interests in Wall Street and a few munition makers. There was even less reason why the nation should have gone to war for the sake of these people than for the sake of the foolish Americans who chose to travel in British ships.

Accepting the premises, it followed that the way to prevent our being tricked into war again was not only to keep Washington's Farewell Address ever in mind, but also to provide legislation to keep under control or to forbid all those activities conducive to our involvement in war which ministered only to the interests of private individuals or special groups.

Consequently, at the very time that the rise of Hitler was posing the same threat to our national security as the policy of the Kaiser had posed a generation earlier, Congress passed a series of acts—the "Neutrality Acts"—designed to prevent our taking interventionist action to contain or overcome that threat. One such act was aimed at the prohibition of all arms shipments to belligerents in case of war. Another prohibited the extension of loans or credits to belligerents.

The practical effect of this legislation was to deprive the opposition to Hitler, in large part, of the advantages inherent in that command of the seas which enabled it to recruit its strength from abroad. By withholding strength from those who might have contained Hitler, it enhanced the threat which his policy posed for our own security. And all this was done on the basis of the isolationist dogma and the isolationist legend that we had no national interest in the victory of one side rather than the other.

This dogma and this legend, in turn, were based on a radical misunderstanding of the causes of our participation in World War I. There is no better illustration of how important a right reading of history is to the shaping of national policy. The historians must bear their share of responsibility here.

The encouragement which our neutrality legislation gave to Hitler, and the impairment of the resistance to him, were appreciable. Fortunately, however, President Roosevelt was able to evade its provisions in substantial measure. And when war finally broke out in Europe, reality once more tended to assert itself against the legend, as it had after 1914. Congress repealed the arms embargo and authorized the sale of arms and munitions to belligerents who would take possession in our own ports and pay cash. A couple of years later, the Lend-Lease Act put a final belated end to the policy represented by the neutrality legislation of the 1930's. We would now have to fight the war that we and the British and the French might have prevented at an earlier stage, if we had allowed ourselves to read the real lesson of the First World War.

XXII • Woodrow Wilson was fifty-six years old in 1913, when he became President of the United States. He was notable for a certain intractability of mind and character. Only the most compelling pressure of circumstances could have educated one who was already so old and so set in his views. As late as 1915 he was still capable of showing himself quite blind to the role of power in international politics. But the pressure of circumstances, at this time, was forcing an impression even on his dogmatic and theoretical mind. Alongside the theoretical, idealistic, Utopian-minded Wilson there was growing up, under the discipline of hard experience, the elements of another Wilson who was the opposite: realistically appreciative of the limits of possibility. From 1915 till his death some ten years later we have two persons in the one person of Woodrow Wilson, for the realist grows up alongside the idealist without displacing him or overcoming the habits of his mind.

A devastating portrait of Wilson at the Paris Peace Conference was later drawn by that realist, John Maynard Keynes, in his *Economic Consequences of the Peace*—a portrait so devastating and so widely publicized that it contributed to the tragedy of Wilson's political downfall and death. Referring to him as "this blind and deaf Don Quixote," Keynes said that "his thought and his temperament were essentially theological not intellectual. . . ." But what dismayed Keynes about the President was not the point of view he represented at the peace table. He agreed with that point of view. What dismayed him was the way in which Wilson allowed that point of view to be defeated by what the others at the peace table—Lloyd George, Clemenceau, Orlando—represented. Keynes, the realist, was horrified to see the unrealistic President abandon, without ever knowing it, the realistic position which he had outlined before coming to Paris. It was because Keynes agreed with Wilson's realism that he was so horrified by his unrealism.

In what did Wilson's Keynesian realism consist?

We get an expression of it as early as February 1, 1916, before the United States had entered the war. Secretary of State Lansing had said that the destruction of Prussian militarism was an essential precondition of peace. Wilson was not sure of this, fearing that the destruction of Prussian militarism might mean the disintegration of German power and the destruction of the German nation.[1] As early as this, and from now on, we find Wilson concerned at the danger of creating what we would today call a "power vacuum" by destroying Germany or making her impotent. This anticipates the realism of both Keynes and, in our own time, of Walter Lippmann and George Kennan.

It was precisely the disintegration of German power and the destruction of the German nation undertaken by the Versailles Peace Treaty which made that treaty seem such a disastrous document to Keynes. "If," he wrote in 1919, "the European Civil War is to end with France and Italy abusing their momentary victorious power to destroy Germany and Austria-Hungary now prostrate, they invite their own destruction also, being so deeply and inextricably interwined with their victims by hidden psychic and economic bonds."[2]

At the conclusion of every major war the task of the peacemakers is twofold: (1) to establish the conditions to which

---

[1] Buehrig, *op. cit.*, p. 144.
[2] *The Economic Consequences of the Peace* (London, 1924), p. 3.

the defeated side agrees or submits, and (2) to re-establish, amid the wreckage of the war, a general international order for the maintenance of peace and security. It is hardly necessary to argue that the primary task, to which the treatment of the defeated side should be subordinated, is that of re-establishing an international order. Simple people, however, are likely to give priority to disciplining and disabling the defeated enemy. They do not readily grasp the larger problem, that of creating such a general international order as may make peace possible. Peace, to their minds, exists of itself until an evil nation flouts it. The way to be sure of peace, then, is to destroy or render helpless the evil nation that has flouted it. This simple view is likely to have an irresistible impelling force at the end of a war, charged as it is with that emotional animus which had supported the victors' drive to victory. There seems to be no conflict between the satisfaction of the animus against the defeated enemy and the establishment of peace. In fact, the two undertakings seem like one.

Wilson took the more sophisticated view, the view that peace depends on the rehabilitation of the defeated nation within the family of nations, and that the achievement of peace is therefore in conflict with the passion to disable the defeated nation. Peace meant that Germany and the victorious allies would have to live together in amity, since they were inescapably neighbors on this earth. Peace could not be established if the victorious powers attempted to keep Germany on its back and helpless in perpetuity. Wilson was clear, therefore, that the enemy which had to be destroyed was the autocratic government of Germany, which could feasibly be abolished, and not the German nation or people, which could not be abolished. With the Kaiser's government there could be no peace; with a government in which the nation and people were democratically represented there could be no acceptable alternative to peace. Here the only realism was reconciliation. A democratic Germany should have an equal place in the family of nations.

When America entered the war, at last, Wilson fixed and

limited the identification of the enemy so firmly, so eloquently, and so insistently as to leave no room for interpreters of his meaning. Addressing the Congress on April 2, 1917, he said: "We have no quarrel with the German people. We have no feeling toward them but one of sympathy and friendship. . . . We act without animus, not in enmity towards a people or with the desire to bring any injury or disadvantage upon them, but only in armed opposition to an irresponsible Government which has thrown aside all considerations of humanity and of right and is running amuck." The only condition he made for an armistice and peace negotiations, for the restoration of Germany to an equal place in the family of nations, was that the Germans should oust the imperial regime and set up a representative regime in its place. This they did.

I shall not attempt to judge whether this statesmanship of Wilson's, more shrewdly advanced at the Paris Peace Conference, might have been made to prevail. A century earlier, when Napoleon had been overthrown, a real peace of reconciliation had immediately been made with a de-Napoleonized France, which thereupon took her full place in the family of nations. That peace had been real and it had endured. But the peacemakers of 1815 were not acting in a representative capacity for the populations of their countries. The peacemakers of 1919 were. Behind them they heard the clamor of their publics demanding that "the Hun" not be let off, that there be no softness to the Germans, that the Germans be required to pay all the costs of the war—irrespective of what kind of government they set up. Clemenceau and Lloyd George represented these people and, flouting Wilson and his Fourteen Points, made the kind of arrangement these people demanded, which was not a peace at all. The unwisdom of the many prevailed over the wisdom of the few, and the new democratic Germany of the Weimar Republic was launched under conditions of such economic oppression and such humiliation that it could not endure. Keynes had not found it too hard to predict the consequences of this even as early as 1919. "Economic privation," he wrote, "proceeds by easy stages, and so long as men suffer it patiently the outside world cares little. Physical efficiency and resistance to disease slowly diminish, but life proceeds somehow, until the limit of human endurance is reached at last and counsels of despair and madness stir the sufferers from the lethargy which precedes the crisis. Then man shakes himself, and the bonds of custom are loosed. The power of ideas is sovereign, and he listens to whatever instruction of hope, illusion, or revenge is carried to him on the air."[3] The result of the process which Keynes here predicted was the usurpation of Adolph Hitler and the doom of a Second World War.[4]

The Paris Peace Conference was the prime agent in that revulsion of feeling which prompted the American people to return to isolationism when the war was over. Expecting the Utopia which the President had promised, having paid the price for it, they saw now how the allies had already bound themselves by secret agreements to what seemed sordid deals based on greed. While they did not, perhaps, understand the grand issue involved in Wilson's defeat at Paris, the tone and tenor of the peace treaty impressed them with its reversion to those selfish power politics which their forefathers had crossed the ocean to escape. And so the United States would not ratify the treaty. In its bitterness it withdrew its influence and washed its hands of responsibility for the fate of a wicked world.

Overcoming our American opposition, the Allies had de-

[3] *Ibid.*, pp. 233-35.

[4] Two statements on the issue involved, one by a lawyer and the other by a newspaper writer, are revealing in their mutual consistency.

1. "Where terms are dictated throughout to the utterly vanquished belligerent at the absolute discretion of the victor, the transaction cannot, strictly speaking, be designated a treaty; it is a unilateral imposition of demands" (Coleman Phillipson, *Termination of War and Treaties of Peace*, [London, 1916], p. 165).

2. "No criticism of the Peace which omits, as Mr. Keynes seems to me by implication to omit, the aspect of it not as a treaty, but as a sentence, has any right to be heard by the European Allied peoples" (*Sunday Chronicle* [London], Dec. 21, 1919).

The real question here, which would come up again in another form when the Nuremberg Trials were held after World War II, is whether the victor, in his moment of victory, is competent to sit in judgment on the vanquished.

cided in 1919 not to negotiate a peace with the Germans but to impose one on them. This was possible only because they were not, in reality, undertaking to make a true peace with Germany. A peace, one supposes, means the restoration of normal, amicable, co-operative relations between former antagonists. Unless the parties reach an agreement on which they can shake hands, such a peace has not been made between them. If one party insists on remaining with his foot planted on the other's neck, such a peace has not been made between them. The other party has not really agreed to it; he will continue to struggle, and when he can once more rise to his feet he will resume the fight. A dictated "peace," or any dictated "agreement," is a contradiction in terms. "Only a peace between equals can last," Wilson had said, "only a peace, the very principle of which is equality, and a common participation in a common benefit."[5]

The posture of the allies was quite impossible. "The dictated peace had hardly been signed before the Germans succeeded in forcing the Allies to the conference table."[6] The actual figure representing the amount of reparations, as well as the terms of payment, having been left open at Versailles, and Article 234 having provided that Germany's representatives should be given "a just opportunity to be heard," the Genoa Conference was called for April, 1922. At this conference, to which Soviet

[5] Address to Senate, January 22, 1917. Woodrow Wilson was not great because he sponsored the League of Nations or because he stood for "self-determination." He was great, rather, in that insight into the need for limited war aims and a magnanimous peace which the few, as opposed to the many, have had since Thucydides. Thucydides has the Spartans saying to their enemies, the Athenians: "If great enmities are ever to be really settled, we think it will be, not by the system of revenge and military success, and by forcing an opponent to swear to a treaty to his disadvantage, but when the more fortunate combatant waives these his privileges, is guided by gentler feelings, conquers his rival in generosity, and accords peace on more moderate conditions than were expected" (translation by R. W. Livingstone, Book IV). General Fuller quotes Theodoric the Ostrogoth as saying: "Those wars of mine have had a successful issue, over the ending of which moderation has presided" (*Armament and History* [London, 1946], p. ix). Sir Winston Churchill provides another example with his precept: "In victory: magnanimity." When this becomes the wisdom of the many we shall have something even better than world government.

[6] Leonard von Muralt, *From Versailles to Potsdam*, (Chicago, 1948), p. 63.

278

Russia had been invited because France wanted her to demand more reparations from Germany out of which to pay the Czarist debts to France, Germany entered into the surprise Treaty of Rapallo with Russia, in which both countries mutually agreed to renounce all reparations, to grant each other most-favored-nation rights, and to resume diplomatic relations. This was a real peace treaty, entered into on a basis of equality by the two major countries that the allies had decided to exclude from the family of nations.

By this stroke Germany regained the freedom of action that made it necessary, at last, to take her views into consideration, to negotiate a peace with her. The result was the negotiation of the Dawes Plan with her in 1924 and, in 1925, the Locarno Conference and her admission to the Council of the League of Nations. 1925, then, may be regarded as the year in which peace was truly concluded with Germany. From 1914 to 1918 the allies had been at war with the old imperial regime, which was finally overthrown by the Germans themselves in the latter year. From 1919 to 1924 they were at war, in a fundamental sense, with the Weimar Republic, which also received its mortal injury at their hands—for it had been so weakened that it could not survive the world-wide economic depression. From 1919 to 1924 the allies had persisted in dealing with the Weimar Republic as an enemy on the anti-Wilsonian premise that the enemy was a nation rather than any particular governing regime. But when the Nazi regime came into power, when Mr. Hyde returned to replace Dr. Jekyll, when it was once more proper, indeed essential, to recognize the German state as a ruthless antagonist, then the former allies, demoralized by their own failures, profoundly ashamed of the Versailles settlement, without confidence in their moral position, watched with fascinated eyes the approaching doom of another war and were incapable of action.

The lesson of the failure to make peace in 1919 was available to the statesmen who, during the Second World War, prepared for another opportunity. It was explicit in the pages of Keynes and many another writer. It had shaped the thinking of that powerful South African statesman, Marshal Smuts. In Britain, Winston Churchill had grasped it from the first. As early as March of 1920 he had written to Lloyd George: "Since the Armistice my policy would have been 'peace with the German people, war on the Bolshevik tyranny.' "[7] Magnanimity in victory was a principle with Churchill. And it had been an American tradition at least as early as Abraham Lincoln's advocacy, in his Second Inaugural Address, of that peace without victory which Wilson was to advocate in a later day.

But this remained the wisdom of the few, which, under the circumstances of war, does not prevail against the passions and the innocence of the many. Our Civil War was not concluded by that peace of reconciliation which Lincoln had advocated. The First World War was not concluded by that peace of reconciliation which Wilson had advocated. And in the Second World War the advocacy itself was abandoned. The United States and its allies were now united in their decision not to make a real peace with Germany and Japan at all, once victory had been won.

I think the explanation for this failure to apply the clear lesson of 1919 is in the overwhelming compulsion of circumstances to which the allied leaders necessarily succumbed. Wartime leadership in the conditions of our day is simply too much for the best and strongest of men. They cannot command the movement of armies and resources, they cannot command the inert and mindless bureaucracies, they cannot command a capricious public opinion, they cannot negotiate agreements with their legislatures, they cannot negotiate international agreements with one another—they cannot simultaneously do all these things with only mortal strength in twenty-four hours a day, and still force through, against the ignorance, the immaturity, or the passion of the masses those measures which represent an essentially recondite wisdom. In any case, while

[7] Quoted by J. M. Keynes, *Essays in Biography* (London, 1951), p. 63.

Franklin D. Roosevelt was a buoyant and optimistic idealist, and a daring practical politician, he lacked those profundities which were to be found in Wilson's mind and which, when allowed play, have given depth to the statesmanship of Winston Churchill. Churchill knew better than to welcome some of the decisions which he had to accept. Roosevelt did not.[8]

But even if Roosevelt had been profound, even if he had been an Abraham Lincoln, I cannot believe that the outcome would have been different. Lincoln himself had written, shortly before his death: "I claim not to have controlled events, but confess plainly that events have controlled me."[9] Even supposing that Roosevelt had been a Lincoln, even supposing that he and Churchill by themselves could have carried through an agreement to make a real peace at the end of the war, it hardly seems possible that they could have taken their Soviet ally into the harmony of such a purpose. Here, in the basic disunity of the allies, was a situation that virtually forbade wisdom and delicacy in the preparation for peace. The winning of the war had to come first, and this meant that the constant struggle to establish relations of some confidence with Moscow took precedence and priority. The whole task, in its range and order, was harder than it had been in 1914 to 1918. It was too much for mortal men.

I cannot believe that the opportunity of 1945 was as good as the one that had been missed in 1919. The allies were divided beyond the capacity of statesmanship to unite, no matter how resourceful and heroic the efforts that had necessarily to be made. The United States and France had not had a common conception at Versailles, but they belonged to the same civilization and could feel secure in each other's company; the possibilities of communicating fruitfully, of understanding each

---

[8] "A constitutional statesman," Walter Bagehot wrote, "is in general a man of common opinions and uncommon abilities." ("The Character of Sir Robert Peel," in *Biographical Studies* [London, 1881], p. 2.) This seems to me to sum up Franklin D. Roosevelt.

[9] To A. G. Hodges, 4-IV-1864—from *The Lincoln Encyclopedia* (New York, 1950), p. 114.

other's points of view, and of subjecting their differences to meaningful debate were there. The element of personal failure appears to have been one significant factor at Versailles. But the United States and the Soviet Union in the 1940's belonged to different worlds, and it is doubtful whether there was any common ground on which they could stand and debate out their difference. What was needed for the establishment of a general peace was peace with the Soviet Union as well as with Germany and Japan; and this was not a peace for which any military victory had prepared the way. As we now see it the United States probably had no choice but to defer the hope of peace and look to her own security.

America and Britain had somehow to maintain constructive co-operation between themselves and Soviet Russia if the war was to be won. The one indispensable bond that united these natural antagonists was their hostility toward a common foe. They could march together as long as they shared this animus and were able to assure each other of their implacable resolve to give it full play to the end. The minute either side showed signs of coming to terms with Germany the precarious coalition would tend to fall apart and its defeat would be threatened. The coalition was, in fact, tending to fall apart because Stalin doubted the Anglo-American determination to fight a total war to a total end, and he had not hidden his suspicion in connection with the dispute over a second front. The maintenance of the coalition appeared to depend, therefore, on the demonstration of our determination not to stop short of total victory, of "unconditional surrender." This surely accounts for one of the motives that, consciously or unconsciously, prompted Roosevelt publicly to commit America and Britain to the objective of totally destroying German and Japanese power, of occupying both countries and making them helpless for an indefinite future.

The greatest strategic mistake which the allies had made in 1919 was to read both Germany and Russia out of the family of nations at the same time. This drove the two outlaws together at Rapallo, in an association from which Germany obtained the negotiating strength to force an allied acceptance of her recovered independence and equality. It is clear now, and was at the time, that the policy of keeping Germany and Japan on their backs after World War II could succeed only by a unanimity of resolve among the victorious powers. Let Russia and the Atlantic powers fall away from each other, and the defeated states, by playing one side against the other, would quickly recover their feet. Just as the wartime unity of the coalition depended on a common resolve not to spare the enemy, so the policy of not sparing the enemy after the war depended on postwar unanimity within the coalition.

The continuance of the wartime unanimity into the postwar period was, however, the one basic precondition, not only of the plan for the treatment of the defeated nations, but of Roosevelt's entire postwar policy. It was the basis on which the United Nations Organization was designed. It was the basis on which the United States opposed Churchill's desire to limit the westward advance of Russian troops in Europe and to divide the Balkans into spheres of influence. It was the basis of those Utopian hopes and plans with which President Roosevelt buoyantly approached the task that had defeated his former chief, President Wilson. Unanimity of the great powers was to be the keystone of the arch, without which the postwar structure would fall.

We see, here, an expression of the indomitable optimism which always enabled Roosevelt to carry on against the greatest odds. But I recall, also, the atmosphere and the context of thought in Washington at the time. In private, everyone shook his head at the slimness of the prospect that we would be able to get along with Moscow after the war, when even under the circumstances of desperate warfare against a common foe it was proving almost impossible. The chances of maintaining unanimity seemed remote. But then it also seemed that, since this was the world's only hope, there was no acceptable alternative. There was, at least, no alternative that a nation with its eyes habitually fixed on Utopia could contemplate. In the absence of any tolerable alternative this unanimity simply had to be. The possibility of failure to obtain it could not be admitted.

Virtually everyone in Washington was uneasy and doubtful of the prospect. But the administration perforce put on a boldly optimistic front for the public. If the public would support the general postwar policy, if the Senate would consent to ratification of the United Nations Charter, then all could look forward to that secure, peaceful, and prosperous world which all had been promised, again in this war as in the last. In November of 1943 Secretary Hull, returning from the Four Power Conference in Moscow, told a joint session of Congress: "As the provisions of the four-nation declaration are carried into effect, there will no longer be need for spheres of influence, for alliances, for balance of power, or any other of the special arrangements through which, in the unhappy past, the nations strove to safeguard their security or to promote their interests." If we were going to put all our eggs in the one basket—and it seemed to us that there were no other baskets—then we might as well do it boldly and confidently, refusing to recognize the possibility of failure. Unanimity of the great powers had to be assumed. Otherwise, everyone might as well cut his throat and get the misery of this world over with.

Given this premise, the lesson of Rapallo had no bearing. One assumed the existence of that unanimity among the great powers which would make it possible to keep Germany and Japan on their backs for the indefinite future. And the devil theory—the theory that war is caused by "aggressor nations"—argued that they had to be kept on their backs. In his Message to Congress of January 7, 1943, President Roosevelt spoke in terms that made the guilt and the threat of the Axis nations independent of the particular regimes that governed them. "It is clear to us," he said, "that if Germany and Italy and Japan—or any one of them—remain armed at the end of this war or are permitted to rearm, they will again, and inevitably, embark upon an ambitious career of world conquest. They must be dis-

284

armed and kept disarmed, and they must abandon the philosophy and the teaching of that philosophy which has brought so much suffering to the world." Hitler, according to this, is but a symptom, and the evil must continue "inevitably" beyond our victory and his demise. Italy, itself, we are told, must "inevitably" embark on a "career of world conquest" if it is not kept disarmed after the war. Even with a new Italy in which Mussolini and fascism have been overthrown we will not dare make a real peace, for the evil is not in fascism or the fascist regime but in the nation itself, which belongs to the species of "aggressor" state that the "peace-loving" states must continue to oppose.

Unconditional surrender was the logical consequence of the doctrine of popular guilt. If Hitler and Hitlerism, Mussolini and fascism, Tojo and Japanese imperialism had been the sources of war guilt, then their overthrow and destruction could have opened the way for a negotiated peace with an innocent successor regime. But a successor regime that represented the people would not do now as in 1918 (when Wilson had refused to negotiate with the imperial government precisely because it did not represent the people), for the people themselves were evil. We could not make peace with the people in these countries if peace meant mutual agreement and reconciliation. We could not make that "peace between equals" which Wilson had called the only peace that can last. We could only require them to put themselves at our mercy, for it would be necessary for us to hold them in bondage pending their re-education, reorientation, and reform.

At last, without agreement among the allies on the ultimate disposition of Germany, came the long-wished-for day when Hitler was dead and a "Commander-in-Chief of the U. S. Forces of Occupation" in Germany (Eisenhower) received a directive from the Joint Chiefs of Staff: (JCS 1067 of April, 1945) on the "Basic Objectives of Military Government in Germany." Part I, 4 provided:

285

"a. It should be brought home to the Germans . . . that the Germans cannot escape responsibility for what they have brought upon themselves.

"b. Germany will not be occupied for the purpose of liberation but as a defeated enemy nation. . . .

"c. The principal Allied objective is to prevent Germany from ever again becoming a threat to the peace of the world."

Surely it is not without significance that the postwar settlements which the allies planned to impose on their defeated enemies in 1919 and 1945 alike had to be abandoned, and in both cases for much the same reasons. In both cases the dominant allied leaders thought that, on the one hand, they could organize a general peace, and on the other hand abstain from making peace with the vanquished. Because we chose, without any real necessity of doing so, to regard the vanquished nations, the peoples themselves, as criminals, whatever regimes they were under, we could not make peace with them, we could not bring them back into the family, we could not seat them at the same table with ourselves. And that meant that we could not make a general peace even though every other circumstance had favored it. A privileged peace for "peace-loving nations" only is not a general peace; by implication it is a tyranny.

It was not feasible for a nation like the United States to project a world in which, for an indefinite period of years, one set of nations were the subjects and another set the masters. For one thing, our subjugation of other peoples would quickly have become unacceptable to us as a matter of conscience, being inimical to our established principles as a nation. Aside from this, however, the master nations, with discrepant views and rival interests, could hardly have been expected to resist the temptation of negotiating with the subject nations, which would then find those who were willing to pay a price for their friendship. When that happened the United States would awaken to the fact that, since national security rests no less on consent than on force, it was not in the national interest to cultivate the continuing enmity of any important peoples on the international scene. The fact that a particular people really did have dangerous tendencies, if such were the case, would make this none the less true. In the aftermath of both wars Russia, by standing apart from us, whether at our instance or her own, brought about the loosening of the enemy's bonds. Twice we refused to make peace with a defeated Germany, only to be forced by the recovery of German independence to go about making it anyway.

XXIII • In an earlier chapter I mentioned that the traditional foreign policy of the United States became obsolete in 1898. It took us fifty years to grasp this fact and adjust our thinking to it. During those fifty years, inevitably, the course of our foreign relations was subject to personal whim or predilection, to sentiment, to the notions of an abstracted morality, to the readings of a questionably relevant international law, to expectations of an impossible Utopia, or to the devil theory of international conflict. For fifty years we could not, as a nation, bring ourselves to face the reality of "a world which we did not make, which we can not alter, which we can not think into a different condition from that which actually exists." In developing our foreign policy we addressed ourselves, instead, to worlds which never were. The result was that we floundered and fell into repeated disaster.

I have examined this half century with some uneasiness at the picture it presents of human blindness, human simplicity, the inability of us men to recognize the real challenges of the world and to deal with them in terms of what they are. I have to remind myself, however, of the special circumstances which make this period exceptional—not exceptional in showing the confusion and inconsequence of the human mind, for that is universal, but in the degree to which the confusion and incon-

288

sequence were uncontrolled. Foreign policy, as I said earlier, must be rooted in dogma and tradition. Therefore it cannot be quickly or easily replaced. All this considered, it may be that half a century was not a discreditably long time to take in moving from the policy of the Farewell Address, which had become obsolete, to the policy which the new times required.

Even at the end of the Second World War we appeared not to have learned some of those lessons which we might have learned from the First World War. We again undertook to make no peace with the defeated nations and, while leaving them in possession of their territories, to make them incapable of defending those territories or playing their indispensable roles in the maintenance of international order. We appear, in the gallant person of President Roosevelt, to have retained the bulk of Wilson's Utopianism while eschewing the essence of his realism. In Roosevelt's person the United States again denied the role of power in international politics and proclaimed the imminent coming of "One World"—that being our new name for Utopia. Apparently we had learned nothing, and perhaps the cycle of disaster would have to take still another turn—what promised, in view of atomic fission, to be its final turn.

I cannot tell to what end, good or bad, the present period of history is moving. Mistakes accumulate in their consequences, and each point of departure for a fresh start is progressively less favorable. We may learn the lessons of our experience, and learn them well, only to find that we have learned them too late. However that may be, my chronicle of the dismal fifty years is over and I can go on, now, with relief, to an account of American resolution in the face of a reality that is at last recognized.

In the fifty years that began with 1898 our foreign policy was generally based on two assumptions which did not fit the realities of the twentieth century. One was that our security in the Western Hemisphere, so far from requiring our intervention in the affairs of Europe, depended on our avoidance of entanglement in them. The other was that the conduct of international relations in terms of power politics, spheres of influence, and the balance of power was inimical to the avoidance of war and the maintenance of international order.

The fact that both of these assumptions were wrong was demonstrated by three successive emergencies in this century, emergencies in which considerations of our own security compelled us, belatedly, to intervene in the affairs of Europe—and to intervene with massive power. Holding the European and world balance of power in contempt, we nevertheless had to mobilize our own power and throw it into the balance whenever, as happened three times, that balance was upset. Both assumptions of our foreign policy survived the First World War virtually intact, despite the vivid and bloody demonstrations of their inadequacy which that war furnished. It is clear that the isolationist assumption did not survive the second bloody demonstration of its inadequacy furnished by World War II. But the other assumption, the assumption that power politics could and should be dispensed with, did survive this second demonstration.

In the limited sense which I have indicated, Franklin D. Roosevelt and his Secretary of State, Cordell Hull, were essentially Wilsonians a generation after Wilson. Their thinking had not advanced substantially beyond his. Like Wilson, they assumed that isolationism was disastrous and that, henceforth, the United States must bear an active part in maintaining the peace of the world. Unlike Wilson, they had the American people behind them in this conception and were able, consequently, to lead the American people into the United Nations where Wilson had been unable to lead them into the League of Nations.

However, Roosevelt and Hull still adhered to the old contempt for power politics as a means of keeping the peace. In his report to Congress on the Yalta Conference, a few weeks before his death,[1] the chief point which the President made was that the Yalta Conference had done away with a threatened recrudes-

[1] March 1, 1945.

290

cence of power politics in the postwar world. Before Yalta, he reported, in connection with the newly liberated areas of eastern Europe, "there actually began to grow up in some of these places queer ideas of, for instance, 'spheres of influence' that were incompatible with the basic principles of international collaboration." "The Crimea Conference . . ." he said, "ought to spell the end of the system of unilateral action, the exclusive alliances, the spheres of influence, the balances of power, and all the other expedients that have been tried for centuries—and have always failed. We propose to substitute for all these, a universal organization in which all peace-loving nations will finally have a chance to join."

The implication here is that international organization and power politics are mutually exclusive alternatives. What did this mean in terms of policy and action? I am afraid it meant that the United States was at last undertaking to assume its international responsibilities with only a partial appreciation of the sacrifices and the burden that an effective discharge of those responsibilities would entail. We were still evading the realities of the twentieth century. We were deluding ourselves that an international organization, based on unanimity among the great powers, could itself keep the peace—requiring of us, by way of our share in the burden, little more than the casting of our vote, the payment of our dues, and perhaps some contribution to an international police force. At the same time that we joined the United Nations we demobilized our armed forces.

So much for the first two emergencies of the twentieth century and our own lagging growth in wisdom.

The third emergency was essentially like the other two—although it was not separated by a generation from its predecessor and it has not eventuated in world-wide military combat. But the Cold War, although fought with different and far more limited weapons, has in a fundamental sense been World War III.

Our involvement in it repeated the pattern of the other two

wars. With the Soviet colossus looming over western Europe and the Mediterranean, as the German colossus had previously loomed, we declined, at first, to participate in the maintenance of that balance of power on which the survival of free Europe depended. We left England alone to attempt to hold the line against expanding Communism in Greece. In fact, we were morally outraged by this example of Britain's imperialism in trying to reimpose an obsolete monarchy on the Greek people by military force. When President Roosevelt, in the speech I have quoted, referred so contemptuously to "queer ideas of . . . 'spheres of influence' " he was rebuking Prime Minister Churchill for the deal whereby Britain's paramount influence in Greece was recognized by Stalin in return for a free hand for Russia in Romania and Bulgaria (both already occupied by the Red army).

As had been the case in the first two wars, we awoke to reality only when western Europe and England were once more on the edge of total collapse. The same danger of a ruthless aggressive power dominating the opposite shore of the Atlantic had again to stare us in the face before we could overcome our aversion to the use of power for the regulation of international relations.

There is a particular irony in the fact that the signal for our awakening was the communication to us by the British, on February 21, 1947, of the information that their own domestic crisis compelled them to abandon Greece, and also Turkey, forthwith. Churchill's comment on this in his memoirs has a tone of satisfaction which I, for one, am willing to allow him. "It did not fall to us to end the task in Greece," he writes. "I little thought however at the end of 1944 that the State Department, supported by overwhelming American opinion, would in little more than two years not only adopt and carry on the course we had opened, but would make vehement and costly exertions, even of a military character, to bring it to fruition."[2]

In 1947, as in 1917 and in 1940, we intervened once more at the last desperate moment with our own power to restore the

[2] *The Second World War* (London, 1954), VI *(Triumph and Tragedy)*, 266.

balance of power in Europe and the world. In 1945 President Roosevelt had uttered the words which I have already quoted about Yalta having put an end to exclusive alliances, spheres of influence, and balances of power. In September, 1947, at Rio de Janeiro, his successor, President Truman, made the following statement: "Our people did not conceive, when we were fighting the war, that we should be faced with a situation of this nature. Our planning for peace presupposed a community of nations, sobered and brought together by frightful suffering and staggering losses, . . . dedicated to the task of peaceful reconstruction. In view of the unfortunate conditions which now prevail, we have faced some difficult problems of adjustment in our foreign policy." What we had faced was the last step in a long course of adjustment from a foreign policy appropriate to our circumstances in the nineteenth century to a policy that addressed itself, at last, to the reality of the twentieth century.

The reality which we brought ourselves to face in 1947 was not, primarily, that of Soviet aggression. More significant than the aggressiveness of the Soviet Union was the weakness that invited and all but compelled aggression—the power vacuum that would not remain unfilled, whether Russia or any other country happened to be the one that was on hand to fill it.

More serious than the physical damage which World War II left in its wake was the destruction, in the occupied and enemy countries, of those political structures which enabled them to function as nation-states. Greece is a good example. At the end of the war Greece was left without an effective governmental authority to regulate forces inside the country. The King of Greece was resident in London; a government in exile had been enjoying the hospitality of Cairo; and the country itself was left to the rival resistance movements, Communist and anti-Communist, which had grown up during the Nazi occupation. There was no legitimate and effective police force to maintain order, no machinery for elections or the adjudication of rival claims. The result, automatically, was bloody civil war among the contending forces—Communists on one side, anti-Communists on the other.

The Communist powers neighboring on Greece, and the British, who depended for their security on maintaining a dominant position in the eastern Mediterranean, alike had great interests in the outcome of the civil war—that of the British being, in a strategic sense, the more vital interest. The British also were involved in the situation to the extent that they had participated in the liberation of Greece and now had a responsibility for setting her back on her feet. Under the circumstances, could one really be too severe on Greece's northern neighbors and on the British for taking an active interest in the victory of the respective sides which they were impelled to favor in the civil war? The British solved the problem temporarily by introducing their military forces under General Scobie into Greece and making a very good deal indeed whereby the Russians recognized (and for a while genuinely respected) the paramountcy of British interest in Greece, while the British recognized the paramountcy of Russian interest in Russian-occupied Romania and Bulgaria. By refusing to make such a deal the British would not have saved the life or liberty of a single Romanian or Bulgarian, but they might well have had to accept the successive enslavement of Greece, Turkey, Iran, and Italy under the Communist yoke, together with Communist domination of the eastern Mediterranean, the Middle East, and North Africa. While we stood on the sidelines crying, "Foul!" the British used an astute combination of force and diplomacy to fill the vacuum and contain the Communist forces that were about to break out into the Mediterranean.

By 1947, however, the British were no longer able to do so. Fortunately, when they notified us, on February 21, that they were withdrawing, when they told us in effect that after March 30 the Communists would be free to move into the eastern Mediterranean and take over, then the shock of reality woke us up from our final dream. In an astonishingly short time—

less than a month—we had reversed President Roosevelt's policy and, with the enthusiastic backing of the nation, had committed ourselves to a course of power diplomacy in Europe.[3]

I said that Greece was only one example of a political vacuum left by the war. A precisely similar example was Poland, but here the Russian strategic interest was paramount. Here the Russians introduced military force to fill the vacuum and establish Communism.

The same was true of Romania, Bulgaria, Yugoslavia, Hungary, and Czechoslovakia. In the case of Germany and Austria, the Russians and the Western allies between them broke them in half along the lines previously agreed to for the temporary military occupation. On their side, the Western allies established that freedom of which the German Federal Republic is an example. On the other side Moscow established the rule of force.

In the winter of 1946-47, however, we discovered belatedly and unexpectedly what a vacuum the war had left, not only in eastern and central Europe, but in western Europe too—in Italy, in France, and in Britain herself. By the spring of 1947 the total collapse of these countries—with the ensuing anarchy and bloodshed, the return to barbarism—was clearly visible on the horizon ahead, almost imminent. These countries were rapidly using up their last financial reserves, and such foreign exchange as they had been able to borrow, in order to keep their people supplied with food, fuel, and other necessities of life. The production with which they might have paid for these imports was not reviving, and now the calamitous end was already in sight.

The Communist vultures, one might say, were already beginning to pick on the flesh of a dying Italy and a dying France. One-third of the electorate in both countries was voting Communist. Communists were in the government coalitions. They

[3] For an able account of these events see Joseph M. Jones, *The Fifteen Weeks* (New York, 1955).

occupied Cabinet posts, and in France had taken over the Ministry of Defense. Britain, in a state of incipient collapse, was rapidly giving up that position in the world which she no longer had the strength to maintain. Already she had got out of Burma and out of India. Now she was getting out of the eastern Mediterranean.

It was quite clear that—with our paper plans for international organization based on unanimity among the great powers, with our repugnance toward power politics, spheres of influence, and balances of power—we were on the way to finding ourselves alone in a Communist world when we at last woke up.

On February 21, 1947, the British told us they were getting out of Greece and Turkey forthwith. On the following March 12 President Truman went before the Congress to request authority and appropriations for immediately taking over these responsibilities from them. At the same time, however, he recognized and announced that Greece and Turkey represented only "one aspect of the situation." That situation had implications which led to the conclusion, he said, "that it must be the policy of the United States to support free peoples who are resisting attempted subjugation by armed minorities or by outside pressures."

Here, then, was the policy of containing Communism by the use of our power—not just in Greece or Turkey, but everywhere. The statement has been criticized, and I think that any diplomatic purist must agree that it was open to criticism. As usual when we reverse our course in foreign affairs, we leaped to an extreme. We assumed a sort of unlimited commitment that we would not be able to fulfill completely and literally. We emphasized, I think too heavily, those ideological considerations that make international divisions or conflicts irreconcilable.

The Europeans and the British, at the same time that they were elated, were rather shocked by the verbal bluntness of our approach. Some of them were sophisticated enough in these matters, from long experience, to know that the best way to use power is quietly. If they had been in our place there would, perhaps, have been no blasts on the trumpet—simply a quiet movement of troops, supplies, or personnel. The One World to which all looked forward had not yet been irremediably divided. The quiet display of the big stick, accompanied by smiles, might still bring the Russians to reason. Instead, we shouted a war cry and proclaimed an ideological crusade.

I think, however, that this may have been a necessity in the relations between our government and our people. In 1947, as in 1917 and 1941, we had to have our emotions aroused by the combination of a great crisis and a great cause if we were going to support the action that had to be taken.

The important fact is that we took the action. That action extended far beyond Greece and Turkey and it involved far more than economic means—although these were primary. Even as we moved to replace the British in Greece and Turkey we addressed ourselves to what needed to be done in the rest of Europe.

The preparation here was somewhat more leisurely and, consequently, more thoughtful. All hands recognized from the start that the financial and economic crisis of the several European states could be met in some degree, though not wholly, by organized co-operation among them—by what came to be called self-help and mutual aid. The European countries could trade out one another's deficits to some extent, so that a consolidated deficit for the community as a whole would be less than the sum of the deficits of its individual members.

For this reason, as well as for moral and psychological reasons, it was essential that the European countries get together to plan and administer their own recovery on a mutual basis. If they did that, then our role could be confined to supplying what would still be wanting—the missing component—when they had done everything they could for themselves. What would still be wanting, as it transpired, amounted to some seventeen billion dollars over a period of four years.

This time we blew no trumpets and were careful to deny the ideological implications of our policy. Secretary Marshall's Harvard address of June 5, 1947, at which he announced what we later knew as the "Marshall Plan," was shouldered off the front pages in the United States by a statement of President Truman on the same day to the effect that the Communist coup in Hungary was an "outrage" which we would not take lying down (though, as it turned out, that is how we did take it).

Secretary Marshall was careful to say: "Our policy is directed not against any country or doctrine but against hunger, poverty, desperation and chaos." He made it clear that our assistance would be available to any country (including Russia or her satellites) that was "willing to assist in the task of recovery." It would not be available to "any government which maneuvers to block the recovery of other countries."

This diplomatic procedure removed from us the onus of finally dividing Europe and the world by granting our aid on an ideological basis. It placed the Russians on the defensive, immediately confronting them with the dilemma of allowing their satellites to be tempted into the Western camp or themselves accepting the onus, by their refusal to co-operate, of dividing the world and depriving the subject peoples under their rule. The immediate result was a weakening of the Russian hold on the satellites, a few weeks of confusion in Moscow, and a final Kremlin decision to go all out against the Marshall Plan and try to defeat it by propaganda and subversion in western Europe.

The Cold War now was really launched—not by us, but by the Soviet Union in its opposition to our plan for the reconstruction of Europe. The Communist parties in Italy and France went all out to create anarchy, to make government impossible, to take over. Using their hold on labor organizations in both countries, they undertook to paralyze commerce and industry, and to prevent recovery, by widespread and chaotic strikes. These efforts failed. Our new policy had encouraged the French and Italians to dismiss the Communists from government and to brace themselves against them. The Italian election of 1948 was fought out on this issue, and the Soviet Union lost. In France the Communist strikes failed, after some anxious days, and finally had to be abandoned. The cost in good-will and prestige to the Communist side was heavy. The Communists had shown their hand and aroused the resentment of French and Italian patriots. From that moment Communism, while remaining strong, was on the decline in both countries. Hope and courage revived throughout Europe.

Sixteen European states now got together in the Organization of European Economic Co-operation to co-operate in their own recovery with the assistance of the United States under the European Recovery Program. How successful that was we may judge when we compare the remarkable prosperity of western Europe a few years later with its economic destitution and hopelessness at the time.

While there had been some preliminary skirmishes, and while the United States had announced in the Truman Doctrine its decision to help the free world resist aggression, the Cold War really began with the Russian decision to fight the European Recovery Program. That decision, I think, was one of several diplomatic blunders by the great realist—as we were so fond of calling him—"Uncle Joe" Stalin. It is a fair guess that if the Russians had joined in the European Recovery Program and handled themselves astutely, there would have been no European Recovery Program and perhaps no European recovery. It would have taken a great deal more than the seventeen billion dollars of American appropriations to have covered eastern Europe and Russia as well as western Europe. Congress might have been less eager to appropriate that money. In any case, there would have been a first-class muddle and frustration.

As if to assist in the passage of the European Recovery Program, Moscow carried out its *coup d'état* in Czechoslovakia just a few days before the Program came up for a vote in the Senate—a piece of diplomatic timing comparable only to Moscow's withdrawal of its representative from the Security Council before the Communist aggression in Korea. By its Cold War policy, in response to our Marshall Plan, Moscow promoted western European and North Atlantic union far more effectively than we could have done by ourselves. And it kept losing the battles that, if they had been won, would in terms of *Realpolitik* have justified its tough and aggressive policy.

If the Russian leaders could have frightened the West into abandoning the West Berliners, in 1948, all the West Germans would have taken note that we could not be counted on to defend them in a showdown, that they had better make the best terms they could with Moscow. The next battle which Stalin launched and lost was the battle to bring the government of Comrade Tito in Yugoslavia a little closer to heel. The loss of this battle was a sort of disaster for the Soviet cause. It set an example for the other satellites; it destroyed the myth of Communist solidarity; it took the main pressure off of Greece and Italy, thereby making the Mediterranean more secure; and it changed the position of some fairly substantial divisions in the balance of military power. Above all, it showed the world that the Communist empire could crumble as well as expand.

But Tito's defection, when it came in 1948-49, was not simply a fortunate accident for our side. It could not have taken place if America had not, in 1947, committed its power and its diplomacy to the containment of Russia in Europe and the eastern Mediterranean.

In 1947, then, the United States finally adopted a new policy to meet the dire necessities of the twentieth century. That new policy was to assume leadership in organizing and directing the power of the free world so as to balance, and thereby to check, the expanding power of the Soviet Union. What this new policy will bring forth in the long future I don't know. Initially, it led to successes of a magnitude which, being so close to these matters as we are, we have hardly appreciated.

Stalin's policy like the Kaiser's policy and Hitler's policy before it, once again brought the weight of the United States into the balance of power. And now the United States would not again turn back from its role and its responsibilities on the international scene.

XXIV • I have ended my account of the actual development of our foreign policy on a heartening note. The fifty years of floundering are over and we see our nation acting, at last, with a degree of worldy wisdom unmatched since the days of the Founding Fathers. But our future is not as secure as this, by itself, might suggest.

Two developments impress me. One is the unprecedented number, magnitude, and complexity of the problems that challenge our policy in the twentieth century. Men and governments are strained almost beyond endurance simply to comprehend them intelligently. Someone recently gave his opinion that our greatest Secretary of State had been John Quincy Adams, our second greatest Dean Acheson. This set me to imagining what the situation might have been if Adams had been Secretary at the mid-point of the twentieth century. The carrying out of the policy represented by the Monroe Doctrine in the circumstances of the early nineteenth century, while not easy, was surely a less exacting task than the carrying out of the policy represented by the Truman Doctrine in the later circumstances. My admiration for both men is deep, but I find it as impossible to compare them in terms of achievement as to compare two mathematicians of whom one has been tested by problems in high school arithmetic, the other by problems

301

in the four-dimensional mathematics of outer time-space. If Mr. Adams has been looking down from the rim of Heaven all these years, he must often have thanked God that his tour of duty did not fall in our day.

But his reason for thanking God would not bear solely on the nature of the external problems that have come to challenge our national society. I suspect that what would really make his cheek turn pale is the thought of the domestic political problems that have tended increasingly to become the first preoccupation even of the Cabinet officer whose field of action is foreign affairs. Mr. Adams, with his austere personality and intellectual distinction, would not have been well equipped to deal with those problems on the scale to which they have grown. He would, I suspect, have been as unwilling as Mr. Acheson was to subordinate the requirements of the external situation. In any case, he would have found that he had less freedom and power to deal with an external environment that had become more difficult.

This brings me to the second development that impresses me. It is no longer possible, as it still was in Adams's day, for six or eight seasoned men, in private rumination and consultation among themselves, to make the foreign policy of the United States. The foreign policy of the United States, today, must normally represent, in the first instance, a consensus among hundreds of diverse persons in the governmental bureaucracy, from speech writers to experts in ballistics. In the second instance, it must represent the consensus, or at least the dominant view, of a vastly enlarged Congress—with the lower, larger, and less qualified chamber playing an increasing role. Finally, it must represent something like a consensus, or at least a general acquiescence, among the far-flung and sometimes agitated American people.

It is one thing to make a foreign policy designed to meet the requirements of the external situation. It may be quite another to make a foreign policy designed to elicit such a wide consensus and acceptance. Whatever is complicated, recondite,

302

abstruse, or subtle must always be excluded from the logic on which such argrement is to be had. That logic must not require a sophisticated understanding or refined knowledge. Where a large enough council of military officers meets to agree on strategy against the enemy a proposal to "clobber them with everything we've got" is more likely to gain acceptance than a proposal to bring limited and selective pressures to bear in connection with a complex of indirect and direct military moves. That is why strategy depends on the authority and decision of individual leaders but gives way before the processes of collective decision. That is why bureaucratic governments are such blunt instruments.

If a policy proposal is to be developed inside the various subordinate staffs of the governmental departments, if it must then be processed through committees, and if it must finally gain the approval of the National Security Council, then it will have to be crude in a degree. This requirement has not lessened with the increasing role, since 1945, of the military and of military organization in the making of our national decisions.

In the field of foreign policy the requirement of crudeness is aggravated where the staffs, committees, and bureau chiefs are not men of professional training or experience in foreign affairs. It is therefore aggravated by our national disposition to believe that government is a business rather than a skilled profession, and that a foreign office may therefore be adequately staffed by lawyers and businessmen brought in from outside. Even in these times it is not unknown for the Secretary of State and the preponderance of those who attend his staff meetings, however able and dedicated they may be in themselves, to be newcomers to the general field of foreign affairs.

The larger the group from which a consensus is to be obtained, the harder it is to obtain one. Consequently, the larger the group the greater the proportion of the leadership's attention that must be given to the objective of obtaining one, of bringing people together, as distinct from the objective of making sound policy. Eventually, only the most vital considerations ulterior to this objective can be allowed to stand in the way. Propositions that would aggravate the difficulty, however valid, must be excluded from consideration. Only the common mind can be welcomed at the council table. Intellectual sophistication must be ostracized for the sound practical reason that, to the extent that it can make itself felt at all, it is disruptive, it tends to make the achievement of consensus impossible. One may question whether, when circumstances like this become extreme, the best minds have a place in government or can make a contribution. One may question whether John Quincy Adams would have been qualified.[1]

We are dealing here with problems of degree for which absolute solutions would be inappropriate. All extremes are dangerous. I would no more have American foreign policy made by one man alone (even John Quincy Adams or Dean Acheson) than I would have it conducted by all men collectively. But the danger, today, is not that one or a few will have too much freedom in making it. The danger is that the few in positions of leadership will be so daunted and oppressed by the pressures of the many that they will break down in hidden ways and abnegate their responsibility. Political leadership almost always involves an ingredient of followership ("My people are going that way and since I am their leader I must follow."), but the danger is that the leaders will at last become followers altogether, that they will no longer attempt to govern the ebbing and flowing tides of opinion but will invariably allow themselves to be carried along, trusting in God for the outcome. (The Psalmist says: "Except the Lord build the house, they labor in vain that build it." But one may properly feel uneasy at that trust in God which is merely a device by which men ease their consciences when they turn away from a labor that is too difficult.) The danger is that they will be directed by an opinion which they no longer attempt to direct.

[1] "Too much intelligence is a handicap for day-to-day management because it hinders conformity and acceptance." Dr. Robert McMurray, American management consultant, quoted in *The Observer*, London, December 21, 1958, p. 10.

There appears to be a natural tendency for democracies to evolve, like parabolic arcs, out of the irresponsible government of tyrants and back again into the irresponsible government of demagogues. The history of Athenian democracy is the classic example.[2] Another is that of the Roman Republic between the destruction of Carthage and the establishment of the Principate. At first the people are inclined to delegate their political power to those who, because of their character and education, have won their confidence. They elect a Pericles or a Washington in the expectation that he will follow his personal judgment, in which they have confided, rather than simply do their bidding. But as they gain self-confidence, as they are encouraged by the rivals for their favor, and as trust in the independent leaders is impaired, the theory of leadership changes. It may be that President Eisenhower was defining this change in his First Inaugural Address when he said that the American faith today "decrees that we, the people, elect leaders not to rule but to serve." The responsibility of the leader is conceived to be that of harmonizing his followers, obtaining a consensus among them, and then giving it expression in action. It is not conceived to be that of seeing to it that the right consensus is reached.

Under this theory the real nature of the external challenges would have a secondary, an incidental, or even only a fortuitous role in the determination of foreign policy—as finally happened in Athens. For the people, however intelligent and conscientious they may be individually, are not in a position to make

[2] "Pericles," wrote Thucydides, "by his rank, ability, and known integrity, was able to exercise an independent control over the masses—to lead them instead of being led by them; for as he never sought power by improper means, he was never compelled to flatter them. On the contrary, he enjoyed so high a reputation that he could afford to anger them by contradiction. . . . With his successors it was different. More on a level with one another, and each grasping at supremacy, they ended by committing even the conduct of state affairs to the whims of the multitude. This, as might have been expected in a great imperial state, produced a host of blunders, and amongst them the Sicilian expedition," from which the disastrous fall of Athens eventuated. The successor to Pericles, Cleon the tanner, denounced educated people in addressing the Athenians, saying: "Ordinary men usually manage public affairs better than their more gifted fellows." (What Cleon called "more gifted fellows" we, in our day, have come to call "eggheads.") (From the translation by R. W. Livingstone.)

such a determination themselves except in the broadest and most general sense—any more than they would be in a position to exercise judgment in the nation's law courts in place of the trained judges who now discharge that function. The external challenges exist beyond the national horizon, in remote and exotic environments. We more often see their effects, like the play of distant searchlights in the night sky, than the challenges themselves. They involve technical and abstruse considerations (just as cases in the courts often do), and they are for the most part hidden by the secrecy or duplicity of other governments. The beams of light represent deliberate deceptions. Any professional adviser to the Secretary of State finds it impossible, with all his professional time devoted to the task, to keep himself adequately informed about any large portion of the external challenges—even where the information is available. How, then, can doctors, shopkeepers, factory workers, farmers, or businessmen, with other uses for their time, keep themselves adequately informed? It is not a question of resistance to knowledge but of the peculiar demands which such an undertaking makes, the intellectual training which it requires, and the maturity on which its success depends.

We have seen such an evolution of democracy not only in America but also in England, where foreign relations were excluded from parliamentary debate until after the First World War. The oligarchical procedure of the American Founding Fathers persisted in the British conduct of foreign affairs long after it had given way in the other fields of government. The members of the Cabinet were like judges in the courts, expected to exercise their own best judgments on the cases that came before them, answerable only in the long run. Since the First World War, however, British governments, though still enjoying a large measure of freedom, have been increasingly gripped by the forces of an unsophisticated public opinion. They have had to labor with increasing difficulty, like men wading through glue. In France it can almost be said that, through most of the 1950's, foreign policy was no longer made at all. On one occasion after another France stood where it found itself, unable to move forward or back, able only to utter protests at the actions of others.[3]

When we feel oppressed by lack of leadership on the national scene our sound and natural impulse is to say: If only the President would go on the air and say this or that, explain this or that! It is primarily in words that political leadership is exercised. The President of the United States cannot gain the support of the American people or the peoples of the world merely by the decisions he makes with respect to the budget, the organization of the armed forces, or federal aid to education. By making these decisions badly he can lose their confidence, but to gain their confidence he must speak to them in words. He must use logic.

Note, now, a paradox. Beginning with the period after Woodrow Wilson, the custom has developed of employing special speech writers to prepare or assist in the preparation of the speeches which our political leaders deliver. This has developed to the point where today it is generally accepted as a matter of ordinary procedure that the President's speeches are written for him, that the words he utters when he addresses the public are not necessarily his own. With all the bureaucratic apparatus of speech writers and public relations experts which is now at the disposal of our Presidents and our Secretaries of State one might expect that this prime function of leadership would be better performed than ever before. Yet I think of no instance in which a truly memorable and statesmanlike utterance has come out of such a combination. One who has, on occasion, been intimately

[3] On February 20, 1958, in the course of a debate in the House of Commons on whether the British government should enter into dangerous and delicate public negotiations with the Soviet Union, Mr. Aneurin Bevan said: "There is a consciousness of a growing gulf between what the public want and what the Government are doing. To some extent the Opposition may share in that guilt unless we make it quite clear we do not consider the Government are following the right course in the present circumstances." The use of the word "guilt" here shows the degree to which it had come to be assumed that the British government had a moral obligation to accept the continuous direction of public opinion in conducting foreign relations.

involved in the process of speech writing for our governmental leaders (and who has seen words of his composition cast in imperishable bronze over the name of a famous statesman) may offer the observation that the fault is not primarily in the ability of the individuals who participate in it. Our Presidents and Secretaries, in recent times, have had speech writers as good as money could hire or patriotic devotion could enlist, men with professional credentials that no Abraham Lincoln or Winston Churchill could match. Yet one cannot say that the consequence has been a growth in the effective eloquence of leadership. On the contrary, I think there is reason to associate this bureaucratic development with a growth in the element of followership, a decline in leadership.

This statement of the paradox suggests its explanation. The primary concern of leadership must be with what needs to be said to the people, with the theme to which a speech must give expression. As a matter of professional training, however, the primary concern of public relations experts and copy writers is with the audience. They are concerned, first of all, with what will appeal to the audience, what will be well received; and what is well received, in general, is whatever corroborates the views that the audience already holds. Where the preparation of speeches is left to them, they will make the theme conform to the audience's intellectual level and inclinations. If the President is to address a labor audience in Detroit on foreign policy, they will not be primarily concerned with the foreign policy subject, on which they are not experts. They will, rather, concentrate on having him avoid such maturity of expression as might make difficulties for those who have not had an education beyond high school; they will have him include statements designed to appeal to important minority groups among them; and they will have him exclude anything that might be unpopular with such an audience, however much it might need to be said. In a sense, then, it is the audience that, by its leanings and limits, writes the speech.

Here is an abnegation of leadership automatically produced

308

by the processes of bureaucracy. The leader, who is merely one piece in this game, does not lift the people up but is brought down, by his staff writers, to their level.[4]

One must look, always, for the problem behind the problem. I cannot say that if our political leaders should dismiss their speech-writing staffs and once more write their own speeches the results would necessarily be better. My occasional regret that some of our leaders have not written their own speeches is matched only by my regret that others have. Few have any literary and intellectual ability approaching that of an Abraham Lincoln, a Woodrow Wilson, or a Winston Churchill. The leader's disability prompts him to resort to speech writers. Without them he might do even worse.

Here is a dilemma that arises, I think, out of the tendency for democracy in its evolution eventually to fall away from educated statesmanship. Pericles, who was schooled in philosophy and literature, had the gift of distinguished and persuasive expression, expression which tended to lift the audience up to his level. But Cleon, the uneducated tanner who succeeded him, did not have it. The gift is a product of that intellectual cultivation to which bureaucracy and, in some phases, democracy are hostile. One understands what Cleon meant when he told the Athenians that "ordinary men usually manage public affairs better than their more gifted fellows." But the history of Athens itself suggests that, as the gifted men retire and the ordinary men step into their places, statesmanship give way to demagogy and leadership degenerates into followership.[5]

[4] This is the same mistake that professional educators make when they write books for eight-year-olds in the vocabulary of an eight-year-old, and with equally undistinguished results.

[5] In a superficial view Abraham Lincoln, who provided the nation with its most notable example of the leadership I am discussing, was an uneducated man. But he was so only in a formal sense. If the criterion is the formation of the mind, he was, perhaps, the best educated of all our Presidents, not excepting Wilson. I recall an occasion when a government speech writer objected to a three-syllable word which I put into the draft of a speech for his chief. He said his chief wanted to use only such simple language as Lincoln used, words of one or two syllables, sentences of five or six words. I offered to buy him a volume of Lincoln's public addresses if he would examine them for

I would not advocate that our leaders, however gifted, consult only themselves in preparing what they will say. But taking the lead in a work of collaboration is different from accepting the completed work which one's staff sets before one. President Washington had the active collaboration of Alexander Hamilton in the preparation of his Farewell Address. But Hamilton was not a public relations man or a professional copy writer: he was himself a bold political leader who happened to share the convictions of the President and was, like the President, intent on giving them an expression designed more to sway the people than to win their applause. If the Farewell Address is great, it is because in its reserved and formal language it expresses the profound personal convictions of a man of strong character who had suffered a long and often poignant experience of public affairs. There is no hint in it of saying what the audience wants to hear.

No one advances, as such, the theory that leadership in our democracy should passively accept popular opinion as it is, without questioning. But approaches to such a theory are advanced, ordinarily basing themselves on the doctrine of Congressional government: the doctrine that the executive branch is subordinate to the legislative branch, which must assume such leadership as is called for because it represents the electorate in detail, as the President does not. The most outspoken statement of the theory was made by Admiral Dewey in 1900 when he announced his candidacy for President: "Since studying this subject I am convinced that the office of the President is not such a very difficult one to fill, his duties being mainly to execute the laws of Congress. Should I be chosen for this exalted position, I would execute the laws of Congress as faithfully as I have always

---

what they revealed about Lincoln's vocabulary and style. This man (and his chief) made the common mistake of equating simplicity with immaturity, a simple style with baby talk. The fact is that this writer's otherwise able chief never gave a speech that contained even one passage which anyone would think of comparing with Lincoln's speeches. What is notable, rather, is the contrast.

executed the orders of my superiors."

The theory would also find a clear expression in many statements by President Eisenhower during his first term and in the period immediately preceding it. But the Congress cannot lead for a number of reasons. For one, when responsibility for leadership is diffused among a membership of over five hundred it tends to be lost. For another, the Congress necessarily lacks adequate means of informing itself on the daily developments that call for action, and it lacks the bureaucratic means of giving effect to its decisions.

The theory that we elect leaders merely to catalyze and represent the consensus on each issue implies that the leaders we elect should have common minds. They should be Cleons rather than Pericleses. But such men have no gift of eloquence in thought or expression. They cannot exercise leadership in the sense of shaping opinion to the necessities of the day. All they can do is to express, before the audience that already holds it, such opinion as already exists and in the standard language of the day. All they can do is to be parrots, to say what everyone is saying; and for this purpose their speeches are best written by professional experts in what the public thinks and says, what language it understands. But this leaves out of account the external situation, that world of reality outside our borders which will not conform to our illusions or defer, of its own accord, to our national purposes and objectives. Here the leadership, under the evolving theory of democracy, is beyond its competence.

The most frequent argument for having a leader's speeches written for him is that, under the pressures of our day, he does not have time to prepare them for himself. But this is too simple. What a man has time for is a matter of the priorities on his time. The man who says he cannot write his own speech because of other demands on his time might have said that he could not meet the other demands because he had to write his speech. An examination of the record would show that in

311

England, during the years of World War II, important state business was sometimes kept waiting for days while the Prime Minister devoted himself exclusively to the preparation of a speech.

Among our own leaders the lack of the necessary priority for speech writing may sometimes reflect the personal reluctance of men who have no gift for composition and nothing to say. But fundamentally, I think, it is a manifestation of something rooted in our culture. We Americans characteristically make an invidious distinction between words and deeds. We prefer to think of ourselves as men of action. Literary composition, together with the processes of thought which provide its substance, seems to us dilettantish or effete, like a preoccupation with court manners and diplomatic protocol. This Cleonesque attitude, as I have noted in an earlier chapter, is an inheritance from our pioneering ancestors, who cleared the wilderness with axes and found scant use for words.

It is inimical, however, to the practice of the highest type of political leadership, as distinct from the practice of demagogy, since such leadership depends primarily on the gift for original words and the intellectual discipline that it reflects. This is true, at least, in a democracy, where leadership is not to be divorced from the use of reason to persuade. The dearth of this gift or its depreciation has constituted a national weakness especially since the end of the Second World War. It has sometimes prevented the national leadership from eliciting popular support for the policies which it found it necessary, in the national interest, to pursue; and so the nation has tended to be paralyzed or to fall victim to demagogues who misrepresented the policy for their own ends.

In a broad sense, what applies to the requirement of leadership in a democracy applies also to that of leadership of a bureaucracy, which may be only less difficult. The President and the Secretary of State, if they are sober and responsible, must consult and listen to the bureaucracy under them. But if they ask it to make their policy decisions for them, then, however intelligent its multitudinous officials, the decisions that emerge will represent only a consensus at the lowest level of understanding. A bureaucracy is essentially uncreative and mindless. It cannot, consequently, take the place of the individual leader, the individual mind. It is a body, not a head.

Nothing would be easier than to exaggerate these difficulties of our democracies, which are essentially no greater than those which have always challenged nations and have often been overcome. It is easy to view them with alarm. But it was quite as easy to view with alarm the difficulties in which our Founding Fathers labored. Our own governmental scene is not, in itself, as dismal as that which met the eyes of Edmund Burke when England, facing disaster, was nevertheless about to enjoy a century of unparalleled success. Surely our political administrations in Washington have conducted our foreign relations more intelligently since the Second World War, and are conducting it more intelligently today, than any administrations since that of Jefferson (which had to cope with the blunder of Jefferson's embargo). It is simply that the external problems have become greater and more dangerous.

In this, however, is the basis for hope. External challenges are essential to the discipline of democracies. Too much prosperity and security dispose all of us to enlarge the smaller difficulties of life, to find intolerable that regime which we cherish only when it is threatened, to become self-indulgent and petty. We become like the overrich, fatigued by small efforts, obsessed with small discomforts, full of complaints. Years of prosperous security preceded the demoralization and breakdown of Athenian democracy. The elimination of the last threat to Roman supremacy by the destruction of Carthage, and the prosperity which followed, contributed to the increasing domestic disorder that ended in the collapse of the Republic and the rise of Caesarism. As the most strenuous efforts of political leadership failed increasingly the time approached when only government by military force was possible.

Anyone who studies Swiss democracy may note one advantage

that it has had over our own. The Swiss people have always been conscious of external danger, of the possibility that their freedom might be snuffed out at short notice by foreign developments against the repercussions of which they had failed to take sufficient precautions. They have been conscious of the need to be self-possessed at all times. Therefore they have disciplined themselves in their own political behavior, making a virtue of moderation and not asking too much in the way of comfort and prosperity. We Americans have hitherto had no like consciousness of danger to our nation. But we have one now. By noting how much more intelligently we have conducted our foreign relations since 1947 than at any other time since the generation of our founding, I pay a tribute of appreciation to the external menace of our times.

XXV • I now bring to a close these chapters on aspects of American foreign policy. Looking back on them, I note that the national limitation has been, in a sense, fortuitous. If I had been in a position to have equal knowledge of British foreign policy—or Russian or Chinese—I might, with any of these as my subject, have written much that was essentially the same as what I actually have written here. For what has concerned me most deeply has not been something underlying the foreign policy of any single country alone, but something common to the foreign policies of all countries, and I have been using the example of our own country to illustrate that something. That something is the human nature of foreign policy. What I have been writing about is the human nature of foreign policy as illustrated by our American experience, with which I happen to be most familiar.

Foreign policy—anywhere, any time—has its birth and its essential being in the recesses of the human mind. Perhaps this is obvious enough without statement. But those of us who study foreign policy are in danger of forgetting or overlooking it precisely because of our necessary preoccupation with technical matters. We are concerned with the international exchange of goods and services, the accumulation of capital for the development of underdeveloped countries, the constitutional provisions of international organization, the formulation of international rules pertaining to civil aviation, and a thousand other technical matters that we isolate from their setting. It is possible to become so preoccupied with these particulars that we never see as a whole the scene in which they occur merely as incidents. So we become technically proficient in the bits and pieces of international relations without ever coming to understand the real nature of international relations. We become expert without becoming wise. We become competent to speak on technical problems, but foreign policy itself, as an expression of the human mind, remains beyond us.

It seems to me that the achievement of wisdom, of the large understanding, must be a prime responsibility of our institutions of higher learning. If one cannot achieve such understanding in the academic world, with its unique opportunities for taking an elevated and comprehensive view, where can one achieve it? Our universities could be centers from which wisdom radiates to our international society as a whole, informing it and guiding it in the determination of policy. I don't know how else the elements of human ignorance and folly, which have been so prominent in the shaping of our policies, are to be reduced.

It is a commonplace to say that the foreign policy of any particular nation addresses itself to the world which is external to that nation. But this is not so. What the foreign policy of any nation addresses itself to is the image of the external world in the minds of the people who determine the policy of that nation. That image may approximate the reality more or less closely, but at best it can never be quite the same thing. And it is generally different in fundamental respects.

None of us can have much certain knowledge of the external world. I cannot know, for example, whether there is such a thing today as a Chinese nation in the sense of a coherent national personality with its own peculiar processes of thought and its own peculiar beliefs about government and society. I don't know what six or seven hundred million Chinese think, or the areas in which there is a consensus among them, or the nature of any such consensus, or the quality of conviction that enters into it. I don't know the political allegiances of these millions. On the one hand I am told that something called "the people of China" longs for liberation from the tyranny of Peiping. Someone else tells me that it hates and fears the rival regime on Formosa. But no one has read the minds of all these people over the vast area of China, and surely many of these people could not read their own minds. All I can get is conflicting opinions among the more or less ignorant or the self-interested on which to base any opinion that I may be so venturesome as to form for myself. Most of the material that comes to me, in fact, is propaganda, deliberately designed to create a legend useful to those who disseminate it.

I face the same dilemma with France, a country which I know better. What do the French (whoever they are) think about the situation in Algeria? I don't know. I don't even know if, on the subject of Algeria, there is such a thing as "the French mind."

Again: I don't know whether the men who wield power in the Kremlin are governed more by the dictates of Lenin or by the requirements of *Realpolitik*. Probably they don't know themselves. Perhaps they would call whatever they do Leninism, though Lenin himself would not recognize it as such if he returned. I don't know under what circumstances these men might risk starting a war. I don't know how much divergence of view there may be among them. I cannot read their minds.

The fact is that none of us has much absolute knowledge of "the vast external realm" to which every nation pretends to shape its foreign policy. But the human mind finds it almost impossible to live with the unknown or the uncertain. Its tendency, therefore, is to fill the vacuum of ignorance by legend, by a view of the unknown world around which belief can crystallize. If you don't know what the thunder is, you tell yourself that it is Thor wielding his hammer. Having accepted this as the explanation, you can be at peace with yourself. If you don't understand the Arabs, you tell yourself that the only thing they respect is force, and again your mind is relieved of a troubling uncertainty. The appeal of dogmatic systems like the Marxist is that they provide a single body of legend which supplies the answer to every question, resolves every doubt. We no longer have to be puzzled by the springs of human behavior: economic determinism makes them clear. We no longer have to strain our minds to understand the causes of war: wars are the product of capitalist conspiracy.

Foreign policy addresses itself, then, to the external world as legend, to the external world that men create in their imaginations.

This brings me to the practical point of this concluding chapter, in which I sum up what seems to me the essential significance of what I have examined in the preceding twenty-four. The root of foreign policy is in the legendary image of the external world to which it addresses itself. In the degree that the image is false, actually and philosophically false, no technicians, however proficient, can make the policy that is based on it sound. Legal experts and political scientists will labor to no avail. Commodity and trade experts will not save the situation. Statisticians, however mountainous their statistics, will not save it. Neither science nor technology can take the place of wisdom, though the whole tendency of our modern world is to try to make them do so. And wisdom resides in a broad, a mature, an informed, a reasonably skeptical, and a humble understanding of the world in which we live.

In the condition of the world as it is at present it seems to me that wisdom is the possession of remarkably few; and those few are not likely to have a determining voice in the policies either of the democracies or of the dictatorships. But this would be a foolish as well as a despairing thing to say if I left it here. For wisdom is not an absolute which some have and some lack. Everyone has a little, and some, I daresay, have a little more than others. It is not unreasonable to believe that we might raise the general level of wisdom by giving thought and by exposing our minds to such accumulated wisdom as is already available—that we might raise it, say, from .7 per cent to .9 per cent, just as we are raising the level of radiation in the earth's atmosphere. That .2 per cent might make all the difference in either case. It may be that if one increased the water in the oceans by only .2 per cent, large parts of our lands would be flooded. Similarly, a very little increase in wisdom might go a long way. Students of international relations, consequently, should not overlook the philosophical foundations of their subject.

The creation of legend is our human response to the unknown or the uncertain. But even measurable aspects of the external world, those aspects that may be understood in terms of arithmetic, may nevertheless assume legendary forms in the minds of the men who determine a nation's foreign policy. My prime example is the view, held by us Americans throughout most of our national history, that the Atlantic Ocean, in and of itself, was a barrier to aggression from Europe. On the basis of this legend, so remote from the demonstrated reality, our foreign policy was often determined with fateful consequences. Most Americans still clung to it even after the German submarine had afforded a glimpse of the reality only less vivid and complete than that of 1814. Yet the true strategic significance of the Atlantic Ocean might have been demonstrated at any time, if not by logical argument then by actual war games. The falsity of the legend might at any time have been proved.

The case is different when we enter the obscure realm of human behavior—of individual and, especially, collective human behavior. Here prediction is not a matter of arithmetic or simple logic. Here the most informed minds know little for sure, and the absence of certain knowledge makes the position of legend the less challengeable. Most social scientists and intellectuals of our day, recognizing this area of ignorance, have a standard response. They say that scientific research into human behavior must be undertaken on a much larger scale than at present. If we would only appropriate as much money and gather together as many scientists to conduct behavioral research as we did to invent the atom bomb, then we would do to human behavior what we did to the atom. We could predict it and by predicting it we could conquer and harness it. Aside from the fact that this is not an appealing prospect to me, I don't share the hopes it holds out for understanding. It seems to me that the so-called "behavioral sciences" can uncover bits and pieces of human motivation and behavior, but that the whole is beyond the kind of research they represent. The analytical view cannot encompass the whole and tends, rather, to destroy it. What is needed is the creative view, the view that integrates rather than disintegrates. In this sense, I think that Shakespeare understood human behavior better than Dr. Freud (whom I do not mean to denigrate); and, consequently, that we would understand it better ourselves by steeping ourselves in the plays of Shakespeare than by studying the works of Freud. In this sense, Tolstoy's *War and Peace* seems to me to have no less value than Professor Quincy Wright's great *Study of War*. So I come back to the difference between wisdom and technical proficiency —in this case technical proficiency in analysis.

The fact remains that those of us whose views bear on the making of foreign policy—and today that includes the masses— know little for sure about human behavior, especially human behavior in the external world to which foreign policy ostensibly addresses itself. Perforce, we have to make mere views do for knowledge. It is the views that we hold in lieu of knowledge that determine foreign policy.

Everything depends, in the first instance, on one's general view of human nature. If one thinks that human nature is predominantly evil, then freedom of the individual will seem dangerous and a primary dependence on force essential. If, on the contrary, one thinks that human nature is predominantly good, one will presumably be inclined toward anarchism and pacifism. Most of us are suspended somewhere between the extremes here. I shall not undertake to say what is the correct

320

view, or to estimate the relative weight of good and evil in human society. But I call attention to what seems to me a basic fallacy, or at least a fallacious tendency, in the thinking of almost all of us. This is the view that mankind is divided into two species, the good people and the bad.

I don't suppose we are actually born with this view, but certainly it manifests itself almost from the start. As soon as his parents begin to tell a child stories they find him asking of any particular situation: Which is the side of the angels and which the side of the devils, which are the heroes and which are the villains, which is our side? I have a nine-year-old son who likes to have the plays of Shakespeare read out loud to him. In choosing which to read I have, with one exception, stayed away from the great tragedies. The exception was *Anthony and Cleopatra,* and it is the one play I have read to him which he could not really grasp. His difficulty was in deciding, as the play unfolded, whether Anthony was the good man and Octavius the bad, or whether it was the other way around. Finally he decided that Anthony was the good man and, consequently, that he would be on Anthony's side. But this made it bewildering and unsatisfactory when the play ended with Octavius's victory over Anthony, whose moral weakness had brought about his defeat. Appreciation of the inner conflict in Anthony, of the contradiction between moral strength and moral weakness in one man, which is the essence of tragedy—this was not possible for anyone who had not himself reached a fairly advanced stage of maturity. Good and evil together in one man, rather than divided between two opposed men, was too sophisticated a concept for the mind of a child. He was not ready for real people yet, or for the real world. I am afraid that applies to most of us grownups as well.

Among the elements of those fictions to which foreign policy is addressed, this fallacy of the two species is prominent. It has a variety of manifestations, not all of them quite as crude as those which occur in the mind of a nine-year-old child. It is never entirely absent from any situation involving conflict, as virtually

321

all international situations do. We believe in the rightness of our own case, and consequently in the wrongness of those who oppose our case. This seems to me unexceptionable and even proper in itself. The fallacy arises only when we identify our rightness on particular issues with a congenital moral superiority in ourselves or our kind. It arises when we equate right and wrong on particular contingent points of dispute with native virtue and native vice. It arises when we cross the line between *right* and *righteous,* between *wrong* and *wicked.* When we cross this line a great and dangerous change takes place in the nature of conflict, for the particular issues that gave rise to it now lose their relevance and any limiting effect they may have had on the conflict.

This consequence of the fallacy of the two species is not confined to international relations. Applied to social classes the fallacy leads to unfounded hopes of Utopia and resort to unwarranted cruelties for bringing it about. Because so many people, at the time of the French Revolution, thought that evil was confined to aristocrats while virtue was the property of the masses they expected that the guillotine would be a sufficient instrument for purging mankind of evil. When only the virtuous were left on earth Utopia would be at hand. But what the French Revolution proved, at a heavy price, was that evil is ubiquitous in mankind, that a Robespierre may be infected with it no less than a Louis XVI. Marxism based itself on this same fallacy, distinguishing "the people" and "the exploiters" as two opposed species of humanity. Suffering and destruction were consequently inflicted on mankind in the name of "the people," the species that represented virtue.

The fallacy of the two species, when it dominates the conflicts of international relations, has the same effect in overriding the particular issues and their limits. In World War II the issue on which Germany was opposed at first was aggression; at the end it was opposed on the grounds that it was of the "aggressor" species, that it was by nature an "aggressor nation." When the line between these two concepts was crossed it no longer became enough to put an end to Hitler's course of aggression. One had to put an end to the German nation itself as a sovereign entity in the community of states.

The plans for the postwar world were uniformly based on the concept that all nations were either "peace-loving" or "aggressor." Since this concept had virtually nothing to do with reality the plans could not possibly bring a settlement of international affairs. Peace, it was thought, could be won by having the "peace-loving" nations disarm the "aggressor" nations—just as the reign of social justice could be achieved by guillotining aristocrats—and so the German and Japanese vacuums were created on either side of the "peace-loving" Soviet Union.

If foreign policy is to be shaped by a legend as remote from reality as this then it will be quite blind and it will not serve to avoid general disaster. A student of international relations, then, or a policy-maker, will not arrive at any constructive solutions of international conflicts by an exclusively technical approach. He has to be a philosopher first. He has to put his fundamental concepts into some accord with the reality of human nature and the world. That done, the technical approach has its place and its indispensable usefulness.

I have simply assumed, so far, that the fallacy of the two species is, in fact, a fallacy, and I do not mean to elaborate, here, an argument in support of that assumption. But these matters have been tested on the historical record in terms that are not too abstruse. One might well have maintained in 1814 and 1815 that France was an "aggressor nation." The Napoleonic aggressions were merely a repetition of the aggressions of Louis XIV, just as Hitler's aggression was a repetition of the Kaiser's. But the victorious coalition did not act on any such concept of France. Consequently, it merely sent Napoleon to St. Helena and left the power of France intact. Within less than a year of Waterloo, France had, in effect, been restored to her full place as one of the great powers of Europe, with the means to discharge her responsibilities as such. The point is that, by the actual test of experience, this turns out to have been a practicable and a useful thing to do. Almost a century and a half have passed since 1815 and France in that time has manifested no tendencies toward general aggression. Apparently the quality of being an aggressor was not, in fact, a fundamental or established element in her national character.

I am, myself, disposed to believe that all good and all evil are to be found in each of us, as individuals or as nations—that we are all like Shakespeare's Anthony, like his Macbeth or his Lear. Certain circumstances bring out the good, others bring out the evil. If one compares the behavior of Switzerland in the 1930's with the concurrent behavior of Germany one sees a contrast between good and bad. But I don't, myself, believe it represents an inherent native difference between Germans and Swiss. I think the real difference is between two sets of circumstances: one set which impelled, tempted, and allowed Germany to smite her neighbors; another which forbade Switzerland to indulge in any like behavior, and which obviated any temptation to do so.

"Behind the great conflicts of mankind," says Professor Butterfield, "is a terrible human predicament. . . . Contemporaries fail to see the predicament or refuse to recognize its genuineness, so that our knowledge of it comes from later analysis—it is only with the progress of historical science on a particular subject that men come really to recognize that there was a terrible knot almost beyond the ingenuity of man to untie. . . . In historical perspective we learn to be a little more sorry for both parties than they know how to be for one another. . . . As regards the real world of international relations I should put forward the thesis (which, if it is true, would seem to me to be not an unimportant one) that this condition of absolute predicament or irreducible dilemma lies in the very geometry of human conflict. It is at the basis of the structure of any given episode in that conflict."[1] Nowhere is this sense of the human predicament more poignantly expressed or with more

[1] Herbert Butterfield, *History and Human Relations* (London, 1951), pp. 17 and 20 (essay on "The Tragic Element in Modern International Conflict").

authority—since it comes from a statesman in the midst of crisis —than by Abraham Lincoln in his Second Inaugural Address, delivered while our Civil War was still being fought.

This seems to me the essence of wisdom. Japan's attack on Pearl Harbor, without a declaration of war or any warning, seemed morally outrageous to most of us Americans. But I don't think that most of us, caught in the predicament of the Japanese —a predicament, granted, which was in part of their own making—would have felt morally bound either to give adequate notice or, if that was not feasible, to refrain from the attack. I share the general horror at what the men who rule Russia did to Hungary in November, 1956, but I don't see what alternative their predicament (which they had inherited) left them—unless they and the whole Communist organization, in Russia at least, were prepared to accept their own extinction. This kind of thing is as much a human tragedy as it is a moral outrage.

We are more likely to gain a realistic understanding of Soviet foreign policy, and therefore to make an effective counter-policy, if we regard the Soviet government as made up of human beings in a predicament than if we regard it as made up of demons whose behavior cannot be explained in human terms.

To my mind it is just as much of a mistake to attribute to our own or any other nation a congenital predominance of virtue, a predominance independent of circumstances, a predominance which gives the nation special rights. This is the aspect of the fallacy at the heart of nationalistic legends. Another aspect of the fallacy was suggested by George Washington when he warned that "the nation which indulges toward another an habitual hatred, or an habitual fondness, is, in some degree, a slave."

I have emphasized this fallacy of the two species, as I have called it. But there are others, many of them related to it, and any of us could make a catalogue of them. I shall not attempt such a thing here. The only point I want to make is that the whole superstructure of foreign policy depends on the substructure of legend, which is generally composed of just such fallacies as these.

When I read the daily press on the foreign policy debates in the United States, or in any other country, I am impressed by this. The opposing sides represent disparate views of the essential nature of the world, and the real issue is here, in these opposed views, rather than in the respective policy recommendations that flow from them. The solution of international problems is also here.

I think, in fact, that the only solution of international problems is here, that here is where the additional .2 per cent in wisdom would be effective. I have already cited one example of the practical bearing that the choice of legend has: Because the allies of 1815 regarded only Napoleon, and not France, as the menace to be got rid of, they were able to make a peace. Because the allies of 1945 regarded Hitler as a mere symptom and the German nation as the real menace they were not able to make a peace. Everything depended on who was considered the enemy.

In the international conflicts of our own day everything depends, similarly, on the identification of the entities that constitute our international world. Mr. Nehru has often spoken as if there were an entity in the international world called "Asia." Mr. Herbert Hoover has spoken as if there were an entity called "the Western Hemisphere," or "the Americas," opposed to another entity called "the Old World." John Maynard Keynes thought in terms of an entity called "Europe." Walter Lippmann has spoken of an entity called "the Atlantic Community." Rudyard Kipling was concerned a generation ago, and Miss Barbara Ward is today, with the confrontation of two supposed entities called "the East" and "the West." In the United Nations—an organization that enshrines the legend of One World in its name—we occasionally hear references to a grouping called "the colonial nations," opposed to another called "the anti-colonial nations." I, myself, have a disposition to talk in terms of an entity called "Western civilization" (from which I do not exclude Asia).

Here are disparate views of the international world which stand opposed to one another at several points. They are all, essentially, legendary views, but some have more reality to them than others. On the choice among them depends the practical solution of our problems.

Let me offer an example. If we think of the world today as being divided between two immutable entities—one "Communism," the other "the Free World"—then a simple, relatively unmanageable, essentially immitigable bipolar confrontation constitutes the situation to which policy must address itself. The possibilities of solution, then, may be summed up in the simple alternatives of *we* or *they*, our survival or theirs. If, on the other hand, we take a more complex view, if we see our contemporary world as made up of many nations and powers, a patchwork—not one entity called "Communism," but rather the Soviet Union, Poland, China, Yugoslavia, Albania; not one entity called "the Free World," but India, the United States, Japan, South Africa, Sweden—if we see the international scene as complex in this sense, then a more fluid and manageable situation presents itself for policy-making.

I do not here judge how much of right or wrong there is, respectively, in these opposed legends of the world to which policy must address itself. I cite them merely to show that it is here, at the level of premises which generally remain tacit, that foreign policy and the effectiveness of foreign policy are determined. If human civilization has a future—and that is a possibility which I do not altogether rule out—it may be because we men of the twentieth century, individually and in our multitudes, have learned to see the world in terms, whatever they may be, that are close enough to the reality to be workable.